A NAVAL HISTORY OF THE PELOPONNESIAN WAR

A NAVAL HISTORY OF THE PELOPONNESIAN WAR

Ships, Men and Money in the War at Sea, 431–404 BC

Marc G. DeSantis

Pen & Sword
MARITIME

First published in Great Britain in 2017 by
PEN & SWORD MARITIME
an imprint of
Pen & Sword Books Ltd
47 Church Street
Barnsley
South Yorkshire
S70 2AS

Copyright © Marc G. DeSantis, 2017

ISBN 978-1-47386-158-9

The right of Marc G. DeSantis to be identified as Author of this work has been asserted by him in accordance with the Copyright, Designs and Patents Act 1988.

A CIP catalogue record for this book is available from the British Library.

All rights reserved. No part of this book may be reproduced or transmitted in any form or by any means, electronic or mechanical including photocopying, recording or by any information storage and retrieval system, without permission from the Publisher in writing.

Printed and bound in England By
TJ International Ltd, Padstow, Cornwall.

Pen & Sword Books Ltd incorporates the Imprints of Pen & Sword Aviation, Pen & Sword Family History, Pen & Sword Maritime, Pen & Sword Military, Pen & Sword Discovery, Pen & Sword Politics, Pen & Sword Atlas, Pen & Sword Archaeology, Wharncliffe Local History, Wharncliffe True Crime, Wharncliffe Transport, Pen & Sword Select, Pen & Sword Military Classics, Leo Cooper, The Praetorian Press, Claymore Press, Remember When, Seaforth Publishing and Frontline Publishing.

For a complete list of Pen & Sword titles please contact
PEN & SWORD BOOKS LIMITED
47 Church Street, Barnsley, South Yorkshire, S70 2AS, England
E-mail: enquiries@pen-and-sword.co.uk
Website: www.pen-and-sword.co.uk

CONTENTS

Acknowledgements vii

Maps ix

Preface xv

Part 1: Introduction 1

Part 2: The Trireme 31

Part 3: The Archidamian War 47

Part 4: The Sicilian Expedition 125

Part 5: The Ionian War 173

Conclusion 235

Notes 241

Select Bibliography 251

Index 253

ACKNOWLEDGEMENTS

There are many involved in the creation and development of a book besides the author. I especially want to thank Phil Sidnell, editor at Pen & Sword, for his belief in me and my idea for the current work, as well as his patience while it was being hammered out on the anvil of thought. Special thanks is also due to Matt Jones, production manager at Pen & Sword, whose expert touch was of enormous help in the forging of this book.

MAPS

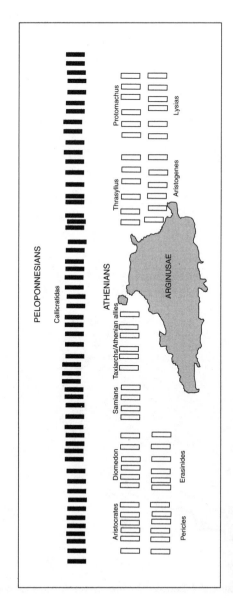

The Battle of Arginusae.

x *A Naval History of the Peloponnesian War*

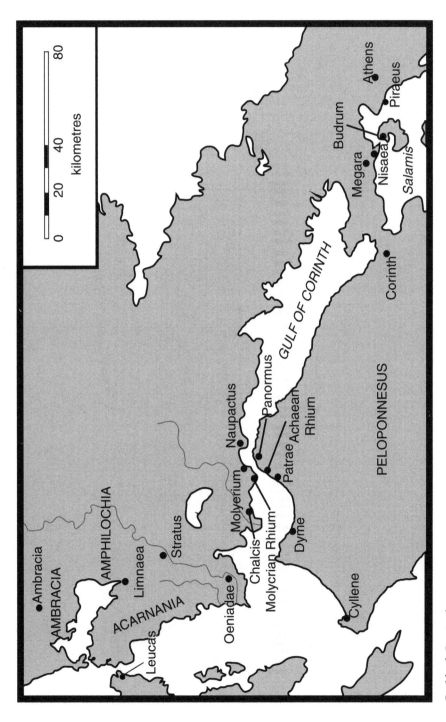

Gulf of Corinth.

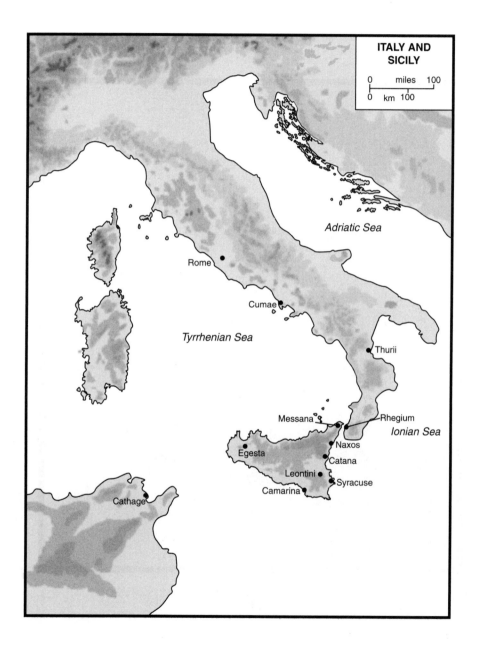

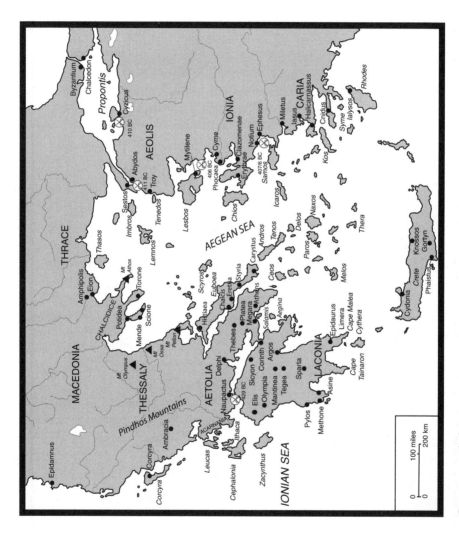

Greece and the Aegean.

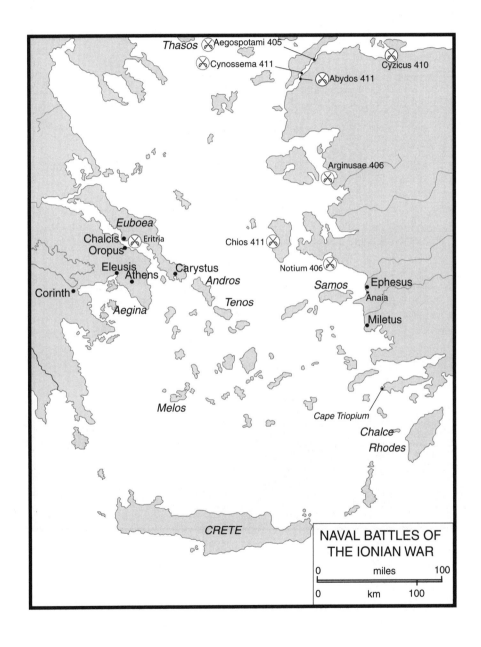

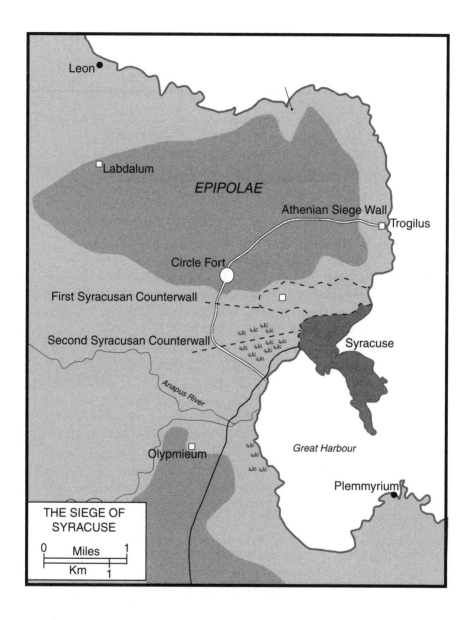

PREFACE

The idea for *A Naval History of the Peloponnesian War* came about as a result of my research for my previous book, *Rome Seizes the Trident*. In that work, I found that it had been possible for Rome, largely ignorant of naval warfare, to meet and defeat the Carthaginians at sea through the application of simple tactics and steadfast resolve. As part of my analysis of the tactics employed in ancient galley warfare, I discovered that in 413 BC, the Athenians had rendered themselves dangerously vulnerable to the prow-to-prow ramming of their Syracusan opponents by bottling themselves up in the Great Harbour of the city of Syracuse. The tight confines of the harbour made it impossible for the Athenians to implement the sophisticated rowing tactics that had made them the past masters of war at sea in the Greek world. Their trained skill was overcome by brute force in one of the greatest and most dramatic encounters of the war. I decided that I must in the future tell the story of the Athenians and how they had been laid low by less talented but deeply motivated foes.

Further research made it clear to me that the Peloponnesian War of 431–404 BC was by and large fought, and certainly decided, at sea. It is important to make this point. Though the sieges of Potidaea and Syracuse, the northern campaign of Brasidas, the battles of Delium and Mantinea and the destruction of Melos loom large in modern consciousness, naval actions determined victory or defeat for the participants. It is a rare thing in a war in any age for engagements at sea to have had such outsized effects, as most often, a naval battle, no matter how spectacular its outcome, will only shift the combat to the land, where the final result must be sought. In this war, the greatest of the ancient Greeks, however, the end came when a Peloponnesian fleet conclusively crushed that of Athens, leaving that city defenceless. Astonishingly, Sparta had made itself master of the sea, while Athens would be ruthlessly starved into submission by an all-conquering enemy navy.

Naval considerations affected the strategic thought of all the major players in the conflict. This was of course fully true for the Athenians, who adopted an almost exclusively naval strategy from the outset to fight the war. It was also true of the Spartans, the leader of the Peloponnesian coalition and the perennial masters of warfare on land. They would try, haltingly at first, and as the war progressed, with much greater success, to wrest control of the sea from the Athenians. With the end of Athens' seapower, her empire crumbled, and the golden age that bequeathed to posterity the likes of Aristophanes, Sophocles and Socrates came to an end. It is worth knowing how and why this happened.

PART ONE

INTRODUCTION

The Athenian historian Thucydides set himself a lofty goal in writing his history of the Peloponnesian War of 431–404 BC. His work was not to be a means of entertainment. 'This is a possession for all time,' he wrote, 'rather than a prize piece that is read and then forgotten.' Of the war's origin between Athens and Sparta, the two great powers of the Greek world, which Thucydides traced in great detail, he said: 'The real cause, however, I consider to be the one which was formerly most kept out of sight. The growth of the power of Athens, and the alarm which this inspired in Sparta.'[1]

The war would be one of contradictions. It was fought to the point of exhaustion between Greece's two most powerful states, but the decisive contribution would be made by a non-Greek actor, Persia. It was a war fought mainly at sea and along the coastal territories of Greece and Asia Minor, but would be won by Sparta, the great land power, against Athens, which had long reigned supreme at sea before it began. It was fought for political dominance in Greece, but perhaps its most notable event would occur far away, in Sicily. The decisive, final battle of the war, a naval one, was not a proper sea battle at all, but one in which the Athenian fleet would find itself caught unprepared ashore and captured almost in its entirety.

The war itself was ruinously expensive, lasting twenty-seven years, with each state making little or no progress against the other for long periods while enduring many setbacks. Yet the combatants would find the means to continue the fighting long past the point where it would have been sensible to make peace. When a peace was made in 421 BC, it proved illusory and fighting resumed in earnest within a few years.

The extreme length and high cost of the war also made it more than just a contest between fleets and armies. It was also a contest between the resources that both coalitions were able to bring to bear to pay for their soldiers and ships. While there was room for outstanding generals to make their mark, national leaders to make ghastly errors of judgment and fine soldiers to win battles against the odds, in the end, money mattered more than any other factor.

At the beginning of the war, and for long afterward, democratic Athens was by far the richer power, the head of an alliance of mostly maritime states clustered around the Aegean. Her seaborne trade flourished, and her culture along with it. With her money she financed a massive navy that protected her trade. Sparta, by contrast, the head of the Peloponnesian League, was a dour military state, oligarchical, parochial, deeply conservative and agrarian. Her citizens engaged in only one occupation, that of the soldier, and money was difficult to come by.

Yet Sparta emerged triumphant at the end of the bloody struggle. Sparta received immense financial aid from Persia that enabled her to overcome the resources deficit she had with Athens and outlast her initially wealthier rival. Money, more than any other single resource, was the fuel of the war efforts of both sides. In this regard, Sparta would come to hold, late in the war, a nearly insuperable advantage in the form of Persian gold.

How this startling turn of events came about is the story of this book, a tale of fleets, seamen and money. It is a naval history, as the war was primarily one fought at sea and along the coasts in amphibious actions. It is a history, too, of how Athens, the brightest city in fifth-century BC Greece, came to ruin, and how culturally backward Sparta came to dominate the Hellenic world. To begin the story, we must make our acquaintance with the pre-eminent historian of the war, Thucydides, son of Olorus.

Ancient Sources

Thucydides (b. *c.* 460 BC, d. *c.* 400 BC) wrote his *History* believing that it would be a war of immense importance that deserved to be chronicled. He did not title this, or specifically call it a history, that being a designation later given to it and used in modern translations of his work.[2] It was nonetheless a history, but with the difference that it was a narrative of contemporary events, not one of tales culled from the distant past. He began his narrative not long after the war began in 431, and he was an active participant in the conflict from its beginning until his exile from Athens in 424 after his failure to prevent the capture of Amphipolis by the extremely capable Spartan officer Brasidas. He was not to return home for twenty years. His involvement included not just holding a major military command. He was also afflicted by the deadly plague that struck Athens between 430 and 427, but was lucky enough to survive, unlike so many thousands of his fellow countrymen.

Thucydides' *History*, in eight books, remained unfinished when he died sometime around 400. The story of the war is taken down only until the winter of 411, and it breaks off in the middle of his narrative in the eighth book. He clearly knew how the war ended in 404, since he included a number of comments showing that he was aware that the Athenians had been defeated in the end. It is thus certain that Thucydides was in the process of composing and editing his work when he passed away. The last book, the eighth, has been criticized for lacking in editing, and as such was almost certainly not the final draft of that part of the history as Thucydides would have intended it. There can be no doubt that Thucydides would have continued the history down to 404 had he lived, but his death ended any chance of that. He would, though, have a number of continuators.

As an incomplete work, the *History* shows signs of revisions that suggest that Thucydides might have made more had he lived longer. It is by no means a first draft, but it is certainly not a finished product as Thucydides would have wanted it, even when considering the books that were finished by the time of his death. It is nevertheless the only source that we possess for many things relating to the war, and when this is not the case, it is still the best. And it holds a special distinction in that, unlike so many histories that survive from the ancient world, the *History* dates from the period that it describes, not centuries afterward.

Thucydides' focused historical survey was, for his day, remarkable. He eschewed the broad gaze of Herodotus, whose wandering narrative contained many extraneous details and digressions, and instead set his sights on the essentials when composing his work.[3] He attempted to write a 'scientific' history, sticking to the facts as best as he could ascertain them, explaining at the outset of his work: 'With reference to the narrative of events, far from permitting myself to derive it from the first source that came to hand, I did not even trust my own impressions, but it rests partly on what I saw myself, partly on what others saw for me, the accuracy of the reports being always tried by the most severe and detailed tests possible.'[4] There is thus something of a dry (though by no means dreary) quality to the *History*, at least in comparison to those of the far more colourful Herodotus. 'The absence of romance in my history,' Thucydides acknowledged, 'will, I fear detract somewhat from its interest; but if it be judged useful by those inquirers who desire an exact knowledge of the past as an aid to the understanding of the future ... I will be content.'[5]

When it comes to the causes of the war, Thucydides divides them into two categories. There were the causes of the complaint (*aitiai*) – the controversies over the allegiance of Corcyra and Potidaea – and the real reason for the conflict (*prophasis*). The intervention of Athens at Corcyra and Potidaea stirred up grievances that gathered momentum of their own. Such grievances were often the proximate causes of wars, but as already noted, Thucydides saw the ultimate cause of the war being Athenian expansionism, and the fear it had generated among the Spartans.[6]

Thucydides was keen to allow the actors in the war to do much of the talking, and so the speech was a common and very important device in the *History*. Thucydides made wide use of speeches in the body of his narrative to explain the viewpoints of the various participants. These were not precise records of what was actually said, since such things 'in all cases [were] difficult to carry ... word for word in one's memory'. Instead, Thucydides meant them to hew as close as could be to 'the general sense of what [the speakers] really said'.[7]

It is often stated that money makes the world go around, and that was true of warfare in ancient Greece as well. The financing of military operations is a recurrent theme in Thucydides, as is his attention to naval power within the larger context of the conflict. Indeed, he begins his work with an examination of the history of naval power among the Greeks prior to the Persian Wars of the early fifth century BC. By his own day, later in the same century, Athens had by far the strongest navy; it would hold this pre-eminent position at the outset of the Peloponnesian War, and retain it for long thereafter. Athenian seapower is repeatedly noted in the historian's narrative, and their opponents, the Peloponnesians, were at a serious disadvantage in this area for a long time. They had far fewer ships, and their efforts to close the qualitative gap between themselves and the Athenians were understood by all sides to be fraught with many practical difficulties. Thucydides makes the maintenance of this edge in seapower one of the critical elements in Athenian early war strategy.

As previously mentioned, Thucydides' *History* breaks off in the year 411. Xenophon, (b. *c.* 428, d. *c.* 354 BC), a conservative Athenian gentleman-soldier, consciously took up the task of completing Thucydides' work, picking up the story more or less where Thucydides had halted. Like Thucydides, Xenophon was a military man and an exile from Athens. After the war, he would accompany Prince Cyrus of Persia on an expedition against his older brother for possession of the Persian throne. In 401, Cyrus, with the help of his Greek mercenaries, was victorious at the Battle of Cunaxa, but the prince was himself slain in the engagement, and the Greeks were left stranded deep inside the Persian Empire. After their commanders were slain through treachery by the Persian *satrap* (provincial governor) Tissaphernes, of whom we shall hear much more later in this book, it fell to Xenophon to lead them out of the empire to safety. Xenophon penned the story of this harrowing journey in the *Anabasis*, or *March Inland*, which he wrote around 379.[8]

Xenophon was a prolific author, and apart from the *Anabasis*, he wrote a work, *Cavalry Commander*, on cavalry tactics, about which he possessed extensive knowledge, as well as a book on horsemanship.[9] The *Hellenica*, his greatest work, records Greek events from 411 down to the Battle of Mantinea in 362 that ended the supremacy of Thebes. For our purposes, it is Xenophon's completion of Thucydides' history of the Peloponnesian War down to 404 that is most valuable, and he supplies the oldest extant narrative for this period. He moves much more quickly than Thucydides did in his work, and the *Hellenica* lacks the fine Attic style of its predecessor. Xenophon of course was not attempting to imitate Thucydides, merely take up where he had left off.

Like Thucydides, Xenophon was attentive to fiscal matters. In 405–404, Persian money would make possible a reconstruction of the Peloponnesian fleet after its devastating defeat at Arginusae, allowing the Spartans to achieve rapid parity with the Athenians despite their heavy prior losses. This rebuilt fleet would prove strong enough to win the decisive Battle of Aegospotami in 405, bringing the war to a close. Xenophon's work is not without its difficulties, as certain problems exist with his chronology of the period of the so-called Ionian War, representing the latter years of the broader war, and as much as possible a plausible chronology of those years has been reconstructed in the present book.

Also of great use for the later years of the war, especially as a companion to Xenophon, is the Greek historian Diodorus Siculus, who composed his *Library of History* in the first century BC. Books 12 and 13 cover the years of the war. Diodorus was in the main a compiler of the written histories authored by earlier historians, and his quality is therefore largely dependent upon the accuracy of the underlying sources that he used. It is known that he relied heavily upon the fourth-century BC historian Ephorus for much of his material. Ephorus is now lost but for fragments, and what has survived largely exists second hand in Diodorus' writings.[10]

Plutarch of Chaeronea (b. *c.* AD 50, d. *c.* 120) wrote in Greek when the Roman Empire was at its height and Greece had been subsumed within its grand imperial structure. He composed a series of biographies,

Parallel Lives, of famous Greek and Roman figures, organized in pairs of one Greek and one Roman, twenty-three pairs of which still survive. Each Greek and Roman in a pair were compared with one another. For the present work, the biographies of leading fifth-century BC Greeks such as the Athenians Themistocles, Cimon, Pericles and Alcibiades, and the Spartan Lysander, contain the most valuable information relating to the naval aspects of the Peloponnesian War.

Also of note is the anonymous work *Hellenica Oxyrhynchia*. In 1906, a lengthy papyrus fragment of a fourth-century BC history was discovered in an ancient garbage heap in the Egyptian town of Oxyrhynchus. It was followed by two further fragments of the same history later in the twentieth century. Each of the three derived from a different copy, from which it may be inferred that the work was a popular one and in wide circulation at some point in time. It was in the latter two fragments that mention of wartime events occur, including an Athenian seaborne campaign in Asia Minor in 409 and the Battle of Notium in 406, while the first fragment dealt with events subsequent to the end of the war. Like Xenophon, the Oxyrhynchus historian, tentatively identified as one Cratippus, a contemporary of Thucydides and an otherwise totally lost historian, was a continuator of Thucydides' history, and it is possible that Xenophon had his work available to him as he wrote his own history.[11]

The Athenians

Athens was an old city even in the Classical era, with an existence dating back to the Bronze Age. The city survived and prospered after the disasters that overwhelmed the earlier Mycenaean Greek civilization in the thirteenth century BC. Human habitation of Athens was never interrupted, despite the calamities that befell other cities around Greece, and the city was likely a destination for Greeks fleeing from other regions.[12] In this period, she came to dominate Attica, a triangular peninsula of about 2,500 square kilometers extending into the Aegean Sea that was geographically supportive of unification. With two sides meeting the sea, and another the mountains, there was an elementary cohesiveness to the region that made it possible for Athens in time to bring all of Attica under its control.[13] This domination was not harsh, and the population came to see themselves as part of the Athenian state even if they did not live in the city proper.

Persian advances towards the Aegean and the Hellespont in the late sixth century BC under the Great King Darius I brought the grain trade from the Black Sea to Greece under his control. He could, if he wished, cut off the flow of grain south through the Hellespont and bring about a famine at Athens, which could not feed itself solely on the produce of Attica. The population of Attica at this time was very large, perhaps 280,000, and growing.[14] Attica had little in the way of arable land, perhaps just 85,000 acres, and the soil was of poor quality. Just 10 per cent of its yield would have been wheat, with the rest being less desirable barley.[15] This made access to overseas markets critical to Athens, which was importing approximately two-thirds of its wheat from overseas at the end of the sixth century.[16]

Though Darius' expedition against the Scythian nomads of southern Russia in 512 BC had been a disaster, Persian domination of the lands on both the European and Asian sides of the Black Sea Straits was firmly established by 500. Egypt, another huge grain-producing region, was also concurrently under Persian rule, and this gave the Great King the ability to shut down much of the food supply of the eastern Mediterranean.[17]

Beyond the physical control of access to these markets, the Great King had one other tremendous advantage, and that was a monopoly on the supply of gold in the ancient world, with most of the metal being locked up in his treasure vaults. If it came down to a contest at auction for the wheat of southern Russia, his agents could outbid the Greeks with gold, which was always preferred as payment.[18]

The Persian Invasions

The origin of Athens as a great seapower may be traced to the Persian invasions of the early fifth century BC. Athens had incurred the ire of the Persian king Darius the Great because it had aided the Ionian Greek cities of Asia Minor in their rebellion against Persia in the 490s BC. One terrible crime committed by the Ionians was the burning of Sardis, the capital of the satrapy of Lydia. Among the many buildings that were torched was a temple to Cybele, and avenging this sacrilege would form a pretext in which Greek sanctuaries would similarly be burned during the later invasions of Greece.[19] When Darius was informed of the destruction of Sardis, and by whom it had been done, he already knew of the Ionian Greeks, and set them aside, since he was certain that they would be punished for their rebellion soon enough. But he did not know of the Athenians, and had to be told who they were. Herodotus says that Darius next asked for a bow, and launched an arrow skyward. While in flight, he uttered a prayer. 'Zeus,' he said, 'let it be granted to me to punish the Athenians.' To prevent himself from forgetting this wish, he designated a servant to repeat to him three times at every dinner the following words: 'My lord, remember the Athenians.'[20]

The first Persian invasion in 490 was repulsed, with the Athenians gaining a famous victory at Marathon. Darius died before he could try again, and the task of punishing Athens was left to his son, Xerxes. It was in the late spring of 480 that an enormous Persian army of perhaps 100,000 soldiers crossed the Hellespont along a bridge specially built for its passage.[21] Accompanying them was a massive fleet of some 1,207 triremes, plus thousands more lighter ships and transports, as reported by Herodotus, though it should be borne in mind that modern scholarship gives a much lower but still indefinite estimate.[22] Fortunately for the Greeks, they had the triremes already in hand with which to defend themselves from this naval assault.

Plutarch writes that it was Themistocles who had laid the foundation for the mighty Athenian navy. Prior to the second war with Persia, 'he was the only man who had the courage to come before the people and propose that the revenue from the silver mines at Laurium, which the Athenians had the habit of dividing among themselves, should be set aside and the money used to build triremes for the war against Aegina.'[23] In 484–483, the revenue derived from the state-owned Laurium mines was especially handsome, some 100 talents, or 600,000 *drachmae*. Two hundred triremes were constructed with this fund, Herodotus says, and he noted that these ships, made for one war, were ready to be used 'for the benefit of all Hellas' against the Persians.[24]

Constructing so many ships to be ready to face a renewed Persian assault required large amounts of materials such as pitch, tar and especially timber. Some of this wood could have been found in the Attic hinterland, but overland transport of big logs would have been very difficult. Macedonia, to the north, was the prime source of shipbuilding timber, where it seems that the forests were nearer to rivers or the seacoasts than were those of Attica. Its tall fir trees made excellent masts. Once the materials were to hand, there was still the enormous task of organizing the building endeavour. Shipbuilding facilities and dockyards had to be built as well. Piraeus became the site of the fleet's dedicated harbours. The wood collected would have had to be cut to size and shaped for assembly. The workers themselves had to be taught how to make the hulls, the ropes, the rowing benches and decks. To lure foreign workers to Athens, Themistocles granted them freedom from taxation. When built, the ships would have been inert if they lacked oarsmen to propel them, and these men had to be trained too.[25]

The creation of a large navy by Athens had the effect, Plutarch says, of setting them on the road to becoming a naval people, turning them 'from steadfast hoplites into sea-tossed mariners'.[26] It was also said that Themistocles, by so doing, 'had deprived the Athenians of the spear and the shield and degraded them to the rowing bench and the oar'.[27] Though the Athenians might have become wedded to the oar, the adoption of a strong naval policy, under the influence of Themistocles, was to augment the political power of the commoners relative to the aristocracy, with Plutarch writing that 'control of policy now passed into the hands of sailors and boatswains and pilots'.[28] This would not be to the liking of the anti-democratic rich, who saw themselves eclipsed by the commoners. The Thirty Tyrants who came to rule Athens after its defeat in 404 believed that 'Athens' naval empire had proved to be the mother of democracy', which they detested.[29]

The transition to a fleet-supported empire had indeed shifted power towards the commoners. Democracy in Athens had its basis in the predominance of hoplite infantry in its army. The hoplite panoply of a bronze cuirass, greaves and helmet, long spear and large round shield had spread across the Greek world around 700 BC. Previously, during the years of the Dark Ages after the fall of Mycenae, military gear had been extremely expensive, and available only to the very wealthy, who formed a tiny military aristocracy supported by their retinues. The hoplite panoply was significantly less expensive, and came within the financial reach of a much larger segment of society, its propertied farmers. Greek armies were thereafter composed mainly of hoplite-style heavy infantry, who had demanded and received a bigger say on how they were governed.

Aristocrats, who typically served as cavalry, and farmers, who fought on foot, were generally more conservative in outlook than the fleet's crewmen.[30] They had something, property, to protect. The *thetes*, in contrast, the lowest social class of Athens and that from which the bulk of the rowers were drawn, had little or no land of their own, and thus little to lose when war came. Instead, they might profit a bit, earning money for their service aboard the state's triremes. Since they had no farms to tend, they could more readily serve away from home on long campaigns.[31] This paved the way for what we today might call popular, even radical, democracy. Long after the Persian Wars, in 462–61, the Areopagus, the ancient aristocratic council that had long been a leading part of Athens' government, was demoted, and the popular Assembly gained vastly in power. The Council of 500 took the place of the Areopagus, but it was subservient to the Assembly, before which it was required to put all motions that had been presented to it. Decision-making in Athens was now in the hands of the broad mass of citizens in the Assembly, where 'the man from the lowest bench of oars' held sway.[32]

As Athens became navalized the franchise was extended to unpropertied men needed to serve as rowers. Aristotle would unflatteringly label them the 'naval mob', and would write that Pericles' push for increased naval power enhanced the political strength of the common people, as sufficient oarsmen for the ships could only be found among the city's less affluent citizens.[33] For Thucydides, the linkage between navy and democracy was very similar. A seaborne empire required a strong navy, and a strong navy required oarsmen. Such men would insist upon and uphold the democracy.[34] When the democracy in Athens was overthrown briefly in 411, the oarsmen of the fleet based across the Aegean at Samos would refuse to be reconciled to the new, oligarchic government, and the fleet became essentially a government in exile until the democracy was restored.

Artemisium

The Greeks were terribly outnumbered by the Persians on land and at sea, but Themistocles persuaded the combined Greek fleet to resist. At Artemisium, a channel lying between the island of Sciathus and Magnesia, the allied Greek fleet of 271 triremes – 127 of them Athenian – met a Persian force many times its number. For political reasons, overall command of the fleet was given to Eurybiades, a Spartan, and not to an Athenian, despite the Athenian contingent being the largest of all. The Persians happily encircled the smaller Greek fleet, which adopted an all-around defence, or *kyklos* formation, and fought hard until the coming of darkness. On the second day, fifty-three additional triremes arrived from Attica to reinforce the Greeks, and together they attacked the Persians and sank some ships.[35]

On the third day, the Persians made the first move to attack, but their large numbers proved a hindrance, with their triremes colliding with one another in the ship-clogged waters. The battle was not decisive, with no clear winner or loser, though the Persians lost more ships than did the Greeks, and both sides retired to lick their wounds. Of the Athenian ships involved, half had been crippled in the battle. Of the combatants, the Athenians had done best among the Greeks, while the Egyptians, serving as part of the Persian fleet (which was itself a multinational assemblage drawn from the maritime satrapies of the empire) were the first among Xerxes' seamen, having captured five Greek triremes together with their crews.[36] Interestingly, the Egyptians were reported by Herodotus to have been heavily armed and armoured; wielding axes, large knives and shields, and clad in breastplates, they were true heavy infantry and comparable in many respects to the Greek hoplite in his bronze panoply.[37]

Once the pass at Thermopylae had fallen at about the same time as the engagement at Artemisium, the Greek fleet withdrew to Salamis, an island nearby to Athens to which the city's population was evacuated. Left largely undefended, Athens was taken by the Persians, who set alight the Acropolis. The Spartans and other Greek contingents wished to withdraw in the face of the gargantuan enemy fleet and fortify the Isthmus of Corinth, and there defend the Peloponnesus by fighting a sea battle there. Themistocles persuaded Eurybiades and the other Greeks to remain and fight a naval battle at Salamis. The strait lying between the island and the mainland was narrow, and would constrict the Persian approach and go a long way toward negating their numerical advantage.[38] With the Greek fleet gathered together in a mass, Salamis was their best chance to defeat the Persians. Had they withdrawn to fight at the Peloponnesus, Themistocles had warned Eurybiades, the various contingents of the Greeks would each go back to their own cities and the united fleet would be a memory. He even threatened to abandon Greece altogether, put the Athenian people onboard ships and sail off to southern Italy to establish a new home there at Siris.[39] Eurybiades, understanding that the loss of the 180 triremes that the Athenians contributed to the fleet would have doomed the defence of Greece, relented and agreed to fight.

At Salamis, a Greek fleet of 380 triremes met the Persian fleet, which entered the strait, thereby sacrificing its advantage in numbers. What ensued was a seaborne brawl, with the Greeks fighting 'in disciplined order' and the Persians failing to 'hold their positions'. The Persian seamen fought hard, knowing that they were doing so under the eyes of Xerxes himself onshore, but the tactical coordination of the fleet itself was non-existent, and Herodotus writes that it 'made no moves that might have followed a sensible plan'.[40] There was simply not enough room, once they had entered the channel to attack the Greeks, for them, especially the talented Phoenician mariners, to enact their manoeuvres. Just trying to conduct a manoeuvre to attack the side or rear of a Greek trireme would have led to it becoming fouled with a friendly warship. In such a confined space, the Persians had sacrificed their advantages of speed and manoeuvrability to get to grips with the Greeks, who generally employed triremes that were heavier and stouter than the swift Phoenician ships.[41]

The result was a clear-cut Greek victory, and though Herodotus does not tell us losses for either side, Diodorus reports that the Persians lost 200 ships while the Greeks lost just forty.[42] But the battle, however much it went in favour of the Greeks, had not ended the war. The enemy had not been destroyed completely, the Greeks understood, and they readied themselves for another Persian attack.[43] Greek victories would follow at the Battle of Plataea in 479, and the Persian fleet would be crushed when caught ashore at Mycale later the same year. But the importance of Salamis was that the Greek triumph there preserved Hellenic civilization in Greece, and made possible the rise of the imperial democracy of Athens.[44]

The Birth of the Athenian Empire

Athens had been put to the torch by the retreating Persians. Its people began to rebuild, but the Persians, though temporarily defeated, were still present elsewhere in and around Greece, and remained a danger. To the Ionians of western Asia Minor, who looked to Athens as their mother city, the Persian War was ongoing. The combined Greek fleet was now under the command of Pausanias, a Spartan officer, and in 478 BC he led his ships against Persian possessions in Cyprus, Asia Minor and Byzantium. Though successful in his conduct of the war, Pausanias alienated the allied Greeks through his imperious style. Having seen how the Persians behaved, and liking what he had seen, he began to behave as a despotic Persian, at least in the eyes of other Greeks. This they could not abide, and they sought a reformed alliance with their Athenian relatives in the lead. Pausanias was recalled by Sparta after being accused of misconduct and medism (treasonous collusion with the Persians), and replacement Spartan officers were sent out to take command of the fleet. These men were rejected by the other Greeks, and the Spartans were happy to be finished with the anti-Persian alliance, which had become a constant headache for them.[45] This was in large part due to the corrupting influence that outside contact was having on the Spartans themselves. 'They feared for those who went out a deterioration similar to that observable in Pausanias,' Thucydides states, and 'besides, they desired to be rid of the war against the Persians, and were satisfied of the competency of the Athenians for the position, and of their friendship at the time toward themselves.'[46] The Spartans were endlessly worried that the Helots of Laconia and Messenia might revolt, and the security of the home territory in the Peloponnesus was its overriding concern, not the Greeks of Asia Minor.[47] Sparta was itself an isolationist power, ultraconservative and uneager to have much in the way of interaction with the outside world. The war, one now fought mainly at sea, interested them very little. Athens could have the alliance if she wanted it, along with its problems, and Sparta bid a less than fond farewell to the troublesome Greeks of the Aegean.

With the Spartans gone, along with the other Peloponnesians, the remaining Greeks needed the Athenians to take the lead in the continuing military effort against Persia. Athens was granted the *hegemonia*, or hegemony, of the allies. A congress was held on the island of Delos, and a new alliance was formed with the League treasury held there.[48] The purpose of the Delian League, as agreed upon by the members of the congress, was to 'retaliate for their sufferings by ravaging the [Persian] King's country'.[49] Though initially welcome, warm feelings toward the Athenians were not to last. The Athenians set about assessing their allies as to what contributions they would make, either in the form of money or in ships. To receive the incoming aid of the League, the office of 'Treasurers of Hellas' was opened at Athens, with the first intake of tribute, as the monetary contributions were dubbed, totalling 460 talents. By the start of the Peloponnesian War in 431, the tribute due from the allies would increase to 600 talents.

Thucydides believed that the other allies were autonomous of Athens at first, but that the supremacy of Athens increased as time passed. He advanced three reasons for this growth in Athenian power over the other League states, writing that it resulted from Athenian actions taken against the Persians; those taken against defecting allies; and those against the Peloponnesians following the formation of the new alliance. During the years 476–467, the archon Cimon led an attack on Eion, on the Strymon River, and seized it from the Persians. The island of Scyros was taken from its inhabitants and colonized by the Athenians. Carystus in Euboea was defeated and surrendered. Around 476, the island of Naxos attempted to escape from the League, was besieged, and brought back in by force, this being the first time that an allied state was treated in this way, creating a precedent in which members would be dragged back into the League by military action.[50]

Cimon was especially aggressive in taking the offensive against the Persians, and Plutarch credits him with ejecting them from Asia Minor 'from Ionia to Pamphylia'. His ships he had inherited from Themistocles' old building programme, and though these were capable, Plutarch says, in terms of their speed and manoeuvrability, Cimon widened them in the beam and built gangways that ran from fore to aft so as to allow the large complement of marines he embarked to fight more easily aboard the ship.[51] In 467, Cimon led a League fleet against the Persians at the Eurymedon River and defeated them in a pair of land and sea engagements. The Persian fleet was comprised of 200 warships, all of which were either captured or destroyed by Cimon's fleet.[52]

Cimon then defeated the Persian army ashore, and learning that a Phoenician reinforcement fleet was stopped at Syedra on its way to link up with the recently defeated Persian ships, intercepted it there. He took it by surprise, destroying the entirety of the Phoenician fleet and killing most of its crews. After this grievous defeat, the Great King agreed to make peace, with the terms including that he would keep his forces a full day's ride away from the coast of Asia Minor and that he would not sail any of his warships west of the Cyanaean and Chelidonian Islands.[53] The peace agreement, negotiated in 449 by Cimon's son-in-law Callias, was not a formal treaty, as the haughty Persians would never agree to such a thing, but it was a durable peace nonetheless. The Great King would remain the formal overlord of the Greek cities of Asia Minor, but the flow of tribute that normally would have found its way to his coffers came to a halt.[54]

The place of Athens in the League went quickly from being that of foremost member to being its domineering overlord. 'Of all the causes of defection,' Thucydides writes, 'that connected by arrears of tribute and vessels, and with failure of service, was the chief, for the Athenians were very severe and exacting, and made themselves offensive by applying the screw of necessity to men who were not used to and in fact not disposed for any continuous labour. In some other respects the Athenians were not the popular rulers they had been at first; and if they had more than their fair share of service, it was correspondingly easy for them to reduce any other state that tried to leave the confederacy. For this the allies had themselves to blame; their wish to get off service making most of them arrange to pay their share of the expense in money instead of ships, and so to avoid having to leave their homes. Thus while Athens was increasing her navy with the funds which they contributed, a revolt always found them without resources or the requisite experience for war.'[55]

Plutarch echoes Thucydides' assessment of the allies' unwillingness to continue to take part in League military operations. 'They soon became tired of foreign expeditions,' he writes, 'for they felt they were no longer needed to fight, and only wanted to live in peace and till their lands', with the Persian menace having been extinguished. At first, the Athenians 'tried to force them into fulfilling their duties, and by penalizing the defaulters and punishing them they soon made the authority of Athens an imposition which was thoroughly disliked.' Cimon had other ideas. 'He did not bring force to bear upon any of the Greeks and he accepted money or empty ships from all those peoples who were unwilling to serve abroad. In this way he let the allies yield to the temptation of taking their ease and attending to nothing but their private affairs, until they lost all their military qualities.'[56]

Towards the Athenians, his policy was very different. '[H]e obliged a large part of the Athenian population to take turns in manning their ships and hardened them on his various expeditions, and thus in a short while, using the funds the allies had contributed, he made the Athenians the rulers of the very men who paid them.' The superior military power of Athens compared to other League states was blindingly obvious. 'Those Greeks who did no military service came to fear and even to flatter men who were regularly at sea or constantly training or under arms, and so before they knew it, they had sunk into a position of tributaries and subjects instead of allies.'[57] As Athens assumed ever greater control over the other states of the alliance, they became more akin to subject states, not even junior allies, and modern historians typically designate the League at this stage as being the 'Athenian Empire' to highlight the commanding position she enjoyed at the top of the alliance.

Athens' allies were not cowards, and a word must be said in their defence. If they may be legitimately called shirkers, then it should also be known they had some sound financial reasons to pay cash instead of sending out their own ships. The primary objective behind the formation of the Delian League, clearing Persian naval assets from the seas, had been achieved by the Battle of the Eurymedon, and continuing to deploy ships for naval service was very expensive. It is estimated that one talent would cover the cost of building and equipping a single trireme (though it must be stressed that is at best a good guess) and that at the early fifth-century BC pre-war pay rate of one-half-drachma per day, a trireme's crew of 200 men would cost an additional half-talent per month to operate. When, in 428, a squadron of ten triremes from the Lesbian city of Mytilene appeared at Piraeus, the expense of these warships to the Mytilenian treasury would have been at least five talents per month for the 2,000 crewmen aboard, and possibly ten talents if they were being compensated at the one drachma per day wartime rate that the Athenian fleet was paying at the time.

These figures are relevant when we consider what the annual tributary payments due from the allied states were during these years. The tribute lists for 430–428, though fragmentary, indicate that most states would have paid less money in tribute than it would have cost them to pay the wages of the crewmen of any naval forces that they would have contributed. A state not in the first rank of payers, such as Abdera, paid ten to fifteen talents to the treasury; Lampsacus, ten; Byzantium, fifteen or sixteen; and Cyzicus, nine. If a hypothetical squadron of ten triremes from one of these states would have cost five talents per month to operate, and we can estimate that it would have seen approximately five months or so of service each year, then the total cost to the treasury of any ally contributing ships would have been at least twenty-five talents, perhaps more if they were to be on lengthier campaigns. This also does not take into account whatever costs would have accrued in building ships or repairing damaged or worn-out vessels. To put such funding into perspective, the costs associated with the Parthenon on the Acropolis were thirty to thirty-two talents each year. While maintaining this grand temple was certainly very costly, this outlay was what the crews of just twelve triremes would have required in wages if paid at the half-drachma daily rate over the course of a single five-month sailing season. With the Persian naval menace quashed by Cimon at the Eurymedon, the 'felt threat' to the Ionians was gone, and it may be readily surmised that the allied states believed, rightly it seems, that paying Athens to handle the naval duties of safeguarding the sea made more economic sense than constructing and equipping their own ships and paying their crews.[58] It is little wonder then that by mid-century the allied states that contributed warships had dwindled to just three, and that the rest had converted their obligations into cash tribute payments.

As for the tribute they paid, it should not be supposed that Athenian tax collectors were showing up at the doors of poor Ionians and demanding money. There is no instance in the historical record of Athens levying a specific tax on the peoples of the Empire. The ancient sources are silent as to how tribute was collected inside a subject state. If what we know about the usual Greek practice concerning tax collection holds for the collection of tribute within a state, then the tribute due from a particular state was paid by the wealthy, not the commoners.[59] For common people among the allied states this was a good deal, as Athens would have brought security without requiring them to serve in person, with the bill being paid by the rich.

Aside from the transformation of the League into a tool of Athenian imperial power, the recession of the Persian threat in the Aegean would have one more effect on the League, and that was to virtually ensure that it was to be short-lived, existing only from 478–404. With no nearby external enemy to scare the Athenians, the League/Empire as an organization would be run mainly for the benefit of Athens, not for the good of all of her allies. The Athenians in effect made themselves into a naval warrior aristocracy supported by the monetary contributions of the subject peoples of the alliance. Though the dominion exerted by the Athenians over their subjects was nowhere near as harsh as that of the Spartans towards their oppressed Helots, Athens' allies would try time and again to be rid of imperial control. This desire to escape was a significant reason for Athens' defeat in the Peloponnesian War and the loss of the Empire.[60]

It is easy to imagine that, had the frontier between Athens and the Persians stabilized somewhere closer to Athens, perhaps in Macedonia, rather than inside Asia Minor, the sense of imminent threat to the Athenians and her Aegean allies would have bound them more tightly together and engendered a sense of common cause and belonging. In such a case, the Athenian Empire would have been perceived as the great protector of all and welcome, and have potentially lasted far longer.[61]

The Figure of Pericles

To its archon and leading citizen, Pericles, son of Xanthippus, Athens owed the golden age of its imperial democracy as well as the coming of the war that ended it. Pericles was an extremely careful general. 'In his military operations,' Plutarch writes, 'he was renowned above all for his wariness. He never willingly engaged in a battle which involved much danger or uncertainty, nor did he envy or follow the example of those commanders who have gained a reputation as great generals by running risks or trusting to exceptional luck; indeed he often used to say to his fellow-citizens that, so far as it depended on him, they could count themselves immortals and go on living for ever.'[62]

It would be a mistake if Pericles should be judged unaggressive or timid. He was at heart a general who calculated his chances very closely and avoided needless risks. Plutarch compares his caution to that of the far less circumspect Athenian general, Tolnides, who led an invasion of Boeotia in 447 BC. Pericles had warned both Tolnides and the Athenian Assembly against going, but could not persuade the

Assembly to prevent Tolnides from departing with his army. Tolnides marched off to his defeat at Coronea, and Pericles, by his correct, if unheeded, appraisal of the danger, gained esteem in the eyes of his countrymen for his foresight and prudence. When Pericles did venture out at the head of the fleet, he had thought through the strategic goals that he was intent on achieving. His campaign in Chersonese in 447 drew praise from Plutarch, who noted with approval that Pericles settled 1,000 Athenian colonists in the area to stiffen the resistance to Thracian incursions and built a fortification across the neck of the isthmus to shut them out. His naval expedition around the Peloponnesus in 453 was a *tour de force* that impressed many Greeks. At the head of 100 triremes, he made descents all along the coast, ravaging the territory all about, as well as undertaking inland raids that caused the Peloponnesians to shut themselves up inside their walled cities when the Athenians approached. Only the men of Sicyon were willing to give battle, and these Pericles smashed at Nemea the same year. After this, Pericles brought his fleet north into the Corinthian Gulf, where he laid waste to Acarnania. 'Throughout this expedition,' Plutarch says, 'he had proved himself a terror to the enemy and at the same time a prudent yet vigorous leader of his fellow citizens, for nothing went wrong, even by accident, from beginning to end of the operation for the men who took part in them.'[63]

Pericles by inclination and experience was the sure hand at the tiller of the Athenian ship of state. He resisted the desires of some other Athenians who, drunk on past success, thought now of reconquering Egypt and launching attacks on the coastal satrapies of the Persian Empire. Others spoke recklessly of taking Sicily, or perhaps Carthage, or Etruria in Italy.[64] Pericles would have none of this dangerous talk, believing that the primary goal of Athenian foreign policy was to restrain and counterbalance Spartan ambitions in Greece. Athenian power therefore had to be focused on Greece and protecting its holdings there, not dissipated in quixotic ventures to distant lands.[65]

League tribute was used by Pericles for other things besides defensive military purposes as originally envisioned by the League. Pericles' own programme of civic construction was, Plutarch says, a source of 'the greatest pleasure to the people of Athens'. His political opponents took a dimmer view, chiding him in the Assembly by saying that he had dishonoured Athens by moving the League treasury in 454 from Delos to Athens. The other Greeks, they said, would be outraged to see that money that had been extracted from them to carry on the fight against Persia was now being used for 'gilding and beautifying' Athens.[66]

Pericles answered his critics by saying that the Athenians were not required to render an account to the rest of the League as to how they spent its money. 'They do not give us a single horse, nor a soldier, nor a ship. All they supply is money,' he explained, 'and this belongs not to the people who give it, but to the people who receive it, so long as they provide the services they are paid for.' The leftover money was for Athens to use as she saw fit. 'It is no more than fair that after Athens has been equipped with all she needs to carry on the war, she should apply the surplus to public works, which, once completed, will bring her glory for all time.' Pericles thereby converted the excess League funds in his possession into a massive public works project of building and temple construction that allowed the common people of the city to receive a share of the national wealth.[67] In 449, he devoted 5,000 talents of the League's collected funds to an ambitious building programme in Athens. The navy was still to be kept up, with ten new triremes to be built each year, and the older ones maintained in battleworthy condition. The new warships were being built at only half the yearly rate as established by Themistocles in 477, and it is probable that the slowing of construction of new hulls was made possible by the conclusion of a peace treaty with Persia in 449 that brought an end to hostilities between it and Athens.[68] The reduction in naval expenditure was thus something of a 'peace dividend' for Pericles.

Threats to Athenian Power

As the head of the Delian League, and then the mistress of an empire in her own right, Athens was firmly established as a maritime power, deriving a large portion of its wealth from seaborne commerce as well as the tribute paid to it by its overseas allies. The navy linked the city with all of her imperial territories, and made it possible for her merchant ships to ply the Aegean safely and for the tribute sent by her subject allies to reach her treasury coffers. Her population had long since outgrown what could be fed solely on the produce of Attica, and she was thus reliant upon grain imported from the farms of the Black Sea region to make up the deficit. With the Hellespont open to Athens since the defeat of the Persians, the Black Sea was one of the four major grain-growing areas producing food for the Mediterranean lands, and as a practical matter it was the only one upon which the Athenians could reasonably rely for the importation of food. North Africa was firmly under Carthaginian control, and Egypt was part of the Persian Empire. Southern Italy and Sicily were potential sources of grain, but they were distant and strongly influenced by the antagonistic Peloponnesian Greeks. Food would have to be sought somewhere else, as the Athenians' strategic calculation was that Athens' security depended upon *not* depending on food supplies from Attica, which was vulnerable to land invasion at any time. As long as food could be brought in from somewhere else, namely the Black Sea, Athens would effectively be an 'island' ensconced behind its Long Walls, and the only way that an enemy could harm her would be to disrupt this sea route via the Hellespont.[69] Her navy had to be potent enough to protect this vital grain lifeline northward across the Aegean to the Black Sea, which was further strengthened through the possession of naval way-stations along the route – the islands of Imbros, Lemnos and Scyros.[70]

This nautical linkage was the source of her power, in that it gave Athens access to money and food that were not available in her immediate vicinity, but it was also her Achilles heel. If the sea lanes connecting Athens with her imperial territories or the Hellespont, through which the Black Sea grain flowed, should ever be cut, Athens might starve. She would also be deprived of the tribute that was used to pay for the triremes that upheld her nautical supremacy. In this regard, Athens was a fragile colossus, immensely powerful but subject to severe shock if the foremost support of her empire, her navy, should ever fail. If the naval strength of Athens ever waned, it was possible, even probable, that unhappy members of the League might seek to escape from her unwanted embrace and go their own way. If such a thing occurred, and one member defected successfully, then not only would she be deprived of whatever funds (or even ships) that state paid to Athens, its example might well encourage others to try the same thing, leading to a snowball effect in which others would fall away, resulting in an imperial collapse.

Athens' hold over her subject empire was enhanced by the planting of cleruchies of Athenian settlers on the territory of allied states. These were not colonies in the formal sense, but settlements of Athenian citizens, who remained such, among the people of the allies.[71] Plutarch says that these, together with genuine colonies, 'relieved the city of a large number of idlers and agitators, raised the standards of the poorer classes, and, by installing garrisons among the allies, implanted at the same time a healthy fear of rebellion'.[72] The empire was thereby shored up by Athenians on the ground even as Athens rid herself of her less than desirable elements. To enhance the security of the mother city, Athens would be given her own form of protection – walls.

Fortifying Athens

Athens, like almost all major port cities, was vulnerable to landward attack. Her enemies were well aware of her weaknesses, and the occupation of Athens would have defeated her powerful navy just as effectively as if it had been beaten in an engagement at sea. The fortification of Athens was thus of immense importance. The city was surrounded by a 6.5km circuit wall begun in 478 BC. This was the doing of Themistocles, enclosing all public and private dwellings in and around the Acropolis.[73] The Acropolis was the heart of Athens, the site of its most sacred civic structures. Athens had grown up first on the Acropolis, which is well inland, Thucydides noted, 'away from the sea' for protection against piratical raids.[74] Being so far from the water presented a problem, in that Athens needed a port where ships could dock and unload their cargoes. This was handled at Piraeus, lying about 6km to the southwest, at which were found the three harbours of Kantharos, Zea and Munychia.[75]

In these harbours the seaborne trade of the Mediterranean made its way into Athens. Piraeus itself was fortified by a circuit wall, but there was much open space between the two cities that was subject to attack. Any people or goods moving between Piraeus and Athens could be intercepted, and a hostile force, should it be strong enough, could in theory cut off Athens entirely from the sea. Thucydides says that the fortification of Piraeus was begun by Themistocles, in his time as archon, who saw this undertaking as the beginning of Athens' bid for seapower: 'For he ventured to tell [the Athenians] to stick to the sea and forthwith began to lay the foundations of the empire.'[76]

Additional fortifications would be needed. Plutarch credits Cimon with beginning the construction, probably around 457, of the Long Walls, called 'the Legs', between Athens and the sea, paying for it out of his own pocket.[77] The initial walls, two in number, ran from the city to the sea. One of them terminated at Piraeus, while the other stretched to Phaleron on the eastern side of Phaleron Bay. A third wall was later added, running parallel with the one connecting Piraeus at a distance of 180 metres. The space between them was enough to accommodate a road.[78]

These structures were to have a profound impact on the Athenian way of war. Their strength must be understood as arising not only out of their physical size, but also out of the ineffectiveness of Greek siege techniques in the fifth century BC. Cities protected by walls were very difficult to capture, and behind its own fortifications, especially once the Long Walls had risen, Athens was virtually unconquerable by a land army so long as her seaborne connection to the rest of her empire, maintained by her formidable navy, was uncut. Given the well-understood advantage of defence over offence in siege warfare of this era, peace terms typically included a provision that the defeated, surrendering city tear down its walls, as this would leave it for all intents and purposes defenceless against attack. For the Athenians, insisting on the tearing down of walls of subject cities meant that it was subsequently easier to bring a defecting allied state back into line because it could not withstand their hoplites once the fleet had landed them outside a city. An ally might even be compelled to raze its walls, as Chios was forced to do with its own new wall in 425/4, on the mere suspicion that it had been planning a revolt against Athens.[79]

Sparta: Fearful Giant

In a work about naval warfare, the army-oriented Spartans are bound to get less attention as a 'background' subject. Nevertheless, it is worthwhile to delve into the history of the Spartans and examine them, as their culture and mindset would be of great importance to the conduct of the Peloponnesian War at sea. If it may be fairly said that all nations and peoples contain contradictions, it is especially true of the Spartans. Famous for their hoplites and their military way of life, the Spartans were not nearly as bellicose as might be presumed. Though Spartan society was geared toward producing excellent soldiers, the Spartans themselves were never in a rush to war, and were certainly less eager to take part in wars than many other Greek states. Sparta may have had capable warriors, but she was not very willing to send them off to battle in the shallow belief that fighting was simply what soldiers did. Sparta was a nation in which the military figured very strongly, but it was not a particularly militaristic state. The Spartan military system was oriented towards achieving victory in war. The army and its interests, however, were not ends in themselves, but instruments to be utilized for the purpose of defending the state.[80] In this regard, I do not mean to split hairs as to the difference between a military state and militarism as an ideology. In modern times, the concept of 'militarism' comes freighted with connotations that are not necessarily applicable to the ancient world.

Notwithstanding this, the entirety of their society was placed on a war footing, and the citizens were organized along military lines. All males were subject to and part of the *agoge*, a harsh public training and education regimen without parallel in other Greek states. At birth, a Spartan infant was inspected by the authorities, who ordered weak babes thrown off a cliff. Boys were taken out of their parents' custody, and each youngster became a member of a squad, which was itself a component of an *ila*, or troop. At the age of 20, Spartan youths entered communal messes, a place of awful food and endless military service to the state. At 30, these men, who had no other profession besides war, were allowed to enter the *apella*, or Assembly.[81]

Sparta's government featured checks and balances. At the apex stood two hereditary kings, who traced their descent from Heracles through the Agiad and Eurypontid families. The powers of the kings were in the main military in nature. The presence of two kings meant that one could act as a check upon the other. Beneath the kings were the *ephors* (overseers), a group of five annually elected magistrates with wide powers who dealt with much of the day-to-day affairs of the citizenry. The Council of Elders, or *gerousia*, was a body of thirty men aged 60 or over. The purpose of the Council was to be a voice of caution and reason in the face of the Assembly's hastier decisions.[82]

The inherent conservatism of the Spartans would find the adventurous, probing spirit of Athenians puzzling and difficult to predict or contend with during the war. The Athenians, in Thucydides' words, saw 'an enterprise unattempted as a success sacrificed'.[83] The Spartans were the temperamental opposite of the quick-to-act Athenians, but not all viewed this cautiousness as a bad thing. In his address to the Spartans on the eve of the war's outbreak, King Archidamus touched upon the main difference between them and the Athenians: 'The slowness and procrastination, the parts of our character that are most assailed by ... criticism, need not make you blush. If we undertake the war without preparation we should by hastening its commencement only delay its conclusion: further, a free and a famous city has through all time been ours. The quality which they condemn is really nothing but a wide moderation; thanks to its possession we alone do not become insolent in success and give way less than other in misfortune.'[84]

'We are both warlike and wise,' Archidamus insisted, 'and it is our sense of order that makes us so. We are warlike because self-control contains honour as a chief constituent, and honour bravery. And we are wise, because we are educated with too little learning to despise the laws, and with too severe a self-control to disobey them.'[85] One might question whether ignorance was a virtue in ensuring compliance with Sparta's ancestral laws and thus her ultimate strength as a society, but the Spartans thought so. Archidamus held up Sparta's native cautiousness as a benefit when making war: 'In practice we always base our preparations against an enemy on the assumption that his plans are good; indeed, it is right to rest our hopes not on a belief in his blunders, but on the soundness of his provisions. Nor ought we to believe that there is much difference between man and man, but to think that the superiority lies with him who is reared in the severest school.'[86]

Sparta's conservatism was so profound that even its military power was something that would be utilized only for limited ends. The Spartan army could win battles, such was the great might of its soldiers, but the purpose for which these battles were fought and won was not expansion, but the maintenance of the fifth-century BC status quo, which suited Sparta.[87]

The political-military alliance of which Sparta stood at the head, known commonly as the Peloponnesian League, was not a true alliance among all the parties involved, but instead was a coalition of multiple states (symmachy) mostly in the Peloponnesus, with each having a bilateral alliance with Sparta, not all with all. The League differed also from the Delian League/Athenian Empire, in that, as Thucydides noted, the 'policy of Sparta was not to exact tribute from her allies, but merely to exact subservience to her interests by establishing oligarchies among them'.[88]

A major problem for the Spartans was their inability to sustain over time the total number of full citizens, or Spartiates, who formed the hoplite portion of their army. Herodotus tells us that in 480 BC, at the time of the Persian invasions, the number of Spartiates stood at 8,000.[89] The decline, as can be traced in our sources, was inexorable and of long duration. In 418, the number of Spartiates stood at perhaps 3,500.[90] The close of the Peloponnesian War would not see the end of the reduction. In 394 there were about 2,500, and at the Battle of Leuctra in 371 there were just 1,500 remaining.[91] Though these figures would not represent the sum total of all the troops that Sparta could actually deploy in the field, it does reflect a constant deterioration of the numbers of men who had undertaken the rigorous military training which made the Spartan hoplite so feared in battle. For Aristotle, the failure to address this perennial manpower problem was unforgivable, as he estimated that Sparta should have been able to sustain some 30,000 hoplites and 1,500 citizen horsemen, a figure that Sparta never came close to matching.[92]

Spartan training was of a kind that was matched nowhere else in Greece, where more typically hoplites were citizens called to serve from whatever other occupation they practised, as was the case at Athens. In Sparta, citizens had only one job, and that was to be a soldier. Yet the manpower problems that Sparta continually experienced caused it to recruit non-citizens into the army on an ever-greater basis. From the time of the wars with Persia, half or more of Sparta's hoplites were non-Spartiate *perioikoi*. *Perioikoi* came from the subject Peloponnesian communities nearby to Sparta, lacking the rights of a full citizen, but not deemed to be lower-ranked Helots. Even Helots were made to serve in the Spartan army on an increasing basis in exchange for their freedom and less than full rights. They would be specifically recruited for service during the Peloponnesian War.[93]

Sparta's naval resources at the outset of the war were minimal, as she was concerned only with dominating the land. The bulk of the Peloponnesian fleet of 100 triremes was Corinthian, having been constructed to fight the war with Corcyra.[94] The Spartans, and the Peloponnesians more broadly, could not compare in either trained crews or existing naval infrastructure, such as the harbourworks and dockyards of Piraeus, which the Athenians had developed over the decades since the Persian Wars. Perhaps most importantly, the Peloponnesians lacked the heritage of victory and the confidence that extensive success brings with it. Ships for their fleet would have to be constructed by the allied states, if they were to take on those of the Athenians, and oarsmen would have to be hired from around Greece to man them.

The physical appearance of the city of Sparta was unimpressive, and nowhere near to that of Athens once Pericles' building programme had made it magnificent. Likening it to Mycenae, the capital of Agamemnon, Thucydides noted that no one now would disagree with the assessments given of its strength by 'poets and by tradition of the magnitude of its armament', even though in Thucydides' day it was a 'small place' and other surviving cities of that era were also now 'comparatively insignificant'. Similarly, he hypothesized, 'if Sparta were to become desolate, and only the temples and the foundations of the public buildings were left, that as time went on there would be a strong disposition with posterity to refuse to accept her fame as a true exponent of her power'. This would of course have been a wildly incorrect judgment. Sparta 'occupied two-fifths of the Peloponnesus and led the whole, not to speak of their numerous allies outside'. The power of the Spartans lay in themselves, not their buildings. '[A]s the city is neither built in a compact form nor adorned with magnificent temples and public edifices, but composed of villages after the fashion of old Hellas, there would be an impression of inadequacy.

Whereas, if Athens were to suffer the same misfortune, I suppose that any inference from the appearance presented to the eye would make her power to have been twice as great as it is.'[95]

The Helots themselves were mainly of pre-Dorian ethnic origin, with most being descended from the Messenians conquered in the late eighth century BC. All of the Greek states condoned slavery, and there were other Helot-like peoples elsewhere in Greece outside of Sparta. What made the Helots different from ordinary slaves is that the owner of the Helots was the Spartan state itself, not individual Spartans. Spartan citizens, the *homoioi* (Equals), made use of the Helots because they came attached to the land that the state distributed to each Equal, and in this were more akin to serfs than slaves.[96] The Helots paid rent to their Spartan masters while living in their own communities. The underlying purpose of 'helotage' was to provide a steady stream of income to the Spartan citizens, who would be freed from the burden of farming the land themselves and thereby enabled to devote themselves to military training full-time.

The use of unfree Helot labour may have allowed the Spartans to become the premier warriors in the Greek world, but the policy towards the Helots trapped them in a never-ending struggle to ensure their suppression. The Spartans suffered in no small measure from paranoia concerning a Helot uprising. Paranoia may in fact be too strong a word, for the Helots genuinely hated their Spartan overlords, to whom they were compelled to turn over one half of their crop. The threat of a Helot rebellion was very real. Helots appear to have outnumbered Spartan citizens by about six to one.[97] By imprisoning the Helots, the Spartans had in a deeper sense also imprisoned themselves in the role of detested masters. Sparta would, until the Messenians gained their freedom after the Battle of Leuctra in 371, be consumed by the need to hold down the Helots of the southern Peloponnesus.[98]

The First Peloponnesian War

Modern historians call the conflict that lasted from 461–446 BC the First Peloponnesian War, to distinguish the periodic fighting from the later, and much larger, conflict that is known more commonly as *the* Peloponnesian War. It was not primarily a war between Athens and Sparta, as was the case in the second war. In the first conflict, Sparta was in the main at war with her bitter Peloponnesian enemy Argos, to which Athens was allied, while for Athens her main enemy was Corinth, her maritime and commercial rival.[99] In 466, the island of Thasos rebelled against Athens, and the Athenians took on the Thasian fleet, won the encounter and landed troops on the island. The causes of the revolt were at base economic in nature. The Thasians and Athenians were in disagreement about markets in Thrace and a Thasian-controlled mine. The Thasians made an appeal to Sparta for aid and the Spartans agreed to give it, but there was an earthquake in the Peloponnesus. A secession crisis soon flared among the oppressed Helots, as well as the Thuriats and Aethaeans of the *perioikoi*, who decamped to Ithome where they made a stronghold. With no help coming from Sparta, the Thasians surrendered in the third year of the Athenian siege under terms in which they tore down their walls, turned over their warships, paid their tribute arrears and agreed to pay tribute in the future. They also relinquished their mainland holdings and the mine.[100]

Relations between Sparta and Athens, outwardly cordial to this point, soured not long afterward. In 462, the Spartans were having difficulty rooting out the Helot rebels in their stronghold at Ithome. They called on their allies, including, at this time, the Athenians, for help. The Athenians sent troops under Cimon. The Spartans understood very well their deficiencies in siege technique and thought that the Athenians, who had much experience in this area of military science, would be of help to them. But when a Spartan assault on Ithome came to nothing, the Spartans got cold feet about the Athenian presence in the Peloponnesus. They were anxious about the 'enterprising and revolutionary character of the Athenians', who were also of 'alien extraction'.[101] They worried that if the Athenians stayed, the rebels holed up in Ithome might persuade them to carry out some kinds of political change. Without explaining why, apart from blandly asserting that their help was not needed, the Spartans gracelessly told the Athenians, alone of all the allies present, to pack up and leave.

The Athenians saw right through this nonsense and were deeply insulted to be dismissed in so brusque a fashion. Once they had returned to Athens, they severed their alliance with Sparta that had been in effect since the Persian invasions and soon formed a new alliance with Argos, a traditional enemy of Sparta in the Peloponnesus.

The Athenian fleet in the First Peloponnesian War was used offensively to land troops along the coast of the Peloponnesus, giving Athens a strategic mobility that purely land forces could never have matched. In 460, a huge fleet of 200 triremes was sent to Egypt to lend aid to anti-Persian rebels, and in 459, the fleet made a descent upon the Peloponnesian town of Halieis and landed troops there. The land attack on Halieis was defeated by the Corinthians and Epidaurians. Not long after, a fleet action occurred, in which the Athenians overcame a Peloponnesian force off Cecryphaleia. Following this, in 458, Athens and Aegina, an island state in the Saronic Gulf, went to war and they fought a major naval battle. The Athenians were victorious, taking seventy Aeginetan triremes as prizes. The Athenians landed troops and began a siege.[102]

The Peloponnesians sent 300 hoplites to help the Aeginetans directly, while the Corinthians brought an army against Megara, thinking that the Athenians would be compelled to lift the siege of Aegina to go to the rescue of Megara. Instead, the Athenians cobbled together an army composed of the old and young men left behind in the city and marched them to the Megarid. This scratch force did battle with the Corinthians and defeated them.[103] It was around this time that construction began on the Long Walls that ran to Piraeus and Phaleron, structures that were to have a profound effect on Athenian strategy in the years to come.

The Athenians and Spartans met in battle in 457 at Tanagra in Boeotia. The casualties for both armies were heavy, but Sparta was victorious. The outcome of Tanagra highlighted for all Greeks the assumption that the Spartan hoplites were the best in all of Greece.[104] This deeply embedded notion (largely correct) would affect Athenian strategic thinking when war came again, convincing many that an open battle with the Spartans was nearly suicidal. The same year, at Oenophyta, an Athenian army defeated the Boeotians and gained control of Boeotia and Phocis. Aegina capitulated too, and by the peace terms was compelled by Athens to tear down its walls, give up its ships and pay tribute.[105]

Elsewhere, in Egypt, conditions on the ground had worsened for the Athenians. In 454, a Persian army had been despatched by King Artaxerxes to Egypt. The Egyptian rebels were defeated in battle and the Athenian garrison at Memphis was expelled. These men took refuge on the island of Prosopitis in the Nile Delta, where they were besieged for eighteen months. The Persians drained the canal lying between the island and the mainland, stranding the Greek ships which were left grounded. The Persians then launched an assault over the dry ground and captured Prosopitis. A relief flotilla comprised of fifty Athenian triremes arrived at the Nile mouth, lacking any knowledge of the reverses just suffered. The Persians fell upon them, and the fleet was attacked by Phoenician warships simultaneously. Most of the fleet was lost.[106]

The port of Nisaea, serving Megara, became an Athenian base in 457–456 when the Athenians built long walls for the Megarians stretching from Megara to Nisaea, earning themselves the deep enmity of Corinth, and emplaced a garrison there.[107] Corinthian distrust of Athens had a long pedigree. Herodotus reports that the Athenians had spread a vile rumour that the Corinthians had fled from the Persian fleet at the Battle of Salamis in 480, though he himself held that the rest of the Greeks believed that they had acquitted themselves bravely in the engagement.[108] More prosaically, Athenian merchants had grown to be fierce commercial competitors with those of Corinth for the trade of Italy and Sicily, even to the point of surpassing them. There was also the matter of the planting of the Messenian colony at Naupactus, which, sitting on the northern shore of the Corinthian Gulf, was a dire threat to Corinth's trade route leading westward out of the Gulf.[109] As a matter of strategic positioning, Athens had secured for itself naval bases near and far from which to mount attacks on the enemy. One such raid was launched out of the Athenian base at Pegae in the Corinthian Gulf in 454, under the command of Pericles. His small fleet made a descent against Sicyon, and his troops defeated the Sicyonians on land and then besieged Oeniadae in Acarnania, but they were unable to capture the place and gave up the siege.

Spartan fear of what the Athenians *might* do caused the Spartans to act in ways that were contrary to their own interests and overall security. The treaty of alliance that Athens formed with Argos soon after their rude dismissal from Ithome and the pact with the Thessalians were products of tactless Spartan blundering, and need not have happened had the Spartans shown greater sensitivity to Athenian feelings. In 451, Sparta and Athens would sign a five-year truce which would bring the warfare in Greece to an end. Though Nisaea would be evacuated in 446 as part of the formal Thirty Years' Peace treaty that ended the war, along with Pegae, Troezen and Achaea, the outline of Athens' maritime strategy was obvious. She would ring the Peloponnesus with bases from which to make raids against all points. Despite the advance warning that Athens could implement just such a strategy by both past practice and apparent inclination, the Spartans were incapable of responding with an effective counter when war came in 431.

The Samian War

In 440 BC, a war broke out between Samos and Miletus over Priene. The Samians had gained the upper hand in the conflict when Athens ordered them to stop fighting and submit their dispute for arbitration in Athens. The Samians rejected this demand, and Pericles led an expedition of forty triremes to the island. Once there, he dissolved its oligarchic government and took 100 men and boys as hostages and placed them on the island of Lemnos.[110] Some of the Samians had escaped the Athenians, and these made their way to Pissuthenes, the Persian satrap of Lydia in the city of Sardis in western Asia Minor. He agreed to provide help, and they raised a force of 700 mercenaries. With these, they returned to Samos and reclaimed it from the Athenians. Next, Byzantium on the Bosphorus joined in the revolt against Athens.[111]

Athens responded quickly, sending sixty triremes against Samos. Sixteen of these peeled off to keep a lookout in Caria for the Phoenician relief fleet said to be on its way (the Phoenicians, being outstanding mariners, provided the bulk of the ships in the Great King's navy) while the remaining forty-four under Pericles and nine other generals engaged a Samian fleet of seventy ships off Tragia. The Athenians won the battle, and once they were reinforced by forty additional ships from Athens and twenty-five others from Chios and Lesbos, the Athenians landed troops on the island and began a siege of the city of Samos.[112]

Word came that the Phoenician relief ships were approaching, and Pericles took sixty of the ships that had been blockading Samos by sea and hurried off to Caunus and Caria to meet them. Once they had gone, the Samians launched an attack on the small force left behind and defeated it before most of its ships could get off the beach. The Samians became 'masters of their own seas for fourteen days, and carried in and carried out what they please', Thucydides says. But once Pericles returned, the siege and blockade resumed in earnest. The Athenian fleet was supplemented by sixty more Athenian triremes and thirty others from Chios and Lesbos. Nine months later, in 439, the Samians capitulated. By the terms of the peace, they were to tear down their walls, turn over their ships to Athens, give hostages and pay war reparations. Byzantium also gave in, and agreed to become subject to Athens once more.[113]

PART TWO

THE TRIREME

It has been noted that the Hellespont link to the grain of the Black Sea region was of paramount importance. Access to the Black Sea by Athenian commerce had been acquired soon after the defeat of the Persian invasions, which meant that food could be brought in from the Black Sea. It was very much needed. The population of Attica had increased greatly, and by the start of the Peloponnesian War was upwards of 460,000, comprising about 250,000 citizens, 100,000 metics (resident aliens) and around 100,000 slaves.[1] Pericles himself commanded a naval expedition in 436 BC to this vital area to demonstrate the power of the Athenian fleet.[2] To enhance the skill of her oarsmen, Pericles would despatch a fleet of sixty triremes on a cruise each year. For eight months the citizen crews would serve, with pay, while they trained.[3] The need for regular practice at the oar was well-understood by the Athenians to be a prerequisite for achieving and maintaining rowing skills at a peak level of performance. Naval movements might also be undertaken in wartime not only for their strategic necessity but also out of a desire to allow the fleet to train.[4] In addition, by having the citizenry serve as rowers, Pericles was putting money into the hands of the common people even as he improved the quality of the navy by constant practice to a level unmatched elsewhere in Greece. The standard Greek warship of the fifth century BC was the trireme (meaning 'three oars' in Latin, with the Greek name being *trieres*), and an investigation of this remarkable ship is in order.

Thucydides credits Corinth as the place where the trireme was first constructed, with the Corinthians themselves being 'the first to approach the modern style of naval architecture'.[5] The fortunate siting of Corinth, on an isthmus, had contributed to the development of her commerce, and with the money that she garnered from trade she was able to acquire a navy and suppress piracy. She was then able to offer merchants markets for both land and sea commerce, and she set about accruing 'all the power which a large revenue affords'.[6]

Alternatively, the trireme may have had its origins among the Sidonians of Phoenicia. The second-century AD Christian father,

Clement of Alexandria, conveyed a possibly much older tradition that it was the Sidonians who were the first to build a three-level ship, *trikrotos naus*, similar to that of the Greek trireme. Sidonians was something of a catch-all term for Phoenicians in general, so it may have simply been that someone among the Phoenicians had begun constructing ships rowed at three levels. If so, the Phoenician possession of larger warships than the two-level, fifty-oared pentecontors standard in the Greek world of the sixth century BC may go far to explain why, despite the victory of the Phocaeans over the Carthaginians (themselves of Phoenician ancestry) at the Battle of Alalia in 539, the Phocaeans soon afterward abandoned their settlement in Corsica and withdrew to southern Italy. Their smaller bireme pentecontors were most likely not capable of standing up to the bigger ships of their opponents. Despite winning, some forty Phocaean ships were lost and another twenty were rendered unfit for service on account of damage to their bronze rams.[7]

Triremes did not become common among Greek navies until the early part of the fifth century BC, in the period immediately before the Persian Wars (490–479), with significant numbers of the new ship type being in service only with some Sicilian Greek tyrants and Corcyra.[8] It would soon become the standard warship of the Greek states. It is not hard to fathom their advantages over smaller ships, such as the pentecontor. With the addition of the third level, a trireme was much taller and would have been much more troublesome for an enemy to board. Missiles hurled from a higher vantage point would have had more force behind them too, and casting missiles at them would have been more difficult. The trireme would also have been able to deliver a more potent ramming attack than a lighter ship, and withstand the same, because of its greater mass.

Though no triremes, or even remnants of triremes, have survived, and no detailed specifications for them in ancient literature either, we can still make a good estimate of their size. The shipsheds at Zea in Piraeus, where Athenian triremes were housed when not in use, still exist. Though only the foundations of the shipsheds, which were covered slipways, have survived, it can be deduced from their dimensions what those of the triremes they were meant to contain were. The maximum dry length of the sheds is 121ft, 5in, and the width between the columns that would have separated one trireme from another is 19ft, 6in. Since a trireme would have had to fit inside, it would have been marginally smaller than these dimensions. The gradient of the shed itself was one in ten, meaning one foot of rise for every ten feet in distance. It took 140 men to pull a trireme up this slope, while 110 could drag it back down.[9] Once out of the water, the triremes could be dried out, protected from the elements, especially in winter, when the ships were not in use, and not subjected to the attack of marine organisms such as the *teredo navalis* shipworm.[10]

In northern Europe in ancient and medieval times, ships were built by means of overlapping planks. A nail or peg was then driven between the planks where they overlapped as a means of fastening one to another. Once the 'clinker-built' hull was complete, frames were added to improve structural rigidity.[11] The longships of the Vikings were made according to this method, which would predominate in Europe until the advent of the frame-first system which affixed planks only after a skeleton had first been completed.

In the ancient Mediterranean, a different method was used for the construction of the trireme. This too saw the hull of the ship created first, but the planks of the ship did not overlap. Instead they were joined edge-to-edge to create a smooth surface. The planks were joined to each other by means of mortises and tenons. An ancient shipwright began his project by first laying the keel. To this he added planks, building up the frame as he went. The mortise was a cut-out portion in the narrow edge of a plank. A tenon was a narrow wooden board that was inserted into the mortise so that half of it remained protruding from the plank. A complementary mortise on another plank was then lowered over the exposed portion of the tenon. There were small holes in both the plank where it had been mortised and the tenon, and these were filled with hardwood pegs to prevent the planks from slipping. Once this was done, the planks were firmly attached and the process was repeated with the next plank, until the hull had been fully formed.

The primary types of wood used to make the hull of a trireme galley were fir (*elate*) and pine (*peuke*). Fir was favoured in the building of triremes because of its lightness, while pine resulted in a heavier timber that found greater use in cargo ships, where speed was not crucial.[12] With the insertion of internal bracing, the galley hull was now reasonably strong, but not altogether watertight. Ancient Greek shipbuilders knew that the watertight integrity of the hull would improve once it had been in water for a while because the woods used for the planking would soak up water and swell, closing any gaps that existed between the planks. For this reason, wood that was only partially dried out was favoured, as this would absorb water well enough to make watertight joints. Completely dry wood, however, was generally not favoured, because it would not absorb water and swell to produce a watertight joint.[13]

The hulls of ancient ships were given a coat of pitch to help preserve their watertightness. Homer would often refer to ships as being 'black' and this must be because of the pitch coating. This was applied by brush, and could also be a mixture of pitch and wax.[14] A measure of water absorption was expected and even needed by a trireme in order for it to function effectively. Too much water was problematic, and would result in a waterlogged, heavy, sluggish ship. The planks drank up the water of the surrounding water very well, and would have to be periodically dried out ashore to return the ship to a high-performing condition. This was, among other reasons, why ancient fleets so often put ashore for the night, hauling their ships out of the water to allow them time to dry. Ships deteriorated quickly if they could not be removed from the water often enough.

Triremes, like all oar-propelled ancient war galleys, had very large crews relative to the size of their hulls, so there was scant space inside the ship for anything else besides the men and some meagre provisions. Food had to be obtained on land, as well as drinking water, and the men needed to sleep, something that was not an easy thing to do while aboard. Travelling at night was extremely difficult with vision so limited. Triremes were pulled ashore usually twice a day, so that the men could eat their lunches and dinners. When morning came, they would rise and take to their ships again. This made the galley a less than ideal instrument of sea control. Naval blockades were porous at the best of times. Galleys could not remain on station for long before having to retire to shore for the reasons just described. Sometimes a faster galley could simply outrun a slower one.

The main weapon of the trireme was the ship itself, and the prow was fitted with a heavy metal ram shaped to smash through the timbers of another ship. An example of the ram manufacturer's craft was discovered in 1980 in the waters off Athlit, Israel. The Athlit Ram, as it is known, was fitted over the prow timbers of a galley, and so is not made of solid metal but is instead hollow. The ram was an extraordinary technological achievement, being made of bronze cast in a single pour. It was composed of 465kg of high-grade bronze, an alloy of 90 per cent copper and 10 per cent tin. Overall, the weapon was 2.26 metres long, 0.76 metres wide and 0.96 metres high. The thickness of the artefact ranged between 7–10mm. The ship that the Athlit Ram belonged to was almost entirely decayed except for a few timbers that remained preserved within the ram itself, and so what class of ship it once adorned is unknown. However, the cross-sectional dimensions of the ram have been compared to those of the sockets found on the Actian Naval Monument erected by Octavian to commemorate his victory at Actium in 31 BC. The Athlit Ram was smaller than any of the rams that once hung on Octavian's monument. From this it can be inferred that the ship it belonged to was on the small side too, with modern scholarship suggesting that it was once fitted to the prow of a *tetreres*, or 'four'.[15] This would have been larger than a trireme, but it is still certainly comparable.

There were other insights besides. Sixteen timbers were extracted from the inside of the ram, and these demonstrated that the ram had been well-crafted to safely channel the shock of a ramming strike into the bottom timbers of its own vessel. Further, the ram was equipped with three fins on each side to prevent overpenetration during an attack, thereby allowing a safer and more effective ramming of an opponent. From an examination of markings found on the weapon, the ram was probably made on Cyprus and its ship likely served with the local fleet of the Egyptian Ptolemies there at some time in the later third/early second centuries BC.[16]

A ramming attack need not have been delivered at high speed for it to be effective. When striking at an angle, the ramming ship needed to achieve only 3–4 knots for success, while a ram delivered amidships required only 2–3 knots for effect. These speed requirements might change depending upon whether the target ships was moving toward the attacking ship, stationary or moving away from it, but the main point is clear. What made the ramming strike so devastating was not the speed of the ship but its mass. The Athlit ram's fins also allowed for a strike to succeed when delivered over a wide range of angles, cutting through longitudinal timbers of the target vessel along their grain.[17]

Surprise Ashore

The need to dry out waterlogged ships, take meals and rest ashore every evening was a necessity, but it also carried with it risks. Once a fleet had disembarked its crews and pulled its ships ashore, it was extremely vulnerable if surprised on the beach by an enemy fleet. This would occur several times during the course of the war, and was a special bane of the Athenians. For example, in Syracuse's Great Harbour in 413 BC, the Athenians, thinking that there would be no more battle for the day, decided to eat their dinners, only to be set upon by the Syracusan fleet as they ate.[18]

Getting war galleys underway in an emergency situation took some time, and a slow-to-launch fleet could find itself caught on the beach or defeated at sea piecemeal if it sailed unprepared and out of formation. A replica of an ancient Athenian trireme, the *Olympias* of the Hellenic Navy, was built in the 1980s, and drills were carried out with its modern crew in boarding and disembarking quickly. *Olympias'* crew typically went aboard with just one gangplank at the stern to reduce the strain on the hull, but depictions of boarding via two gangplanks is found on vase paintings and in ship inventories surviving from antiquity. The Hellenic Navy was able to put a complete crew aboard *Olympias* and run out the oars in just 90 seconds when using two gangplanks and moving at the double. It stands to reason that an experienced ancient crew could have done so at least as quickly. This is of import when we come later to consider why several ancient Greek fleets were either surprised ashore or slow to launch. This is almost certainly because their seamen were allowed to wander about far from their ships, as they were not expecting to do battle any time soon, and chaos reigned as thousands of men frantically sought out their ships, not because getting aboard in itself was particularly problematic.[19]

Proper reconnaissance and the employment of lookouts might seem to be an obvious answer to the threat of being taken unawares in such situations, but since galleys could not remain continuously at sea, there was always the chance of such an occurrence. Even a major port such as Piraeus, which served Athens, was not protected by a continuously-at-sea squadron of ships, and so surprise might be achieved against even the most important of shore targets.[20]

Military Harbours

The construction of military harbours distinct from the 'civilian' harbours open to merchants ships was a fifth-century BC phenomenon. At Piraeus, two lesser harbours, Zea and Munychia, and a section of the bigger commercial harbour of Kantharos, were set aside for the fleet's warships. In the latter fourth century, there were slips enough at Zea to house 196 triremes, and 82 at Munychia.[21] It is probable that the military dockyard was walled off from the rest of the city and access restricted. But the citizens of Athens would nonetheless have had cause to enter very often when serving as oarsmen in the ships. Security was a major concern, since the ships were so vital to the survival of Athens. Arson was a major crime, and in Rhodes, a subsequent naval state of importance, merely entering the yard illegally was a capital offence. Second-century BC Carthage took naval security so seriously that its military harbour was hidden behind a double wall so that it was not even visible from inside the adjacent civilian harbour.[22]

Best Triremes

Some triremes were judged better than others, or were used for different purposes. Newer ships were superior to older ships. A handful of triremes were considered to be *exairetoi* ('selects'), while others were said to be 'firsts', 'seconds', and 'thirds'. This ranking system in Athens corresponded to the speed of the trireme, with the ships in the best condition, presumably the newest, with full crews, said to be 'fast triremes'. With dried-out hull timbers they would have been lighter, and with a complete set of oarsmen would have had maximum propulsion at sea. It is probable too that the fast triremes were specifically fitted out for swift manoeuvring in battle, carrying no passengers or other unnecessary weight.[23]

Worn-Out Triremes

Triremes eventually wore out from years of service. Some were converted into troop transports. One such ship was called the *stratiotis* ('soldier ship') which could carry upwards of eighty-five soldiers. Seventy-four such *stratiodes* were used to transport a force of 6,400 troops from Corcyra to Sicily in 415 BC. Apart from these converted units, there was the troop transport known as the *hoplitogogos*. Horses were moved in an old trireme converted for the purpose, a *hippagogos*.[24] Before the war, horses were transported in whatever vessels were available, but in 430 Pericles embarked 300 horses on such ships.[25] These were, Thucydides says, 'for the first time made out of old triremes'.[26] Once the useful life of a trireme with the battlefleet had expired, it could thereby still perform some service in a role in which speed and manoeuvrability were not required.

Shipworms

Wood is an organic material, and is subject to decay which can, over time, result in a loss of strength and consequently hull integrity, so endangering the ship. It was susceptible to living creatures too. The *teredo navalis*, or shipworm, was a seaborne pest whose action could bring a ship to ruin if its crew was not careful. The teredo mollusc larvae floated around the summer seas of the Mediterranean seeking out wood. The type of wood itself did not matter, and the shipworm would latch on to anything from driftwood to the hull planking of a trireme. After attaching itself, the teredo would use its shell to drill inside, ever deeper, with its mouth affixed to the outside, where it drew in water. As the hole grew, so did the teredo, and in a month it could reach a foot in length. At that point, it would release a new batch of larvae into the surrounding waters, which then went in search of wood. Left unchecked, the teredo might bore so many holes in a ship that its hull integrity could be fatally compromised, and a ship could suffer a catastrophic break-up while at sea.[27] The dangers of shipworms were real, and preventing their infestation of a ship's hull required ceaseless inspection. It is a wonder then that a trireme, properly attended to, might survive in service for over twenty years, with one Methuselah lasting twenty-six.[28]

Tactics

War galleys had two main means of propulsion, and this would have profound significance for the tactics that were employed. The first was by the wind, and all galleys were equipped with two masts. The larger of the two was the mainmast, set at midship. The foremast was set near to the bow of the ship, and was raked slightly forward. Reliance upon wind propulsion was beneficial because it did not tire the crew. The winds of the Mediterranean were, however, often fickle, and when a ship found itself becalmed it still required a means to move itself. Oars then came into their own as they could deliver propulsion regardless of the wind. They further enabled the galley to move in any direction at any time. This was of enormous importance in battle, where the ability to manoeuvre rapidly was paramount. To save the strength of the rowers, triremes typically relied upon their sails for long distance movement, and then quickly switched to oars when battle was in the offing. Sails and masts were ordinarily taken down before battle, or even left ashore, when a confrontation was certain. Sails and masts were just useless, dead weight in a fight between galleys, and there was no reason to carry them if they could just as easily be removed.

There were two main manoeuvre tactics used by triremes during combat. The first was the *diekplous*, or breakthrough, in which a trireme would attempt to penetrate the enemy battleline, come about – which was called the *anastrophe* – and ram hostile ships in the stern. While the *diekplous* was taking place, the trireme would sometimes bring itself close enough to sideswipe an opponent and shear off its oars before turning to deliver a ramming strike. The *periplous*, or envelopment, was an attack around the flank of the enemy line. Once in the rear of the opposing fleet, the triremes would be directed against the vulnerable sterns of the enemy ships.[29]

To deliver a ramming strike, then 'back water' to pull the trireme out and repeat the process against another enemy ship, required a very high level of skill amongst the rowers of a ship. Oarsmen had to row in time with the others onboard to achieve a useful ramming speed. They also needed to be able to turn themselves around on their benches and row in the opposite direction to 'back water'. When an enemy vessel approached with the intent to smash the oars, the rowers had to be able to pull them inward lest they be snapped off.[30] To do all this proficiently required extensive training. The Athenians were willing to make the investment in their crews to allow them to achieve an impressive degree of skill at the oar. Most other Greek states paid much greater attention to their armies, and their navies rarely equalled that of Athens in tactical ability.

Ramming, as can be intuited, was one of the primary means to attack an enemy trireme. It was heavily favoured by the Athenians, who constructed their ships to be light and swift so as to be better rammers in combat. It was not the only one. The other means of fighting was to simply bring a ship into contact with the enemy and try to board. This had been the usual way that combat at sea was conducted. It was not elegant, and required very little of a ship's crew in terms of skill. Once contact with an opposing ship had been made, the soldiers aboard, whom we will call marines, would either attack or defend against enemy marines. Thucydides recounts one such engagement that occurred just before the outbreak of the Peloponnesian War. Fought between the Corcyrans and Corinthians off Sybota, he was unimpressed by the brutish way in which it was fought, lacking, as he believed, the tactical sophistication to be found in the Athenian fleet.

Shipboard Fighting

Shipboard fighting was the role of the embarked marines (*epibatai*), of which there were ten, and four archers (*toxotai*). The archers were seated while aboard the trireme, and their place, at the stern, suggests that their duty there was to protect the *trierarch* (the ship's captain) and the *kybernetes* (the helmsman). The *epibatai* fought as hoplites, armed with a spear and shield and body armour. Their place was the deck of the ship. Since the Athenians much preferred to ram and avoid boarding fights, the *epibatai* were present mainly to do battle if the trireme that carried them could not disengage. In addition to fighting, they may also have been put aboard to keep the oarsmen in line. The *epibatai* were highly regarded soldiers, drawn from men aged from 20 to 30.[31] Thucydides considered such men to be in 'the prime of life' and lamented when 120 such *epibatai*, fighting on land under the command of Demosthenes, perished in battle against the Aetolians in 426 BC.[32]

There was a sonic element to fighting at sea. With oars moving and dipping into the water, and the sound of the waves, and above all the shouts of the men themselves, hearing the commands of the captain and boatswains was difficult. Such was the confusion and panic among the Peloponnesians at Chalcis in 429 that their commands could not be heard at all, making an orderly response to the Athenian assault impossible.[33] Not long after the same battle, the Athenian admiral Phormio reminded his men to be 'sharp at catching the word of command … [and] in action think order and silence all important – qualities useful in war generally, and in naval engagements in particular'.[34] In the last days of the war, when a much-deteriorated Athenian fleet faced off against an improved Peloponnesian naval force, this superiority manifested itself in the ability of the enemy seamen to obey the orders of their admiral in complete silence.[35] Modern experiments have shown that there was little trouble in giving orders verbally in a ship as big as a trireme so long as silence in the ship was maintained.[36]

Funding a Fleet

The maintenance and operating cost of a wartime fleet was enormous, if we are to believe the numbers supplied to us by Thucydides. In 428 BC, he noted the vast size of the Athenian navy, which in the summer of the fourth year of the war stood at 250 triremes, the most that she had ever deployed at one time. He set forth the pay of the hoplite that made up the backbone of the Athenian army, who was paid one *drachma* per day, and said that the ships, meaning the crews, were all being paid the same, that is, one *drachma* per day. There were altogether 200 rowers, hoplites and sailors aboard a single trireme. There were six thousand Athenian *drachmae* to a talent. The cost to the Athenian treasury for just one month to keep that ship in service was thus an entire talent, since each member of the ship's complement would be paid one *drachma* for each of the month's thirty days. Multiplying that across the 250 warships in service, we come to the total upkeep cost of over eight talents per day for the whole of the fleet.[37] This was hugely expensive, even for a wealthy state such as Athens.

The expenses of the fleet were not borne solely by the state. Wealthy citizens were required to spend their own money to ensure that their personal triremes were properly equipped with gear, such as sails and oars, that they had complete crews and that they remained in seaworthy condition while out on campaign. It was generally the case too that the trierarch would serve in person as the captain of his trireme.[38] The financial cost to an individual citizen could be very heavy, especially if the trierarch was assiduous in recruiting full crews of the best oarsmen so as to make his ship faster and more capable. One such trierarch, on trial after the war for embezzlement, claimed to the jury that he had spent six talents (an Attic talent was some 57lb, usually of silver coins) as a trierarch with the fleet, a sum above and beyond what would have ordinarily been expected of a trierarch. It was a testament to the quality of his crews and his ships that over the course of seven years of campaigning, his trireme would be commandeered by higher-ranking generals in command of the fleet for their personal usage on at least three separate occasions.[39]

While the need to find 200 crewmen for a trireme might not sound like an insurmountable challenge for an Athenian trierarch, his efforts were hindered by competition from other captains who were recruiting from the same talent pool. Just finding full crews for thirty ships (not counting the marines in the total) would have required assembling 5,580 men, and this would likely have represented one of the largest hiring drives in the city of Athens when compared to other contemporary sectors of the economy.[40]

Though the monthly cost of keeping a trireme in service would remain the same even after many years of war, Athens' ability to pay for them would decline, resulting in serious financial problems for her.[41] Collection missions on numerous occasions had to be mounted to bring in tribute to pay for the maintenance of her fleet and the wages of her oarsmen. Not that a rower's full wage was paid all at once. In practice, it was Athens' policy to pay just half of the one drachma per day salary, or three obols, with the remainder to be paid later once the ship had returned home to Piraeus.[42] Thucydides preserves the advice given by Alcibiades to the Persian satrap Tissaphernes in 412/11 to reduce the in-hand payments to the crews of the Peloponnesian fleet in the same way, from one drachma to three obols, saying that the more experienced Athenians did this to 'prevent their seamen being corrupted by being too well off, and spoiling their fitness by spending money upon enervating indulgences'. The payments should also be made, Alcibiades said, irregularly, as this would deter desertion since the men would not depart without the money they were still owed.[43] But even with this measure, Athens found itself struggling to find money later in the war as her coffers were drained by years of fighting.

Skilled oarsmen were in high demand, and there was something of an 'international' market for them. Athens normally relied to some degree or another on hired help, mercenaries, to fully crew their triremes, even in peacetime. The enlistment of mercenaries could imply that Athenian manpower, in the form of citizens and metics, was insufficient on its own to fill the fleet's ships, especially in periods of large deployments. The Corinthian ambassadors urging the Spartans to war in 432 would note specifically that the Athenian navy relied heavily on mercenary rowers to make up its numbers.[44]

The use of mercenaries, however, could simply have been an expedient used when trained oarsmen were not readily available. Hiring men who could handle an oar would quickly put experienced men on the benches. The Athenians ordinarily numbered among their 'best ships' those that had full crews, and so mercenaries that filled out a crew would represent one straightforward method to improve the speed and handling of a trireme. Mercenaries in every age have been seen as an expedient if not inexpensive means of bulking up armed forces in a hurry, and Athens' employment of them need not have been any different. Mercenaries had clearly been enrolled in peacetime, and their use may have been a means of allowing citizens and metics to get on with their economically productive lives while war was not ongoing.

Regularly hiring mercenaries made Athens a known employer among the community of oarsmen in Greece, and it also prevented them from seeking service elsewhere with Athens' rivals. At the outset of the war, Pericles acknowledged the possibility of Athens' foreign sailors deserting her to serve in Peloponnesian ships, but dismissed it as unlikely, saying that none 'would consent to become an outlaw from his country … for the sake of a few days' high pay'.[45] This estimation runs directly counter to the Corinthian insistence at the war's beginning that the Peloponnesians might use funds borrowed from the treasuries at Delos and Olympia to hire away mercenaries from Athenian service with higher pay.[46] The Peloponnesians would in time use the lure of higher pay to entice skilled oarsmen into their service over that of Athens' fleet.

Ensuring that individual Athenian triremes were properly equipped and had full crews was the responsibility of the trierarch. The standard term of service for the trierarch was twelve months. After his term was completed, the trierarch would hand the job to his successor, and was spared further duty as a trierarch for one or two years hence.[47] The trierarchy was composed of wealthy citizens, each of whom had the obligation to perform civic *leitourgia* (liturgy) such as paying for, out of their own pockets, choruses, banquets or supervision of athletic contests. Paying for the outfitting of a trireme, recruiting its crew and commanding it on campaign was a liturgy itself.[48]

One of the foremost benefits of the trierarchy as a system was that it needed little in the way of state supervision to function effectively. The trierarchs themselves could be counted on to work out any problems that arose concerning maintenance expenses for their ships amongst themselves. An unlucky trierarch could find himself spending extra while on extended campaign, and he might demand that his successor reimburse him for his costs.[49]

Apart from the need to pay for wages accruing from extended duty or necessary repairs, there were the ordinary costs that the trierarch had to bear, and these were not negligible. Every trireme required a degree of standard equipment, and this consisted of, among other things, 200 oars (170 for rowers and thirty spares), two rudders, a mainmast, a shorter boatmast, a big sailyard, a boat sailyard, the *hypozomata* hull-girding cables, sails, ropes and two anchors.[50] These items, purchased by individual if wealthy citizens, were all part of the ultimate cost of a trireme, and the trouble that the Athenians, as well as the Peloponnesians, would experience in financing their fleets has to be understood in light of the fact that the expense of building a trireme was not a one-time cost, but also included the continuing expenses necessary to keep the ship in a battleworthy condition.

Other Officers

Though the trierarch was indispensable for financing a trireme and keeping it running, he was not the only vital officer aboard. The tactical handling of the ship in battle was the job of the *kybernetes* (variously helmsman/steersman/pilot). The *kybernetes* steered from the stern of the ship, and had to rely on the *prorates* on the foredeck to keep a watch on the sea ahead of the trireme and convey what he saw to him. Other shipboard duties were the province of lesser officers, such as the *keleustes* (boatswain). The main task of the *keleustes* was to establish the timing and rhythm for the oarsmen. This was signalled by calling 'O-opop-o-opop'; and when the speed was to be increased the *keleustes* cried 'rhypapai' or 'arrhy'. The *keleustes* ensured that the rowers were quiet so that orders could be heard. When a stealthy manoeuvre was required, the *keleustes* would not speak aloud, and instead conveyed his orders by tapping two stones together. Command of the ship was of course left to the trierarch.[51]

Overall command of an Athenian fleet was placed in the hands of the ten annually elected *strategoi*, or generals, who held command of Athens' land forces. There was no distinction made between generals at sea and those commanding armies.[52] The situation among the Spartans was of course different, given their much more limited experience with the sea. Sparta appointed a special officer to command its fleet, a *navarch* (admiral).

Payment on Campaign

Placing money directly into the hands of the crews was critical, especially when on campaign. If the need to pay soldiers and sailors on the spot seems surprising, it must be remembered that the troops were responsible for securing their own food. Typically, this was obtained at local markets wherever the fleet put in. With limited space aboard a trireme for storing food or eating it, stopping frequently ashore was the surest way that the men could find food. Such a market, for example, was established immediately upon arrival of the Athenian fleet outside Syracuse in 415 BC.[53] Coined money was necessary to enable the crewmen of the triremes to purchase their sustenance, and so the flow of metal specie into Athens was critical if it were to keep up its war effort. Special markets would often be set up just outside a city at the request of the fleet's commander, so that the men could find food and eat right beside their ships. Local merchants could reap a genuine benefit from feeding the crewmen, since a fleet of sixty ships would have carried some 12,000 hungry men aboard it.

Propulsion

A trireme's motive power was provided by her oarsmen. These were seated at three staggered, superimposed levels, with one man to an oar. The full rowing complement of a trireme crew was 170. In the hold were seated fifty-four thalamian oarsmen (*thalamioi*), with twenty-seven men per side. Above them were fifty-four zygian rowers (*zygioi*), again with twenty-seven men on each side. At the topmost level sat the sixty-two thranite oarsmen (*thranitai*), with thirty-one men per side. Each man pulled on a wooden oar while facing toward the stern of the ship. The stresses on the trireme as it cut through the waves were very great, and additional reinforcement was needed to keep the hull rigid. Strong cables (*hypozomata*, meaning 'undergirds'), weighing about 250lb and around 300ft long, were attached in pairs to the hull and were passed from the stem to the stern, under tension, to strengthen the hull.[54]

The Hellenic Navy's *Olympias* reconstruction provides us with an invaluable look at what rowing an ancient trireme was like. First putting to sea in 1987, *Olympias* underwerwent a series of trials in that year, 1988, 1990, 1992 and 1994. The crews of *Olympias* varied in ability year to year, and they were not always full. Still, during her sea trials, *Olympias* was capable of long-distance voyaging speeds of about 6 knots, 7 knots while moving at speeds appropriate for battle and about 9-knot bursts when delivering a ramming attack.[55] It is reasonable to presume that a trained crew, with its full complement of oarsmen, would have been able to meet or slightly exceed these figures.

These assessed speeds of the replica ship correspond well with the estimated speeds of ancient triremes. The records of a handful of voyages made by triremes survive, and from them the travel times of triremes can be inferred. One found in Thucydides was of an unhurried voyage from Piraeus to Mytilene, over a distance of 201½ nautical miles, giving an average hourly speed of 5.9 knots. Xenophon records a 129-nautical mile voyage between Byzantium and Heraclea which was completed in a single day's movement. Assuming that the journey was made at a time of maximum daylight, and factoring in also that an hour would likely have been spent by the crews taking their meals, then we have a period of about 17½ hours in which the voyage was completed. The average speed of the trireme would then have been 7.37 knots.[56] The maximum speed of a trireme under oars would have been about 10 knots.[57]

PART THREE

THE ARCHIDAMIAN WAR

Corcyra

The island of Corcyra's importance may be explained by its position on the trade route to Italy. The western trade was of interest to Athens as it needed access to Sicilian grain. If this could not be had, she might become dangerously reliant upon grain shipments from the Black Sea region, which was liable to being cut by Persia or any other power that could close either the Bosphorus or the Hellespont.[1] Epidamnus in western Greece was a colony of Corcyra, which in 435 BC requested help from Corcyra against an alliance of exiles and barbarians who were raiding its territory. Corcyra refused, and Epidamnus then sought aid from Corinth, the mother city of Corcyra. Epidamnus, on the advice of the oracle of Delphi, surrendered itself to Corinth. Corinth agreed to help, and a relief army and some settlers marched for Epidamnus. Corinth was now risking war with a potential opponent, Corcyra, that was not to be trifled with. Corcyra was a very powerful state, writes Thucydides, one that 'in point of wealth could stand comparison with any' and that 'possessed great military strength'. Corcyra 'sometimes could not repress a pride in [its] high naval position of an island whose nautical renown dated from the days of its old inhabitants, the Phaeacians. This was one reason for the care that they lavished on their fleet, which became very efficient; indeed they began the war with a force of 120 triremes.'[2]

Corcyra was angered by the Corinthian move and sent a flotilla of twenty-five ships to Epidamnus to insist that the exiles be allowed to return to the city. The Epidamnians refused to comply and were attacked by a Corcyran fleet of forty ships, and Epidamnus was then placed under siege. In response, the Corinthians assembled volunteers to form a colony at Epidamnus, with protection for the convoy provided by Corinth, Megara, Pale, Epidaurus, Hermione, Troezen, Leucas and Ambracia.[3] An effort to arbitrate the matter peacefully by the oracle of Delphi fell through, and Corinth declared war, sending seventy-five triremes and 2,000 hoplites to Epidamnus. This force met a Corcyran fleet of eighty galleys and was worsted in the Battle of Leucimme, losing fifteen ships. Epidamnus was captured on the same day.[4] The Corcyrans erected a trophy to commemorate their victory, and killed all of their captives except for the Corinthians, who were kept as prisoners of war.

With the Corinthians defeated, the Corcyrans were left unopposed on the sea. They attacked Leucas, a Corinthian colony, and burned Cyllene, the harbour of Elea, which had itself sent ships and money to support Corinth. Corinth's allies were harried mercilessly by Corcyran warships, forcing it to take belated action. In 433, two naval stations were established, one at Actium and one at Chimerium, to provide protection for her allies. Corcyra set up a station of its own at Leucimme.

Corinth also reconstituted its fleet, building new ships and recruiting oarsmen from across Greece with high pay, indicating that a real effort was being made to turn the fleet into an effective fighting force. Corcyra was aware of the Corinthians' building programme, and not being a member of any pre-existing league, asked Athens for an alliance. The Corinthians learned of the move and hurriedly sent envoys to Athens to prevent it from helping Corcyra. The two sides presented their appeals to the Athenian Assembly. The Corcyrans argued that it was in Athens' interest to aid them. Corcyra possessed the second-largest fleet in Greece (after Athens) and their naval strength would enhance that of Athens and strengthen it against Sparta, with which a war was coming, they warned.[5] They further noted that keeping Corcyra free would prevent their ships from falling into the possession of Corinth, which if combined with the Peloponnesian fleets would pose a formidable threat to Athens' navy.[6]

The Corinthians responded to the Corcyran presentation by saying that they had always been regarded with contempt by their colony of Corcyra, and this had now flared into outright hostility over Epidamnus. The Corcyrans had no cause for complaint over how Corinth was acting in regard to Epidamnus. They had only taken an interest in Epidamnus after Corinth had. The proposed naval alliance that Athens might form with Corcyra, the Corinthians argued, was a mirage. Whatever advantage that might accrue by pairing their naval forces together would never be worth the disadvantage of having Corinth as an enemy.[7] The truth of this point was difficult to establish at the time, but would prove to be accurate in the long run.

Both sides had presented sound, if self-serving, advice to the Athenians. The Assembly afterward held two meetings to discuss what they had just heard. The initial meeting seemed to favour Corinth, but popular feeling had changed by the second, and a Corcyran alliance was formed, albeit one with caveats as the Athenians did not want the pact to constitute a breach of the treaty that existed between them and the Peloponnesians. The alliance was cast as a defensive one in which Athens would not be obligated to take part in any attack on Corinth, and would only help Corcyra resist an invasion. But for the Athenians it also seemed that a much larger war with the Peloponnesians loomed threateningly, just over the horizon, and 'no one was willing to see a naval power of such magnitude as Corcyra sacrificed to Corinth'. It was also thought that if both Corcyra and Corinth fought each other, this would weaken both and make fighting Corinth and the other Greek naval states easier for Athens if and when a general war came.[8]

Athens was certainly in a bind. To allow the Corcyran fleet, should Corcyra be defeated, to come under the control of a potentially hostile state was nothing that any Athenian wanted to see. Yet to side with Corcyra against Corinth risked creating the ill will that any sober state would wish to avoid inculcating in another. Athens' decision was therefore an example of Machiavellian *realpolitik*. War was coming, or so many of her people thought, and the least dangerous course of action would be to support Corcyra, and thereby prevent her navy from falling into the hands of an enemy. Corcyra would not, as it turned out, prove to be of very much value to Athens as an ally over the course of the war.

So with an alliance formed, Athens despatched ten triremes to Corcyra under the command of Lacedaemonius, the son of Cimon, the former archon of Athens. These ships were instructed not to do battle with the Corinthians unless they tried to make a landing on the island or struck at her possessions. In those cases, the Assembly authorized them to do whatever was necessary to stop the Corinthians. Thucydides asserts that these instructions were given out of anxiety to avoid a breach of the Thirty Years' Peace Treaty.[9]

Battle of Sybota

The Corinthian building programme, in the meantime, had borne fruit, and a fleet of 150 triremes was fitted out. These had been supplied not only by Corinth, which furnished ninety, but also by Elis (ten), Megara (twelve), Leucas (ten), Ambracia (twenty-seven) and Anactorium, which sent a single vessel. The fleet stopped just across from Corcyra at Chimerium in Thesprotis. The Corcyrans emerged with 110 ships, and accompanied by the ten Athenian triremes, took up position near one of the Sybota Islands.

The Corinthians stowed three days' worth of provisions aboard their ships and left Chimerium at night. At dawn they spotted the Corcyran fleet, and both arrayed themselves for battle. The Corcyrans formed themselves with their right wing extending out to sea, where sat the Athenian ships with ample room to manoeuvre. The Corinthians put their allies towards the land on their right wing, but stationed themselves on their left, with their best crews opposite the Athenians and Corcyran right wing.

The battle commenced with the raising of signal flags. The triremes of both fleets had numerous hoplites embarked to fight as marines, together with large complements of archers and javelineers. With both sides prepared to fight boarding actions, the battle was fierce, with little in the way of manoeuvring. There were too many galleys doing battle in a confined space, and once they had rammed or been rammed, the press of the ships made escaping by backing water to mount another ramming attack extremely difficult. So the decision was to be had among the hoplites, who would fight just as if they were on land. There was no opportunity to try a *diekplous* because the crowded waters would not allow it.

Thucydides described the tactics used by the Corcyrans and Corinthians as being out of date, and his description of the fight is worth citing at length. 'Both sides had a large number of hoplites on their decks,' he writes, 'and a large number of archers and javelin throwers, the old imperfect armament still prevailing. The sea fight was an obstinate one, though not remarkable for its science; indeed it was more like a battle by land. Whenever they charged each other, the multitude and crush of the triremes made it by no means easy to get loose; besides, their hopes of victory lay principally in the hoplites on their decks, who stood and fought in order, their ships remaining stationary. The manoeuvre of passing through the line [the *diekplous*] was not tried: in short, strength and pluck had more share in the fight than science.'[10]

For Thucydides, 'science' meant the sophisticated manoeuvre tactics of the Athenian fleet. At Salamis in 480 BC, the Greeks had been outclassed by the Phoenicians in the enemy Persian fleet in knowledge of manoeuvre tactics, and had won the battle after stiff fighting consisting of boarding actions. Once the Phoenicians had entered the channel, they had given up any chance to employ their ships as weapons, and had to instead rely on the power of their marines, an area in which the Greeks largely had the advantage. But in the decades since then, the Athenians had made naval strength the basis of their military power, and it was thus the foundation of their maritime empire. So, subsequent to the Persian Wars, they had chosen to train their crews to a high level of efficiency, capable of enacting the *diekplous* or *periplous* manoeuvres as her fleet's commanders so chose and making her navy better than any other. Not every state in Greece would be so eager to put so much stress and effort on manoeuvre tactics, which required extensive training of oarsmen. Most, in fact, would not. It made sense for the Athenians to do so, given their reliance upon seapower to maintain their empire. As long as Athens' generals were prudent, and did not throw away the advantages that a fleet manned by highly trained crews brought, her navy would possess a near-insuperable edge over her enemies.

The small Athenian contingent had mostly hung back from the combat, but would close whenever the Corcyrans were in trouble. Their approach scared the Corinthians, even though the Athenians did not take an active role in the fighting because of their orders from the Assembly. On the Corinthian right wing, their allied ships broke and fled, pursued by twenty Corcyran galleys. The Corcyrans followed this up by attacking the Corinthian fleet encampment and put it to the torch.

It was a different story on the other end of the line, on the Corinthian left, where the Corinthians were winning heavily. The Athenians saw that the Corcyrans there were in real trouble, and intervened to take a more active part in the encounter, involving them in direct combat with the Corinthians.

The Corinthians were nonetheless victorious on their left, and spent much of their time killing the men who had fallen into the water between the ships. Some of these unfortunates were their own seamen, but they were slain anyway because the Corinthians did not yet know that their right wing had been routed. They forced the remaining Corcyran ships to beach themselves, and then turned their attention to recovering their wrecked triremes and their dead. After this they made for Sybota, where they dropped off their damaged ships and dead, and sailed out again to face the Corcyrans.

Later the same day, but by now with the light fading, the Corinthians were ready to renew the battle, singing the *paean* as they rowed to signal the attack, when they halted their forward movement and began to back water. In the distance, someone had spotted twenty Athenian triremes approaching. The Athenian Assembly had become worried that the ten galleys previously sent out would be too few to be of sufficient assistance to the Corcyrans and that the Corcyrans would lose. These twenty late-coming ships had been despatched from Athens to reinforce the original contingent of ten. With darkness falling, and the Corinthians unwilling to fight again, both fleets retired to their camps.[11]

On the next day, the Athenians went to sea with their thirty triremes, together with the Corcyran ships that could still fight, and sailed to Sybota's harbour to draw out the Corinthians. The Corinthians were willing to come out, but would not take any offensive action against the Athenians. The Corinthian ships were encumbered with prisoners taken during the fight of the day before, their ships were in need of repairs which could not be performed in this location, and they were also worried that the Athenians would judge that the Thirty Years' Peace Treaty of 446 had been breached and refuse to let them return to Corinth.[12] They sent a few men in a boat to hold a parley with the Athenians. They accused the Athenians of breaking their treaty by interposing themselves between them and the Corcyrans. The Athenians responded, saying that they were not beginning a war, merely coming to the aid of their allies. The Corcyrans were eager to have the Corinthian messengers killed, but the Athenians allowed the Corinthian fleet to depart, as long as it did not make for Corcyra. The Corinthians, with their damaged ships, wanted to return home in any case, and after setting up a trophy at Sybota, they sailed away.[13]

The battle was over, but the Athenian intervention would have dreadful political consequences. Initially, the Athenians sent too small a force to keep the peace between the warring sides, but it was large enough to incense the Corinthians with their meddling. Had the Athenians sent thirty triremes at the outset, the same number as they would have on hand at the end of the affair, the battle might never have taken place. Alternatively, if the small Athenian squadron had taken part in the fighting from the beginning of the engagement, they and the Corcyrans might have won the battle and prevented the much larger Peloponnesian War from occurring at all.[14]

Plutarch explains the smallness of the Athenian squadron by attributing to Pericles a desire to 'humiliate' its commander, Lacedaemonius, who was known to be sympathetic to Sparta. Should Lacedaemonius be defeated, his pro-Spartan sympathies would likewise be discredited. From the first, the 'paltry size of the force he had sent' brought severe criticism upon Pericles, and this spurred him to send the additional twenty ships afterward, but these arrived too late to make any impact in the battle.[15] It is hard to accept that the high-minded Pericles would have been so petty, as well as so myopic, to risk *any* ships and seamen on such a mission solely to disgrace a political opponent. Instead, it is more likely that the tiny squadron represented Pericles' hesitancy about becoming embroiled in what was still only a conflict between two states on the other side of the Balkans.

Potidaea

The Corinthians believed they had won the battle, and their victory might have been more conclusive had the Athenians not belatedly intervened. This intervention on behalf of the Corcyrans was a blatant provocation to war. Soon after, while Corinth was plotting some kind of revenge for this, Athens moved to interrupt a possible defection by Potidaea that might take the rest of Athens' allies in Thrace with it. Potidaea was a Corinthian colony, but an ally of Athens, and the Athenians ordered the Potidaeans to knock down their walls, deliver hostages and expel their Corinthian magistrates. Corinth sent a force of hoplites and mercenaries under Aristeus to defend Potidaea, but he was overmatched by the Athenian force, together with seventy ships that arrived outside the city. Not long afterward, an additional 1,600 Athenian hoplites under the command of Phormio appeared. With the siege looking hopeless, Aristeus made a breakout from Potidaea, sailing his ships out of the harbour straight past the blockading Athenian triremes.

Each side saw itself as having a justification for war. The Athenians believed themselves aggrieved because the Corinthians had incited a tribute-paying ally of theirs to defect from the alliance, while Corinth saw the siege of its colony as a severe affront. This was the second means by which Athens antagonized Corinth in this period, and it would bring about great harm. Corinth would now be an implacable enemy, and would remain fervently anti-Athenian for the duration of the upcoming war.

The Corinthians lost no time in lining up support for themselves against Athens. During the winter of 432/1 BC, a Corinthian delegation went before the Spartan Assembly and complained that their inaction had made Athenian aggression possible. Their disappointments with Sparta went far back in time. Sparta had allowed Athens to fortify itself, they complained, and then put up its Long Walls to Piraeus. By doing nothing to curb growing Athenian power, Sparta had allowed the Athenians to enslave Greece. '[T]he true author of the subjugation of a people,' they said, 'is not so much the immediate agent, as the power which permits it having the means to prevent it; particularly if that power aspires to the glory of being the liberator of Hellas.'[16] The Corinthians asked the Spartans to come to their aid at Potidaea by sending an invasion army to ravage Attica.

There were Athenian envoys engaged in other business in Sparta at the same time that the Corinthians were urging war, and they were summoned before the Spartan Assembly. The Athenians said that they should not forget Athens' pivotal role in defending Greece against the Persian invasions. They cited the victory at Marathon in 490 and the contribution of the bulk of the ships of the fleet that had won at Salamis in 480. The role of Athens in those wars fought on behalf of all the Greeks justified her empire now, they said. Sparta had its own empire in the Peloponnesus and organized those states as it saw fit. Why should Athens not do the same elsewhere in Greece? The attack on Potidaea was merely Athens asserting her right to control the states within her own sphere of influence.

When both sides had finished their presentations, the Spartans debated what they had heard, and judged the Athenians to be the aggressors. Though most were resolved for war, at least a few doubted this course and asked the Assembly to reconsider. King Archidamus, 'a wise and moderate man', stood forth and warned that they could not know how this major war would turn out. It was one thing to pit Sparta's strength against other Peloponnesian states, whose power was of the same kind as that of Sparta, but another thing entirely to embark on a war against a faraway enemy possessing 'an extraordinary familiarity with the sea, and who are in the highest state of preparation in every other department; with wealth private and public, with ships, and horses, and hoplites, and a population such as no other Hellenic place can equal, and lastly a large number of tributary allies'. To begin such a war against such a powerful enemy would be unforgivably rash.[17]

Sparta was not the equal of Athens in ships, and would need time to build them. It would need time too to learn how to master the art of rowing them to achieve any sort of parity, Archidamus said. Further, Sparta lacked the money, whether from its own treasury or from private sources, to carry on a war against the wealthy Athenians. Sparta's hoplites might be employed to devastate Attica, but Athenian seapower would still allow them to import whatever they needed from other parts of their empire. If Sparta tried to turn Athens' overseas allies away from them, these states would have to be supported by Spartan ships, which it did not have. 'What then is to be our war?' he asked. 'For unless we can either beat them at sea, or deprive them of the revenues which feed their navy, we shall meet with little but disaster.'[18] Archidamus urged caution and advised that Sparta should bide its time while building up its own naval and financial power over two or three years. Then Athens might be more inclined to back down.

Archidamus' speech seems to have made an impression on some of the Spartans, because when a vote was taken the shouts of the side in favour of war could not be distinguished from the side against it. But when the members of the Assembly were made to physically divide themselves by groups, whether for or against war, the party that believed that the treaty had been broken and that war should be declared was in the comfortable majority.[19] The Spartans were still uncertain about taking this action, and sent an embassy to Delphi to ask the oracle of Apollo whether war was the proper course. The oracle responded that victory would be had 'if they put their whole strength into the war' and that Apollo would be on the side of Sparta in the conflict.[20]

The Spartans were still unwilling to fight without a firm commitment from their allies in the Peloponnesian League, and these were summoned to Sparta for a congress, where the majority was for going to war. The Corinthians were of course very much in favour, and they argued that the league's naval power could be increased out of the resources they already had, while more money could be obtained via loans from the temples of Olympia and Delphi. This money could then be used to hire foreign sailors away from the Athenian fleet through the promise of higher pay. The Athenian edge in seapower was real, but precarious. Just one loss by the Athenians at sea would mean their defeat, and even if they fought on, the Corinthians said, that would mean that there would be more time for the Peloponnesians to gain experience. Then, 'as soon as we have arrived at an equality in [naval fighting], we need scarcely ask whether we shall be their superiors in courage.'[21]

The Corinthians saw the upcoming war as one that must strike against Athenian revenue, because money was what paid for the food and ships of Athens, a strategy of economic strangulation. This would be done by peeling away her allies. They also advocated setting up fortified places in Attica from which to harry the enemy. '[T]he tyrant city that has been established in Hellas has been established against all alike, with a programme of universal empire, part fulfilled, part in contemplation; let us then attack and reduce it, and win future security for ourselves and freedom for the Hellenes who are now enslaved.'[22] The Spartans then held a vote of all of the Peloponnesian allies, and most voted for war, but since very few were ready to undertake military action, there was little that could be done right away. These preparations were nonetheless made energetically, and the Peloponnesians would send troops into Attica in under a year from deciding on war.

The Spartan government was not eager to make war, even though the Assembly had voted for its declaration, and it sent a delegation to Athens to try to negotiate a way out of the looming conflict by making a handful of demands. The Spartans offered that war could be avoided if the Athenians would agree to lift the Potidaean siege, respect Aegina's independence and revoke the Megarian Decree which had closed Athenian harbours and the market of Athens to the Megarians, this last being the Spartans' chief demand. They further demanded that Athens allow the Greeks their independence.

The advancement by the Spartans of the demand that the Megarian Decree be rescinded is a difficult one to square with the other material presented by Thucydides revolving around the origin of the war. The roles of Corcyra and Potidaea in igniting the conflict received heavy attention from him, and then, seemingly out of nowhere, the Megarian Decree surfaces and is made Sparta's foremost demand to avoid war. The date of the Decree is not certain, though it was likely promulgated between late 433 and the middle of 432. The underlying purpose of the embargo is not certain either. The exclusion of Megarian goods from imperial harbours would have had a devastating effect on Megarian trade, and it is possible that Athens, sensing that war with Sparta was coming, was using economic pressure to force Megara back into an alliance with her, as she had been from 460–446. Just recently, twelve Megarian warships had taken part in the Battle of Sybota alongside the Corinthians, and a friendly Megara would have been an effective means of protecting Attica from invasion via the Isthmus of Corinth.[23]

Athens Considers War

The Athenians in their Assembly discussed the Spartan proposals, and there were arguments made for and against them. The most powerful voice belonged to her most prominent citizen, Pericles, who took a strong position against acceding to any of Sparta's demands. He noted that the Spartans had failed to submit the dispute over Potidaea to arbitration, as required under the Thirty Year's Treaty.[24] Pericles was not completely against reaching a settlement with the Spartans over the issues dividing them, but he was adamantly against making any concession unless the matters at hand were submitted to arbitration as stipulated by the treaty. The Megarian Decree was not a 'trifle', he insisted, but a matter of principle. 'If you give way, you will instantly have to meet some greater demand, as having been frightened into obedience in the first instance; while a firm refusal will make them clearly understand that they must treat you as equals.'[25] Giving in once would merely encourage further unreasonable claims. The Athenians had to resist the overbearing Spartan demands. Only by doing so, Pericles argued, would Sparta treat Athens with the respect due to her.[26]

Pericles then went on to list the advantages that Athens held over the Peloponnesian League. Since the Peloponnesians were farmers, they had to personally take part in cultivating their lands, had little money and no experience of fighting wars at sea, where Athens held a vast advantage. The agrarian nature of the Peloponnesian economy made it impossible for them to leave their fields behind for any length of time. 'Capital, it must be remembered,' Pericles said, 'maintains a war more than forced contributions. Farmers are a class of men that are always more ready to serve in person than in purse. Confident that the former will survive the dangers, they are by no means so sure that the latter will not be prematurely exhausted.'[27] They were without money to pay for a protracted war, and though 'in a single battle the Peloponnesians and their allies may be able to defy all Hellas', this would not be the case over an extended period of time. The Peloponnesians lacked the unified command authority that Athens had, and had to make do with an unwieldy congress of the allied states in which each would strive for its own selfish goals.[28] Pericles was here simply noting the inherent inefficiencies of coalition warfare.

There was nothing to fear from the Peloponnesians' navy, Pericles continued, and there was little possibility that they might establish fortified places within Attica. Such fortifications would not be able to stop Athenians from sailing against the Peloponnesus and setting up fortifications there. 'For our naval skill,' Pericles said, 'is of more use to us for service on land than their military skill is for service at sea. Familiarity with the sea they will not find an easy acquisition. If you who have been practising at it ever since the Persian invasion have not yet brought it to perfection, is there any chance of anything considerable being effected by an agricultural, unseafaring population, who will besides be prevented from practising by the constant presence of strong squadrons of observation from Athens?'[29] A lack of practice would make the Peloponnesians clumsy and timid at sea. 'It must be kept in mind that seamanship, just like anything else, is a matter requiring skill, and will not admit being taken up occasionally as an occupation for times of leisure; on the contrary, it is so exacting as to leave leisure for nothing else.'[30]

The money that the Peloponnesians might obtain from Olympia and Delos might enable them to lure away some of the foreign sailors serving in Athens' fleet, Pericles argued, but this was unlikely, since it would make them outlaws, all for just a few days' worth of higher pay. Even if they did bolt, Athens would be a match for the Peloponnesian navy if she recruited her own citizens and resident aliens for fleet service, and Athens' native sailors and coxswains were better than any others in Greece.

If the Peloponnesians invaded Attica and laid waste to its fields, this would hurt Athens less than if the same happened to only a small portion of the Peloponnesus, Pericles said. The Peloponnesians would have to make up for any lost resources by battle, but Athens would still be able to supply itself with the produce of its overseas lands. Athens must never give battle, no matter what the enemy did to her people's homes and fields in Attica. Even if Athens won a victory on land, it would scarcely dent the numerical advantage of the Peloponnesians, and a defeat would embolden her allies to defect. Athens would remain safe so long as it guarded its overseas empire, the real source of its power. To do this she would have to maintain her strength at sea and stay within the protection of her Long Walls. 'The rule of the sea is indeed a great matter,' Pericles said. 'Consider for a moment. Suppose that we were islanders: can you conceive a more impregnable position? Well, this in future should, as far as possible, be our conception of our position. Dismissing all thought of our land and houses, we must vigilantly guard the sea and the city. No irritation that we may feel for the former must provoke us to a battle with the numerical superiority of the Peloponnesians.' Fighting on land against the enemy had to be avoided, as it brought little chance of reward, but carried great risk. 'A victory [on land over the Peloponnesians] would only be succeeded by another battle against the same superiority: a reverse involves the loss of our allies, the source of our strength, who will not remain quiet a day after we become unable to march against them.' Pericles painted the outlines of his strategy in the starkest terms: 'We must not cry over the loss of houses and land but of men's lives; since houses and land do not gain men, but men them. And if I thought I could persuade you, I would have bid you go out and lay them waste with your own hands, and show the Peloponnesians that this at any rate will not make you submit.'[31]

War was necessary, Pericles told the Assembly. For now, Athens must forget embarking on any new efforts at conquest and concentrate on avoiding mistakes. 'I am more afraid of our own blunders than of the enemy's devices.'[32] Pericles foresaw that the coming war would be a long one, and that in a long war, Athens, with the advantages it derived from its overseas possessions and its impregnable position, would have the edge over the Peloponnesians.

Plutarch writes that the archon had foreseen a 'war bearing down on Athens from the Peloponnesus'.[33] It seems likely that Pericles was at no time trying to avoid a war that he judged to be in any case inevitable, either right now, or at some point in the future. The defensive strategy that he urged on his fellow Athenians would not do much to intimidate the Spartans from going to war themselves, since it promised little immediate hurt to them. It was instead a plan meant to see the Athenians through a lengthy conflict by making the best use of its maritime advantages over its land-bound rival.

The essence of the Periclean war strategy was thus to sit tight, almost completely on the defensive, and make only small naval raids and landings against the Peloponnesus to irritate the enemy and demonstrate to them that the Athenians could inflict much more damage whenever they wished.[34] It seems indisputable from Pericles' own words that he did not promise victory over Sparta so much as assure his countrymen that they would survive Peloponnesian attacks and wait for the storm to pass. Precisely what Pericles hoped to achieve with his defensive strategy of avoiding land battles and conducting limited naval raids against the Peloponnesus has been questioned by modern scholars. Some have believed that it was meant to tire the Spartans, who would then come to their senses and seek out a peace agreement. Others have criticized it for offering no certain route to victory in the conflict. At most, Pericles' chief objective seems to have been to fight for a stalemate, not the defeat of the enemy.[35]

One major flaw in Pericles' strategy was that it ignored the possibility of Persian intervention on the side of the enemy. He seems not to have anticipated this happening, but King Archidamus had broached the idea of seeking Persian assistance as early as 432, prior to the war. Not long after the war's start, the Spartans would send an embassy to Persia to request assistance from the Great King.[36] In the careful calculus of power, Pericles had neglected to account for the introduction of Persian forces or finances on behalf of Sparta. Persian resources were far greater than those of Athens. The annual tribute sent by the many satrapies of the Persian Empire to the royal court in the time of Darius the Great in the early fifth century BC was 14,560 talents. This dwarfed the yearly income of the Athenians, which was only 600 talents at the start of the war.[37] Though Persia would not commit itself until the war had dragged on for many years, when it did so it was one of the deciding factors, perhaps the deciding factor, in the war's outcome.

The Athenians voted just as Pericles advised, telling the Spartans that they would not accede to any of their demands, but were ready to have the dispute arbitrated.[38] Plutarch writes that because of Pericles' adamant opposition to what were reasonable Spartan attempts to avoid war by having the Decree against Megara rescinded, later 'it was he alone who was held responsible for the war'.[39] The Spartans were surprised and irritated by Athenian unwillingness to come to a peaceful understanding. When a Spartan delegation came to Athens to talk about lifting the Decree, Pericles is said to have raised a specious objection to doing so, saying that there was a law forbidding him from taking down the tablet on which the Decree had been inscribed. To this nonsense one of the forthright Spartans replied, 'Very well then, there is no need to take it down. Just turn its face to the wall. Surely there is no law forbidding that!' Pericles remained unmoved by either Spartan practicality or humour, and Plutarch speculated that he held some undisclosed enmity towards the Megarians that prevented him from making any concession on the subject of the embargo.[40]

So Pericles would come to be blamed for his intransigence, but the Spartans had certainly backed him into a corner as well, by making an ultimatum and refusing to arbitrate their dispute, as was clearly required under the peace treaty. Much later, when the fortunes of war had turned against them, the Spartans would blame themselves for their failure to adhere to the treaty terms and see this as one of the causes of their wartime disasters.[41]

The Rival Coalitions Form

War did not erupt immediately thereafter, but it became unavoidable at this point. Interaction between the rivals was limited to that conducted by heralds, and an unmistakable breach came in 431 BC when the Boeotian city of Plataea, an ally of Athens, was attacked by a small Theban force (Thebes lay just 8 miles away) that was captured and then executed. Though the Athenians had wished for the lives of the Thebans to be preserved, their messenger reached Plataea only after the deed was done.

A period of coalition-building began as Athens and Sparta sought to entice other states to join their side in the conflict. Naval preparations were an important matter for the Spartans, as this was an area of serious weakness for them. Sparta sent orders to her Italian and Sicilian allies that they should build 500 ships, with the number of ships to be contributed based upon the size of the city, and provide a set contribution of money. Until these ships were ready for action, these states were to remain outwardly neutral, but deny Athenian shipping access to their harbours.[42]

Overall, Thucydides writes, Greek opinion greatly favoured the cause of the Spartans, who had cast themselves as the defenders of Greek freedom. 'So general was the indignation felt against Athens, whether by those who wished to escape from her empire, or were apprehensive of being absorbed by it.'[43] Both sides also had high hopes for victory and displayed great energy in their war preparations. 'Zeal is always at its height at the commencement of an undertaking,' Thucydides noted wryly.[44] This would hold true for many other wars, ancient and modern.

The Athenian coalition was composed of Chios, Lesbos, Plataea, the Messenians of Naupactus, the majority of the Acarnanians, Corcyra, Zacynthus and several cities in Caria, Thrace, Ionia, the Hellespont, the eastern islands between the Peloponnesus and Crete, and the Cyclades with the exceptions of Melos and Thera. Of these allied states, triremes were provided by Chios, Lesbos and Corcyra, with the rest supplying infantry and money.[45]

The Spartan/Peloponnesian alliance included the states within the Peloponnesus except for Argos and the Achaeans, who remained neutral, and Pellene, an Achaean city which nonetheless joined the Peloponnesian cause. In wider Greece, Megara, Locris, Boeotia, Phocis, Ambracia, Leucas and Anactorium declared for Sparta. Of this alliance, warships were provided by Corinth, Megara, Sicyon, Pellene, Elis, Ambracia and Leucas.[46]

In early 431, a Spartan army under King Archidamus was sent to invade Attica and destroy as much Athenian property as it could. In Athens, Pericles, one of Athens' ten elected generals for the year, repeated to the people his earlier advice against going out to meet the enemy head-to-head. Instead, they were to bring all of their property within the area protected by Athens' walls and prepare for fleet service. He also listed for them the financial strengths of the Athenian state, and his assessment of the funds available to Athens sheds light on why he anticipated outlasting the Peloponnesian coalition. Tribute from the allies brought in 600 talents each year. There was some six thousand talents of uncoined silver in the treasury on the Acropolis. In addition to this, there was uncoined gold and silver, war spoils, sacred religious vessels and other wealth totalling 500 talents. In an emergency, the forty talents of gold that adorned the statue of Athena on the Acropolis could also be used. This money would be sufficient to see them through the war against the Peloponnesians.[47]

The available military power of Athens was also tremendous. She had an army of some 29,000 hoplites, 1,200 cavalry and 1,600 archers. Her stout protective walls, the Long Walls to the Piraeus and the Phaleric Wall, as well as the city walls themselves, encompassed many square miles of territory. The fleet had 300 triremes ready for action.[48] There is some modern dissension concerning this figure. Thucydides notes that later in 431 the Athenian Assembly voted to create a 'special fund' of 1,000 talents subtracted from the money stored on the Acropolis. A 'special fleet' of 100 of the 'best ships of each year' was to be funded with this money, and this fleet was to be set aside for use against the 'same peril', if one of sufficient magnitude should arise.[49] Some historians believe that this fleet of 100 triremes should be added to the 300 previously mentioned, giving a total of 400, while others favour the position that these 100 warships were drawn from the 300 already in existence. It seems more reasonable that the smaller figure should be preferred. A major financial and logistical effort would have been needed to build 100 additional ships, and Thucydides does not mention such a programme. He does say, however, that these 100 'best ships' were voted to be 'set aside', with the obvious meaning being that these ships were already in existence and were being sequestered in reserve for use in an emergency.[50] Whatever the case, Athens' military resources were undeniably vast.

How Long a War?

The wealth of Athens at the start of the war was considerable, but for how long did Pericles think that Athens would have to fight this defensive war? He gave no set prediction of its length, but some rudimentary calculations can give some insight as to how long he thought it could be maintained. The first question that arises concerns how much money Pericles anticipated spending per year fighting the Peloponnesians. A useful guide to what Pericles may have had in mind is to consider the cost of the Samian War of 440–439 BC. To conduct that year-long war, Athens borrowed 1,404 talents from the treasury. To this figure should be added the 600 talents that came in from the Empire in the form of tribute, it being most likely that the Athenians would have spent this money before they ever resorted to borrowing additional funds from the treasury. So it stands to reason that since the cost of the Samian War was about 2,000 talents, Pericles probably estimated that a war against the Spartans would cost about as much per year.[51]

At the war's inception, the Athenians would have had a total of 6,000 talents on hand. From this figure must be subtracted the 1,000 talents that the Athenians would set aside in a special emergency fund later in 431, to be used only if they needed to defend the city from an enemy naval attack, leaving 5,000 talents immediately available. The annual tribute per year was again 600 talents, and at least early in the war the arrival of this money from overseas would have been ensured by Athens' control of the sea. So at the beginning of the first year of the war, the Athenian treasury would have held some 5,600 ready-to-spend talents, from which must be subtracted 2,000 talents in annual war expenditures, leaving 3,600 at the end of the first year. In the second year, 600 more talents would come in, giving the treasury 4,200 talents. Expenditures would again be 2,000, and the amount left would be 2,200 talents. In the third year, 600 more talents in tribute would arrive, giving 2,800. 2,000 talents would again be spent, leaving the Athenians with 800. However, in the fourth year, even with the addition of the 600 talents of tribute, the treasury would be holding only 1,400 talents, not enough to cover the full annual 2,000 talent cost of conducting the war as we assume Pericles foresaw it. There was still the special fund of 1,000 talents, but this presumably would not have been touched by the Athenian Assembly in order to continue with the defensive war strategy. Following this line of thinking, Pericles must have envisioned a war that would not have lasted for more than three years.

Naval Raid on the Peloponnesus

Though Pericles had advised his people to stand on the defensive, Athens was not completely passive in this period. With the Spartans busy ravaging the Attic countryside, in 431 BC, Athens sent out a fleet of 100 triremes with 1,000 hoplites and 400 archers aboard to raid the Peloponnesus. The Spartans departed Attica soon afterward. This cruise was a major undertaking, representing a force of 21,400 seamen and troops aboard the ships. In conjunction with an allied fleet of fifty Corcyran ships, they attacked Laconia and a descent was made against Methone. An enterprising Spartan officer in the area named Brasidas organized a relief force of 100 hoplites and came to its aid. With these men he drove off the besiegers and secured himself in Methone. Thus stymied, the Athenians departed and sailed off to continue their voyage. The fleet stopped once more at Pheia in Elis, the countryside around which they ravaged over two days. A force of 300 men from around Elis was defeated, but a storm came up, and the Athenians, not wishing to remain in a place with no harbour, took off and anchored in the port of Pheia. Pheia itself would be taken by Messenians and some men who had been unable to get aboard the ships. The Athenians sailed back and picked up all of these men, and left. Pheia was thereby evacuated as the main Elean army was closing in.

The cruise around the Peloponnesus continued. Elsewhere, a squadron of thirty triremes under the command of Cleopompus was sent against Opuntian Locris, which was attacked. Thronium was seized and hostages were taken from the town.[52] It seems that the Athenians at this early stage of the war were not yet interested in capturing and holding naval bases, and instead sought only to conduct hit-and-run attacks against the Peloponnesus. As noted above, the size of the fleet involved, 100 ships embarking over twenty thousand men, was enormous. A descent made by such a force was much bigger than what might be conventionally considered a 'raid'. The point of the attacks made by this fleet may have been to display the full extent of Athenian naval power and the impotence of the Spartans to prevent the attacks, in the belief that this would cause the Spartans to seek out a negotiated peace.[53]

Elsewhere, the island of Aegina, which like Athens was a strong maritime state, had long been considered a threat, and its population was expelled and replaced by colonists drawn from Athens. The exiled Aeginetans were settled by Sparta at Thyrea.

Withdrawal to Athens

To minimize the loss of life among the civilians of Attica, the Athenians brought their families and property out of the countryside and within the safety of the city walls. This was not done easily. The Athenians were attached to their country homes, and the conditions of the move were far from ideal. Many had to find whatever unbuilt spaces they could in which to make their new dwellings. The city soon became overcrowded and uncomfortable with all of the refugees inside it. To leave their ancestral lands undefended in the face of Spartan invasion was nearly intolerable to the mass of Athenians who discontentedly sought the protection of the walls. The distress, Thucydides says, was so great because they had to 'bid farewell to what each regarded as his native city'.[54]

The defensive strategy as advocated and implemented by Pericles at the beginning of the war engendered terrible frustration and anger among the dispossessed citizenry, who saw their lands outside the walls ravaged by the Peloponnesians. For Pericles to have weathered this upsurge in popular discontent, his strategy must have enjoyed the support of many influential Athenians apart from Pericles himself. These men would have been willing to accept whatever damage the Spartans could inflict on their property in Attica while providing Pericles with political support to survive the wrath of the unhappy public.[55]

To ravage a rural countryside meant, in its simplest form, to destroy the crops of the enemy populace. The thought of their farms being despoiled by the Peloponnesians made the Attic refugees furious. They could not abide that the Athenian army did not march out to stop them. The Spartans too were certain that the Athenians would come to fight them in a big battle once they started destroying farmland. That they stayed behind the safety of their walls was utterly unexpected. The Greeks were an agrarian people, and the struggle for land was of huge consequence. Yet they remained on the defensive in Attica and did not give the Spartans the major battle that they wanted, and expected, to win. Leaving farms undefended would seem to have been a recipe for Athenian disaster, but physically destroying crops is much harder than might be thought. Olive trees are extremely difficult to chop down, and vineyards are likewise difficult to ruin. Further, fields of grain and fruit trees do not burn easily. The Spartans were incapable of doing lasting damage to the agricultural lands of Attica during their relatively brief stays in the countryside, especially while being harassed by Athenian cavalry, and in time they also found that much of what they had destroyed in previous invasions had grown back. The true harm of the Spartan attacks was not the actual damage done, but the harm imagined in the minds of the Attic farmers huddling inside the shanty towns of Athens. They could not stand the thought of their life's work going up in flames unchallenged, and this resulted in a severe political problem for Pericles.[56]

The Plague

The teeming, squalid conditions inside Athens were right for an outbreak of disease, and this followed soon after the arrival of Archidamus' second Spartan invasion of Attica in the spring of 430 BC. Thucydides writes that the disease had erupted first in Ethiopia, moved on to Egypt and Libya, and then assaulted the Persian Empire. It made landfall on the island of Lemnos and in other places in the Aegean, and then it arrived first in Athens' neighbourhood in Piraeus. '[A] pestilence of such extent and mortality was nowhere remembered,' Thucydides said.⁵⁷ The historian himself fell ill because of the disease and tells us that 'people in good health were all of a sudden attacked by violent heats in the head, and redness and inflammation in the eyes, the inward parts, such as the throat or tongue, becoming bloody and emitting an unnatural and fetid breath.'⁵⁸

Other symptoms were sneezing and hoarseness, followed by coughing. Upset stomach was also common, as was vomiting. The afflicted felt extremely hot and could not tolerate even the lightest of clothing upon their bodies. Sleep was impossible. The last stage usually involved severe diarrhoea, and then death ensued. The entire course of the disease from onset to end was seven or eight days.⁵⁹

What caused the plague? That is uncertain. It is possible that the accumulation of people and animals within Athens, brought inside to escape the hurts of the Peloponnesians in the Attic countryside, encouraged the transmission of pathogens. Unsettled conditions prevailing during wartime, together with the congregation of peoples from different areas, have been known to be a fertile breeding ground for disease. That being said, the disease is clearly stated to have wound its way across the Mediterranean world, broadly moving from east to west, before it struck the city, so its origination cannot have been solely due to factors specific to Athens. It is also speculated that the severity of the plague owed much to it having been an unfamiliar infection to which the people of Athens would have had no prior exposure, and thus little or no resistance. Hippocrates, whose life was contemporaneous with that of the plague, shows no evidence in his writings of a knowledge of either smallpox or measles, diseases which would later go on to cause many deaths.⁶⁰ This is not to imply that it was one of those illnesses, but it does suggest that at this time, in the latter fifth century BC, there were still many deadly afflictions that had not yet been encountered by the people of the Mediterranean, and this may explain the especially heavy toll that the plague took when it arrived at Piraeus in 430. It is also consistent with Thucydides' firm attestation that the disease that struck the city was a new one.

As mentioned above, candidates for the plague illness include smallpox and measles, as well as typhus.⁶¹ The advent of smallpox in the New World, brought by the Spaniards, would fell huge numbers of Aztecs in 1521, and in large part ensure the Spanish conquest of Mexico. In its lethality, the plague certainly behaved like a precursor of the later smallpox epidemic that struck the Valley of Mexico in the sixteenth century. Also like the Aztecs, the Athenians would have had no previous experience of the disease, and thus no acquired immunity.

At this remove, certainty is impossible, but the plague itself, which would recur in 427, would be a terrible blow to Athens. Both outbreaks taken together would kill about one-third (4,400) of the city's 13,000 hoplites that Pericles had stated Athens had at the war's outset, as well as one-quarter (300) of her 1,200-strong cavalry corps. It may be presumed that the mortality rate for the civilian population as a whole was about the same as for the military, and thus around one-third of Athens' population perished.[62]

Pericles would suffer a heavy political cost as the plague took the lives of the Athenians. His enemies, Plutarch reports, would go around telling the people that 'the plague was caused by the herding together of the country folk into the city. Here, in the summer months, many of them lived huddled in shacks and in stifling tents and were forced to lead an inactive indoor life, instead of being in the pure open air of the country, as they were accustomed. The man responsible for all this, they said, was Pericles: because of the war he had compelled the country people to crowd inside the walls, and he had given them no employment, but left them penned up like cattle to infect each other, without providing them with any relief or change of quarters.'[63] In their misery, the stunned, plague-ridden Athenians would now bitterly recall an old oracle which had predicted that 'A Dorian war will come, and with it pestilence'.[64]

In early 430, around the time that the plague was establishing itself in Athens, Pericles led a naval expedition against Epidaurus while a Spartan army was once more busy ravaging Attica. For this campaign he took with him 100 triremes, 4,000 hoplites and 300 cavalry in horse transport triremes. This force was supplemented by fifty more ships drawn from Chios and Lesbos. Just before the armada was to depart, while Pericles stood upon the deck of his personal trireme, Plutarch writes, there was a solar eclipse. This was a dreadful omen, and in the darkness panic tore through the oarsmen and soldiers. His helmsman was terrified by the eclipse, but Pericles held up his own cloak in front of the man's eyes, and asked him if he was scared by this and if it was a dire omen. The helmsman said no. 'What is the difference, then,' Pericles asked, 'between this and the eclipse except that the eclipse has been caused by something bigger than my cloak?'[65]

Landing at Epidaurus, the Athenians ravaged the lands around it, but Epidaurus would not succumb. Plutarch says that the Athenians were hampered by the effects of the plague, with the sickness felling Pericles' men and those with whom they came into contact. Both Thucydides and Plutarch place the organization of the expedition to the period after the emergence of the plague. For Pericles to have undertaken this massive project in the midst of a deadly pestilence appears foolhardy. Plutarch writes that the mission was conceived by Pericles in the 'hope of relieving these troubles' arising from the plague and 'at the same time doing some damage to the enemy'. If this were so, the disease could only have just made itself felt at Athens, since it must be presumed that the thousands of trireme crewmen and 4,300 other embarked troops in the expedition were still healthy when they went aboard their ships. Pericles would not have seen any value in a naval expedition on this scale composed of sickly men. Plutarch's later statement that the attack on Epidaurus was 'frustrated by the plague' indicates that the disease must have became problematic for the fleet only after it had left Athens.[66] The Peloponnesians stayed in Attica for forty days, in what would prove to be their invasion of longest duration, but they hurriedly departed when they saw that the Athenians were suffering so badly from the disease.[67]

Whether the Epidaurus expedition should be thought to represent a significant alteration to Pericles' original strategy depends on how much weight should be given to the strict letter of his plan as enunciated at the war's start. For one, it is not fair to lock Pericles into a set strategy and see everything that does not fit neatly into it as a serious deviation. He may well have adopted a 'wait and see' approach in which Athens would react to the enemy's moves and form effective counters. For that matter, much of what comes to be labelled 'strategy' is done so only retrospectively, and often fails to capture the contingent and improvised nature of decision-making in war. Pericles need not have remained wedded to his initial, highly defensive posture as set forth at the start of the war if he saw an offensive opportunity had presented itself that made good strategic sense to pursue.

Second, Pericles had in fact explicitly contemplated establishing fortified posts in enemy country when he explained his strategy to the Assembly.[68] A fleet of 100 ships had already been despatched earlier in the war. The Athenian component of the current allied fleet of 150 triremes was 100, and so would have required Athens to find and pay approximately 20,000 crewmen, not to mention the embarked hoplites. The expense would have been substantial, and this expedition could hardly be deemed a mere raiding force. Plutarch has Pericles undertaking the mission as a means of lessening the hurts of the plague, while at the same time wounding the Peloponnesians, but it is hard to believe that had Epidaurus been captured that the Athenians would not have retained it afterward.[69] It is more likely that the assault on Epidaurus was a move fully consistent with his earlier belief that Athens might well establish fortified positions in enemy country.

Pericles' motives in launching the venture against Epidaurus may have been mixed, seeing it as a way to relieve some of the pressure in the city caused by the plague in addition to taking a strategically located city. This can hardly have been an abandonment of his strategy, as it is difficult to give credence to the notion that a naval expedition against a city on the Peloponnesian coast was what Pericles truly had in mind when he warned his countrymen against fresh conquests. From the context, it would seem that Pericles was actually worried more about the grandiose, even megalomaniacal, schemes to conquer Sicily, Etruria or Carthage that were being so loosely talked about by his countrymen in the pre-war period. These were far cries from operations directed toward the seizure of single cities, even one conducted by a very large fleet, and Pericles would not lightly have rejected the idea of implementing a strategy that had proven successful before against Sparta.

Another expedition that same summer was mounted against the Chalcidians in Thrace and against Potidaea, where the siege was still going on. The expedition's commanders, Hagnon and Cleopompus, brought 4,000 hoplites to supplement the Athenian forces already on site. They deployed their siege engines against the city but failed to capture it. Their efforts were stymied by the plague, which tore through their men. In about forty days, the Athenian expeditionary force lost 1,050 of the 4,000 men they had brought with them, and Hagnon went back to Athens, leaving the original troops in place to continue the siege.

Periclean *Realpolitik*

The people of Athens had by this time, after two years of war and with a frightful plague scything down citizens, thoroughly soured on Pericles, whom they thought to be the 'author of the war and the cause of all their misfortunes'.[70] Peace envoys were sent to Sparta, but these made no headway, which is understandable when one considers that the Spartans must have now seen Athens as a hobbled, pestilence-ridden state. With dissatisfaction surging, in the summer of 430 BC Pericles called an assembly in which he tried to reassure the people about their chances in the war. He told them to stick to his original war strategy, and not diverge from it. The war was being fought in two spheres, he said: land and sea. Do not worry about losses such as land or houses, since these were insignificant, he urged. On the sea, Athens reigned supreme, and their 'naval resources are such that your vessels may go where they please, without the King [of Persia] or any other nation on earth being able to stop them'.[71] So long as Athenian liberty was preserved, they could recover whatever they might lose on land, he said, but if they succumbed, they would lose everything.[72]

The Athenians, he argued, could not stop fighting. They could not relinquish their empire. In a remarkably candid manner, he warned: 'You should remember also that what you are fighting against is not merely slavery as an exchange for independence, but also loss of empire and danger from the animosities incurred in its exercise. Besides, to recede is no longer possible, if indeed any of you in the alarm of the moment has become enamoured of the honesty of such an unambitious part. For what you hold is, to speak plainly, a tyranny: to take it perhaps was wrong, but to let it go unsafe.'[73]

Thucydides says that as a community the Athenians were convinced by Pericles, but as private individuals their wartime losses stung so badly that they would not relent until Pericles had been slapped with a fine. Once this had been done, their anger dissipated; the people elected him as general again and gave him the supreme command of the war. In his judgment of Pericles, Thucydides praises him for correctly assessing the strength of Athens, and said that the 'correctness of his foresight became better known after his death'. Pericles had advised the Athenians 'to wait quietly, to pay attention to the marine [the navy], to attempt no new conquests, and to expose their city to no hazards during the war'. If they adhered to this sensible policy, they would survive.[74] The Athenians would, as the war unfolded, and deprived of Pericles' guidance, fail to keep to Pericles' advice, and Thucydides blames this for Athens' eventual defeat in the war.

Though the Athenians were clearly dominant at sea, the Spartans themselves were not always on the defensive there, and they launched a strike at Zacynthus in 430. This attack was an acknowledgement that the strategy of invading Attica and wrecking the crops to make the Athenians either fight a stand-up hoplite battle or surrender was making no progress. The naval descents made by the Athenian fleet in this, the war's second year, had done great harm to Sparta's coastal allies, who were understandably worried about further attacks. If Spartan protection failed them, then there was the strong likelihood that they might break from the alliance with Sparta. Spartan strategy in assaulting Zacynthus rested on the belief that Athens' naval expeditions would be hindered if the bases her triremes required to operate effectively in the waters off the western Peloponnesus were taken from her. If the west could be made safe from seaborne attacks, then the available Peloponnesian forces could be more effectively stationed in the east to dissuade Athenian naval raids.[75] With the Spartan admiral Cnemus in command of a fleet of 100 triremes and 1,000 hoplites, they tried to capture Zacynthus, but were repulsed and failed to achieve anything besides ravaging the land about, and returned home.[76] The strategy was sound, albeit one that had failed in its implementation. Also, it is likely that in response to this move against Zacynthus, the Athenians would send a small squadron of twenty triremes to Naupactus in the Gulf of Corinth in late 430.[77]

The Passing of Pericles

In 429 BC, Pericles would himself die of the plague, as had so many of his fellow Athenians. His particular form of the illness was different from the sudden, acute onset that had felled most others, it being a 'lingering fever', writes Plutarch. As he lay on his death bed, his friends gathered around, talking about his 'famous exploits and the number of trophies he had set up'. As the supreme commander of Athenian military forces he had won nine victories. His admiring friends thought that Pericles was unconscious, but he had been listening to all that they had said about him, and he spoke. 'He was astonished, he told them, that they should praise and remember him for exploits which owed at least as much to good fortune as his own efforts, and which many other generals had performed quite as well as himself, while they said nothing of his greatest and most glorious title to fame.' Pericles explained, 'I mean by this that no Athenian ever put on mourning because of me.'[78]

The Battle of Chalcis

In 429 BC, a major Peloponnesian expedition involving 1,000 hoplites was sent to Acarnania in northwestern Greece under Cnemus, commanding a handful of ships, with additional ships being readied in other League states. The Ambraciots and the Chaonians had told the Spartans that if they made a move by land and sea, the Acarnanians on the coast would remain in place, and that the islands of Zacynthus and Cephallenia would be quickly subdued once Acarnania was taken. The strategic benefit of such an expedition was that this would make the long voyage around the Peloponnessus much more difficult for the Athenians. There was also the hope that the Athenian base at Naupactus might be captured. Naupactus was Athens' key naval base in the Gulf of Corinth. She had gained control of the city from the Ozolian Locrians in 457–456, settling rebellious Helots there, and these new inhabitants were reliably anti-Spartan in their outlook. Taking it away would remove a painful thorn in the side of Corinth and deal Athens a heavy blow. The Spartan ships made their way past the Athenian flotilla at Naupactus, which was under the command of Phormio, and landed troops in Acarnania.[79]

The Acarnanians appealed to Phormio, but he had his hands full with the fleet in Corinth that was getting ready to sail and had to remain in place to defend Naupactus. When the Peloponnesian fleet of forty-seven ships was ready, it moved along the coast to reinforce Cnemus in Acarnania, but this was prevented by Phormio's small, twenty-ship squadron, which had them under observation. Phormio was following them closely, waiting only for the chance to strike at them in open sea where his manoeuvring would be more effective. The Peloponnesians had not organized their fleet for a battle, as they were intent upon going to Cnemus' aid in Acarnania, and they hardly expected that Phormio's ships, being so few in number, would dare to challenge them.[80]

The Peloponnesians were unprepared for a fight, and their ships were heavy with troops for the land campaign. They spotted the Athenian squadron pacing them, on the other side of the Corinthian Gulf, while they themselves were hugging its southern (Peloponnesian) coast. When the Peloponnesians reached Patrae in Achaea, they tried to cross northward to the mainland, but this move was seen by the Athenians, who had taken up observation positions at the Evenus River and at Chalcis, which lay on the northern shore of the Gulf. The Peloponnesians halted their movement, and waited until nightfall to try again. The darkness was of little help, as the Athenians saw them in any case as they weighed anchor. Phormio's ships caught up to them and forced them to fight a night battle midway between the two shores, where there was plenty of room in which to manoeuvre.

The Peloponnnesian fleet was a composite force drawn from several states, and each contingent within it had its own native commander. The Corinthian ships had three – Machaon, Isocrates and Agatharchidas. They clearly lacked confidence in their chances against the Athenians, encumbered as they were with troops, and instead of deploying in formation in which to fight a conventional battle, they arrayed their triremes in a circle, bows pointed outward. Within this circle they put all of the small ships that had accompanied them, together with the five best-performing ships in their fleet. The job of these five triremes would be to act as a 'fire brigade' to reinforce any section of the circle that came under pressure from the enemy.[81]

This formation, known as the *kyklos*, had one great advantage in that by providing an all-around defence, it precluded any chance at a strike at the vulnerable stern of a trireme. But the disadvantage of using this formation off Chalcis on this day was that it ceded the initiative completely to the Athenians. The ensuing sea fight was thus more like a siege on land than a naval battle in the ordinary sense. The twenty Athenian triremes adopted a line formation, each ship behind the one ahead of it, and again and again sailed around the immobile Peloponnesian ships. Each time that the Athenians circled the enemy they would feint an attack, causing the Peloponnesian ships to be drawn inward in defensive reaction. Phormio had ordered his captains not to press their attacks home, thinking that in time, with repeated feints, the enemy formation would contract so much that their ships would become fouled amid the cramped space in the ever-contracting *kyklos*.[82]

Apart from his holding the initiative, Phormio also knew that the wind would soon turn to his advantage. The wind usually picked up in the morning, blowing from the direction of the Gulf, and he thought that his ships would handle this better than the bunched-up Peloponnesians. Once the wind had arisen, a strike at the disorganized and static enemy triremes would have the most effect. When the wind did rise, it played havoc with the Peloponnesian fleet. Their triremes were too close to each other, and they and the small ships collided inside the confines of the shrunken *kyklos*.[83]

The dangerous press also impeded the Peloponnesians' ability to redeploy their ships. The collisions that were now occurring brought about such panic and shouting that no one could hear the commands of the trireme captains or the boatswains. The Peloponnesians were also at a severe disadvantage in rowing; in the roiling seas, they were unable to lift their oars far enough above the water to move their ships. With the *kyklos* collapsing in total confusion, Phormio at this moment ordered his triremes to go on the attack.[84]

The Peloponnesians were incapable of mounting any defence in their stricken state. A trireme belonging to one of the fleet's many commanders was the first to be sunk, and several more were disabled. The remainder of the Peloponnesian fleet turned south and ran for the safety of Patrae and Dyme in Achaea on the Peloponnesian coast. The Athenians pursued them, and captured twelve of their ships. They then sailed to Molycrium, where they erected a trophy on the promontory of Rhium in honour of their victory and dedicated a trireme to Poseidon. After this, Phormio led his squadron back to his base at Naupactus, having suffered no losses at all. Once the Peloponnesians had caught their breath and collected themselves, they coasted to Cyllene, where Cnemus was waiting for them with his ships and those from Leucas. Phormio sent an urgent request to Athens for more ships to reinforce his still outnumbered squadron.

The sharp defeat inflicted by a small flotilla of Athenian warships off Chalcis does not seem to have properly registered on the minds of the Peloponnesians. Instead of admitting that their crews were inferior and their ships less skillfully handled, they thought that misconduct of some sort must be the reason for the loss, not Athenian experience or a concomitant deficit in experience among themselves. The Spartans sent a three-man commission composed of Timocrates, Brasidas and Lycophron to assume control of the fleet and take it back into battle. They also called up additional ships from the League's naval states and prepared the ships on hand for renewed combat. Receiving Phormio's appeal for reinforcement, Athens sent twenty ships to rendezvous with him at Naupactus; these did not hurry to meet him, but instead sailed first to Crete to attack Cydonia on an irrelevant mission, and spent so much time there that they would not be a factor in the next encounter. Phormio would be on his own.

Waiting Game

The Peloponnesian fleet emerged from Cyllene and coasted to Panormus in Achaea, where it linked up with a land army which had marched in support of its operations. Phormio, on the northern coast of the Gulf, sailed to Molycrian Rhium, where he anchored with his twenty triremes. On the southern shore opposite it on the Peloponnesus stood Achaean Rhium, and there the reinforced Peloponnesian fleet, now numbering seventy-seven triremes, dropped its anchors. The distance between the two Rhiums was only three-quarters of a mile. The Peloponnesians desired to fight a battle within the narrow confines of the Straits of Rhium, since this would necessarily restrict the manoeuvring room available to the Athenians. The Athenians for their part wanted to move out into the open water to fight, where they would have more space to manoeuvre. The Peloponnesians would not oblige them, recalling very easily the drubbing they had just received off Chalcis.

For a week the two fleets practised and readied themselves for battle, but neither budged. Cnemus and Brasidas expected that reinforcements would be arriving soon from Athens (unaware that this Athenian fleet had, because of bad winds and poor weather, found itself stuck at Crete) and decided to chance a fight. Morale among their shaken crews was very low, however. They spoke to their men and sought to re-instill some spirit in them.

There had been insufficient preparation for the last fight, they told them, and they had not been organized as a true fleet ready for battle but just an expeditionary force meant to convey troops. There was also the matter of their own inexperience, and they admitted that the Athenians were more capable. It had not been for want of courage that they had lost the battle. For the upcoming fight, they assured, the Peloponnesians would be fighting close to a friendly shore with an army of hoplites in support, and 'previous mistakes ... will teach us better for the future'.[85] For their own part, Cnemus and Brasidas promised the men that they would be at least as well prepared as their original commanders.

The Athenians on the opposite side of the narrows had their own issues with morale, despite their earlier triumph. The twenty ships of Phormio's squadron had never been reinforced, and the Peloponnesian fleet of seventy-seven ships greatly outnumbered them. Phormio insisted that these numbers were meaningless, that there were no odds too great for them. There was still a sense of dismay at the sight of a Peloponnesian fleet that was almost four times as large as their own. Phormio called a meeting of his crews. The Peloponnesians were wrong, he told them, to think that the same ingredient, courage, that worked for them so well on land would work just as well in naval combat. But the Athenians had the edge in confidence, and neither were they inferior in courage. The Peloponnesians were putting their faith in their superior numbers, not in their own resolve.

Then there was the matter of tactics. Phormio gave a brief summary of what Athenian naval power was all about. He promised that he would not, if at all possible, give battle within the strait, acknowledging 'that in a contest between a number of clumsily managed vessels and a small, fast, well-handled, squadron, want of sea room is an undoubted disadvantage. One cannot run down an enemy properly without having a sight of him a good way off, nor can one retire at need when pressed; one can neither break the line nor return upon his rear, the proper tactics for a fast sailer; but the naval action necessarily becomes a land one, in which numbers must decide the matter.'[86]

There was much at stake in the approaching battle. 'The issues you will fight for are great – either you will destroy the naval hopes of the Peloponnesians or you will bring nearer to reality the Athenians' fear of losing control of the sea.' But Athenian prospects were good. '[Y]ou have defeated most of them already; and beaten men do not face a danger twice with the same determination.'[87]

The Battle of Naupactus

With the waiting game having gone on a week, the supposed reinforcement fleet expected soon and the Athenians refusing to budge, the Peloponnesians blinked first. They set sail eastward along the Peloponnesian coast, heading back into the Gulf. The right wing was in the lead, with twenty of the fleet's fastest triremes, the thought being that if Phormio suspected that they might attempt a strike at his unprotected base at Naupactus and rushed to defend it, the speedy ships of the Peloponnesian right wing would be able to cut him off. Phormio did just that, and after getting his men aboard their ships coasted along the northern shore of the Gulf toward Naupactus in single file.

The Peloponnesians, seeing that Phormio had done as expected, executed a turn to the north, with the right wing leading again, making straight for the Athenians. They were still not fast enough to catch the entire squadron, and the first eleven Athenian triremes evaded the manoeuvre. The rearmost nine, however, were trapped and driven ashore, with some crews killed and others making an escape to the land. Their triremes were tied with cables and hand-hauled away by the Peloponnesians. One still had an Athenian crew within it, having been unable to escape before the enemy had set upon them. But the other ships were rescued by some intrepid Messenians who rushed into the waves in full armour, clambered aboard, and took back possession of the ships.

At this point the battle had been a one-side affair, completely in favour of the Peloponnesians. But Athenian tactical acumen would enable them to turn the tables on the enemy. The leading eleven Athenian triremes were still being pursued by the Peloponnesian right wing of twenty ships, and of the eleven, all managed to reach Naupactus. There they turned their ram-equipped prows outward, with their sterns close to the shore in a defensive stance. When the Peloponnesian ships finally arrived, they were out of formation, and their crews could be heard singing the *paean* to celebrate their victory. Just one Athenian ship had not yet made it into Naupactus' harbour, and she was being hunted by a lone Leucadian trireme (the Spartan Timocrates was aboard) that had ranged far in advance of the others.

In the roadstead leading into Naupactus was an anchored merchant freighter, and the Athenian trireme used its presence to execute a daring manoeuvre. It sailed around the merchantman, using it to protect its sides as it turned, and then fell upon the Leucadian trireme, ramming it amidships. The Leucadian ship sank, and the rest of the Peloponnesian fleet, in hopeless disarray, panicked and came to a full stop, while still others grounded themselves, so limited was their knowledge of the local waters.[88]

The fighting spirit of the Athenians inside Naupactus was rekindled at the sight of this minor victory, and they surged out of the harbour. The Peloponnesians turned and fled westward, in the direction they had just come. Not all would escape. The Athenians claimed six of the nearest Peloponnesian ships, and recovered the ships that had been previously captured or driven aground. Timocrates' body (he had taken his own life) was later found washed ashore in Naupactus.[89]

Both sides exchanged their dead and erected trophies in honour of their respective victories in the Battle of Naupactus. The Athenians did so at Naupactus to honour their startling recovery, while the Peloponnesians, a little less convincingly, set up a trophy for the initial portion of the battle in which they had driven a few Athenian triremes ashore and captured one other. This ship was dedicated by them alongside the trophy. Still expecting Athenian reinforcements, the Peloponnesians, with the exception of the Leucadian contingent, made for Corinth. The twenty laggard Athenian triremes of the reinforcement fleet appeared at Naupactus not long afterward.[90]

After landing an expeditionary force of several hundred troops in Acarnania during the winter of 429/428 BC, Phormio led his squadron back to Athens.[91] Unhappily for the Athenians, their great admiral seems to have died not long after his masterful triumphs at Chalcis and Naupactus, and with the exception of this minor Acarnania campaign, took no further part in the war. The Athenians would erect a statue of him on the Acropolis in appreciation of his sterling service to his city.

The recall of the Athenian squadron from Naupactus at this time is puzzling. It is probable that the Athenians believed that after the two defeats of the Peloponnesian fleet and its break-up, keeping a squadron on station at Naupactus was not required by strategic circumstances, though a continuing naval presence in the Corinthian Gulf would certainly have been of real value to Athens as the war went on.[92] The Athenian ships based at Naupactus had also seen extensive action, whether in the battles in the Gulf or on the long voyage there by way of Crete, and perhaps bringing back these ships for repair at Piraeus seemed advisable. The delivery of the prisoners taken by Phormio and the captured ships would also have been necessary, and continuing to pay the ships' crews of the Naupactus squadron cost money. These ships had originally been sent to the Gulf in late 430, as an answer to the Peloponnesian fleet's attack on Zacynthus, and by the time that they had gone back to Athens in early 428, the expense to the Athenian treasury of their long deployment would have amounted to at least 240 talents. This must have been an expense the Athenians thought that they could do without.

The outcomes of the battle of Chalcis and Naupactus in 429 show how extremely effective the Athenian navy was, especially when the conditions of battle were in its favour. At Chalcis, it was able to row circles around an opponent that huddled in a defensive *kyklos* formation and relinquished the initiative utterly. Perhaps even more impressive than its performance at Chalcis was the resilience it demonstrated at Naupactus. Even though the squadron of twenty was heavily outnumbered, it was able to regain its balance despite losing nine ships in the run to Naupactus. That the commander of a single trireme could make such clever use of the moored freighter outside Naupactus to deliver a deadly ramming attack on its pursuer highlights the quality of Athenian trierarchs, helmsmen and crews. The bold act of this trireme also gave heart to the dispirited Athenian ships already inside Naupactus, and when they emerged it was to resume the fight with renewed vigour. The Athenians truly were, man for man, far superior to the Peloponnesians.

The Peloponnesians had much work to do. If they had any hope of defeating the Athenians, their crews and tactics would have to improve. That being said, they had performed well enough, all things considered. Their fleet at Chalcis had been organized as a transport force, not a battlefleet, and at Naupactus they had shown that they could row with sufficient speed to catch a substantial segment of the Athenian squadron as it raced home to Naupactus. Their decision to threaten Naupactus with assault was a sound one in that, although it allowed more sea room to the Athenians in which to manoeuvre, it compelled them to travel home rapidly in a single column that was more vulnerable to attack than a proper battle formation. The Peloponnesian defeat at Naupactus was brought about by a fatal bout of overconfidence. Thinking the battle won, they believed it was already over when it was not. They allowed their ships to fall out of formation and were no match for the Athenians when they returned to the fight. Timocrates must bear some of the blame for this, since it was his own trireme that had rowed so far ahead of the rest of his ships.

The Peloponnesians certainly seemed to have learned the lesson that it was folly to go head-to-head with the Athenians in an engagement on the open sea. The Athenian conception of naval warfare was predicated upon three things. First, that the Athenians had better crews than their opponents. Second, that their ships were faster and more manoeuvrable. Lastly, that there was adequate sea room in which to utilize to the full the manoeuvre tactics made possible by their better oarsmen and nimbler ships. At Chalcis, Phormio had all three. At Naupactus, he had only the first two, and the engagement was a close-run affair, with the day saved only by a daring manoeuvre executed by a single trierarch. If any one of these elements did not exist, the system of Athenian naval tactics was liable to fail, as it nearly did completely in the waters off Naupactus.[93] The Corinthians especially, with their own longstanding naval tradition, recognized the weakness of the Athenian system, and would never again give them the chance to manoeuvre as freely as they did at Chalcis. Chalcis would also prove to be the first and only time that an admiral had a fleet so skilled that he could deploy the rams of all the ships of his fleet at once, at his command, as a single tactical unit. After Chalcis, other fleet commanders would have to leave the tactical handling to the individual trierarchs, who would execute their ramming attacks as the chance appeared.[94]

Phormio's achievement in the Gulf went far beyond the matter of the destruction and capture of a few warships. He had blunted the Peloponnesian offensive against Acarnania and prevented the valuable naval base at Naupactus from falling into enemy hands, to remain a thorn in the side of Corinthian commercial traffic. By displaying Athenian nautical skill in so outstanding a manner, he deterred for a long time further enemy naval ambitions as well as thoughts of defection among Athens' own allies.[95]

The Athenian decision to send the reinforcement fleet of twenty ships, which were desperately needed by Phormio at Naupactus, first to Crete to attack Cydonia, has never been given a convincing explanation. There is no doubt that in war mistakes are made as to strategy, and sometimes directions are taken that are of limited value, or perhaps even self-defeating. The diversion of the squadron to Crete is something worse, however. It was a mistake that impacted an ongoing operation in the Gulf and delayed the arrival of the ships at Naupactus until after the battle had been fought. Suppositions that explain the move run the gamut from civilian incompetence, to trading interests in the eastern Mediterranean, to a desire to provoke an anti-Spartan insurrection on the island.[96]

The simplest reason for the detour is that the Athenians must not have believed that the voyage to Crete would detain them for as long as it in fact did. There is also the possibility that Athenian finances were not up to the task of sending out more ships at the time, and that the diversion of the fleet meant for the Gulf was done because there were no other ships with crews to hand. This does not excuse their shocking lack of urgency, since Phormio must have made it abundantly clear that he needed help right away. Thucydides writes that in addition to the military operations on Crete (Cydonian territory was laid waste by the Athenian force), the Athenian ships were kept there because of 'adverse winds and stress of weather'.[97] The Cretan adventure at this harrowing time was thus an ill-considered move made much worse by bad weather.

Attack on Piraeus

The Peloponnesian fleet was still extant, though dispersed, and had found safety at Corinth and elsewhere in the Corinthian Gulf. The Megarians managed to convince Cnemus, Brasidas and the rest of the Peloponnesian fleet commanders that they should make a descent upon Piraeus, which had been left unprotected. The plan they outlined called for the fleet's ship crews to carry their oars, rowlock thongs and seat cushions across the Isthmus of Corinth and march to Megara on the other side. Seat cushions were routinely used as a buffer between an oarsman's bottom and the wooden bench upon which he sat. One dire affliction commonly seen among rowers was the fistula of the anus. If corrective action was not taken, the fistula could end up penetrating the wall of the rectum. Various remedies were applied, including water mixed with honey for its antimicrobial properties, powdered hartwort root, linen plugs and myrrh. Failure to treat the condition could result in the death of the afflicted man.[98]

Waiting for these rowers in the docks of nearby Nisaea were the forty triremes that they would board and sail against Piraeus, which was unready for an attack.[99] The plan was not a poor one, and might have worked had it been carried out as formulated. Having made it over the Isthmus to Nisaea, the fleet did not sail on to Piraeus directly, but instead it seems that the Peloponnesians got cold feet, or perhaps a contrary wind hindered them. Their ships were not in the best condition either, and seem not to have been in the water for some time. This would have badly affected the galleys' performance. When the timbers of a trireme dried out too much, they shrank, creating gaps between the planks, and the vessel would no longer be watertight. Lacking confidence in their chances, the Peloponnesians went first to the point of Salamis opposite from Megara. They stormed the Athenian-held Fort Budorum that kept watch on Megara and captured the three triremes stationed there, and then began to ravage the island.[100]

None of this much mattered, however, as the all-important advantage of surprise had been lost. The Athenians panicked, thinking that the Peloponnesians had somehow entered Piraeus. But this was not the case, and the Athenians quickly rallied and sent their fleet to Salamis. The Peloponnesians ran away, carrying off their loot and captives before the Athenians could catch them. The Athenians next took precautions to guard Piraeus and closed the harbours there. One must ask why the Athenians did not have a small patrol squadron watching over the approaches to Piraeus, as it seems extremely lax of them to have left themselves so open to a surprise attack. Thucydides attributed the lack of a defence to the Athenians' overconfidence in their navy, but it was the nature of ancient war galleys themselves that made a constant guard so hard to keep up. The hulls of the ships, as noted earlier, became saturated with water very quickly, and the wood itself was always subject to the potentially devastating action of the *teredo* shipworm, so they had to be taken ashore very often to get them back into a good fighting condition and prevent the shipworms from fatally weakening their timbers.[101]

The triremes' crewmen also needed to eat and sleep, and keeping ships on alert with rowers seated at their benches was trying for the men. Then, too, the Peloponnesian movement came at night, when any movement by ships would have been especially difficult and thus unexpected. Ironically, in the attack on Piraeus, the Megarian ships would suffer from the opposite problem of having timbers that were *too* dry, and thus their ships were leaky. The Megarians, it may be presumed, had kept their ships out of the water prior to the attack so as to keep the Athenians from learning of the strike, and these vessels became too dry to remain watertight. When a wooden ship has been kept out of the water for too long, its seams need to be recaulked, and this was an extremely labour-intensive task that would have been impossible to hide from Athenian eyes. The hazards that ships left in the water were prone to, and the length of time that it took to get them back into proper fighting condition when they needed to be used, goes a long way to explaining why there was no fleet sitting outside Piraeus when the Peloponnesians came, and Athenian fleets would remain challenges to deploy over the course of the war. We have seen how the Athenians had to send their triremes to Crete in 429 BC, despite the desperate need for them in the Corinthian Gulf. It may be presumed that there were no other ships on hand ready to send to accomplish both missions at once. Similarly, in 428, a fleet that was to conduct raids against the Peloponnesus was deployed instead against rebellious Mytilene in Lesbos, and another fleet heading to Sicily in 425 would be diverted to deal with a problem on Corcyra.[102] Further, these diversions do not take into account the delays experienced when new ships had to be built to make up for losses to augment the ships already on hand.

The Piraeus raid had failed, but the Peloponnesians can't be faulted for trying. Had the daring strike succeeded, it would have been a noteworthy victory and a deep embarrassment to the Athenians, unable to protect their home against attack. That being said, it is unlikely, even in a best-case scenario for the Spartans, that the attack would have appreciably altered the balance of power in the war. The Athenian ships in port might have been destroyed, but Athens had many others and would have built more. The force of forty triremes was itself insufficient to transport enough troops to seize Piraeus, so the venture would have been at most a tactical success, not a strategic one, and so more akin to a major raid than a serious assault. The Spartans would need more than a single bold stroke to defeat Athens so early in the war, and this would require a different strategy than a surprise attack on Piraeus or annually raiding the farms of Attica. This successful strategy would be a long time in coming.

The Revolt of Lesbos

Dissatisfaction among the people of Lesbos with their place in the empire had engendered a desire among them to escape even before the war had erupted. The Spartans had not been interested in accepting them into their own league, and the beginning of the war caught the Lesbians unprepared. They hurriedly started to build ships and defensive moles across their harbour mouths, and purchased grain from the Black Sea region to shore up their food supplies. The Methymnans were the sole people on Lesbos who remained loyal to Athens, and they alerted the Athenians to the mounting danger.[103]

The Athenians could not afford to lose Lesbos. As Pericles had advised, it was imperative that Athens preserve its overseas empire, which was where her true strength lay. But at first they could not countenance the idea that any of the Lesbians were thinking of revolting. Their wishful thinking ended abruptly when a delegation to Mytilene discovered that the Mytilenians were compelling the other Lesbian cities to join them in an island-wide union. The Athenians knew that the Mytilenians were currently holding a festival in honour of Malean Apollo outside Mytilene itself, and sent forty triremes to strike the city in what they hoped would be a surprise attack. Ten Mytilenian triremes and their crews that had previously come to Athens as part of the alliance were interned, and the fleet set out. But the Mytilenians were warned of the mission by a man who had taken passage out of Athens aboard a merchantman, and they desisted from going to Malea to hold the festival.

With the security of their mission fatally compromised, the Athenian triremes found the city expecting their attack and the Mytilenians unwilling to negotiate. The Athenians and the Mytilenians fought a small battle just outside the harbour, the Athenians having the better of it. The Mytilenians requested a parley, hoping to extricate their ships from their predicament. The Athenians were willing to talk too, since they worried that their strength would be insufficient to take on the entire island. With an armistice in place, the Mytilenians sent envoys to Athens to try to have the Athenians withdraw their fleet. At the same time, hedging their bets, they despatched a trireme to Sparta with a delegation aboard to secure aid.[104]

The Spartans were convinced by the delegates' presentation to allow Mytilene into their alliance. The Spartans, urged on by the Mytilenians, decided to mount another attack on Attica, and this would be by both land and sea. They brought up machines to pull their ships based at Corinth on the far side of the Isthmus over to the Athenian side, but the ardour of their allies did not match that of their own people. Their allies were, Thucydides said, 'both engaged in harvesting their grain and sick of making expeditions', and their turnout was very slow.[105] The Athenians were aware of the activities at the Isthmus, and understood that the Peloponnesian move had been occasioned by a belief in Athenian vulnerability. Seeking to prove them wrong, the Athenians found crews for 100 additional triremes with which to harry the Peloponnesian coasts. These ships were a supplement to the fleet at Lesbos, which had been neither withdrawn nor reduced. Apart from these fleets, there was already a force of thirty triremes abroad that was raiding the coasts of the Peloponnesus. Taken altogether, Athens had some 250 triremes at sea in mid-428 BC in various theatres, and this would be the most ever put into service at any one time during the war.[106]

While this was an impressive logistical achievement, Thucydides bemoaned the outrageous cost of such a gigantic navy. Since crewmen drew one drachma per day as pay, and there were about 50,000 men serving with the fleet, the total *daily* cost of keeping so many ships at sea was about 8.3 talents. This was a genuine haemorrhage of money. The siege of Mytilene would prove to be very expensive, and the need to pay for it occasioned the first imposition of a capital levy (*eisphora*) on the Athenian citizenry in 428/7.[107] This war tax raised the enormous sum of 200 talents, Thucydides writes, but even this was not enough, and an Athenian squadron of twelve triremes under the command of Lysicles and four other officers was sent overseas to collect money from the allies.[108] Athens' need to sail abroad for money to sustain its military operations would become ever more pressing as the war dragged on and drained its treasury.

The Voyage of Alcidas

In the summer of 427 BC, a Peloponnesian fleet of forty-two ships, commanded by Alcidas, headed for Mytilene, while at the same time Attica was again invaded. But Alcidas seems to have been in no hurry to reach Lesbos, and the Mytilenians surrendered before he could render assistance. Learning of the surrender upon touching at the island of Myconus, he made his way along the coast of Asia Minor, hearing the full story of what had occurred at Mytilene only after reaching Embatum. Other officers in the fleet still wished to use their ships against the enemy in some way. One advised making a sudden descent upon the satisfied Athenians at Mytilene, judging them to be unwary after having just taken the city. Others pleaded with Alcidas to seize an Ionian city to use as a base for supporting an Ionian uprising against Athens. Thucydides believed that this strategy had merit, as it would cut off the flow of tribute to Athens from her allies.[109] It is certain that if such cities could have been detached from Athenian orbit, this would have made it harder for Athens to sustain its fleet, and if it had trouble keeping up its naval strength, then it would have had a much more difficult time holding down its empire.

But Alcidas would hear none of either plan, and now that it was clear that he had been too late in getting to Mytilene, he wanted nothing more than to sail straight back to the Peloponnesus. He raced homeward, in fear of being chased by Athenian ships. His triremes, now numbering forty, were spotted by Athens' state galleys, the *Salaminia* and the *Paralus*, while he was anchored at Clarus, but Alcidas ran so fast that he easily outpaced them. But near to Crete his ships were struck by a storm and were scattered. The Peloponnesians next made their way to Cyllene. In the harbour waiting for them were thirteen Leucadian and Ambraciot triremes. Numbering fifty-three ships, Alcidas sailed for Corcyra.[110]

Second Battle of Sybota

In 427 BC, a revolution had upended the government of Corcyra, with an anti-Athenian faction seizing power. The Athenian squadron based at Naupactus, comprising twelve ships carrying 500 Messenian hoplites, arrived at Corcyra. Soon afterward, the fifty-three Peloponnesian ships from Cyllene, where they had been blown by a storm after fleeing from Lesbos, approached and anchored off Sybota. To counter this new threat, the Corcyrans launched sixty ships in great haste, ignoring the advice of the Athenian admiral Nicostratus to let his own ships depart first from the harbour. The Corcyrans rowed out in terrible disorder. Two of their ships immediately deserted, while fights among the crewmen erupted aboard two others. With the distress of the Corcyrans obvious to the Peloponnesians, Alcidas chose to place just twenty of his triremes against the Corcyrans, and set the remaining thirty-three against the twelve Athenian ships, which included the state galleys *Salaminia* and *Paralus*.

Among the Corcyrans organization was nonexistent, and they attacked haphazardly in small groups instead of a concentrated battle formation. The Athenians were wary of striking directly at the Peloponnesians ranged against them, and mounted a flanking attack on the enemy wing, where they sank one ship. Just as they had at Chalcis in 429, the Peloponnesians went into a defensive crouch, forming the *kyklos* for protection. The Athenians repeated Phormio's old trick, rowing in circles around the Peloponnesian ships in an attempt to disrupt their formation. But the Peloponnesians had seen this happen before and had learned something from the earlier encounter. The entire detachment of twenty sent to fight the Corcyrans turned away and went to help the ships doing battle against the Athenians, and Nicostratus' twelve ships were presented with the combined strength of the entire Peloponnesian fleet. The Athenians decided to withdraw, but did so slowly so that the Corcyrans, still in a mess, could make their escape while all of the attention was focused upon themselves.[111]

The Peloponnesians refused to follow up after their victory against the Corcyrans, and departed with the thirteen Corcyran triremes they had taken in the battle. Warning came not long after of the approach of an Athenian fleet of sixty ships, and Alcidas hurried away by night, even going so far as to haul his triremes across the Isthmus of Leucas to avoid being spotted going around it.

This battle shows plainly the enormous respect that the Peloponnesians had for the Athenian navy. Thucydides makes it clear that the Corcyrans were of no account in the engagement, so the actions of the Peloponnesians were occasioned solely by their wariness of the Athenians. The sinking of just a single trireme on the wing had caused the Peloponnesians to retreat into a *kyklos* formation, even though they heavily outnumbered the Athenians. That the Peloponnesians had come to understand that a purely defensive tactical stance was hopeless is illustrated by the extraction of the twenty ships initially apportioned to fight the Corcyrans so that they could lend help against the Athenians. There were in this section of the encounter roughly fifty or so Peloponnesian ships taking on just twelve Athenian triremes, approximately a four-to-one advantage. Despite this substantial numerical superiority, the Peloponnesians were unwilling to press their advantage once they had rescued their comrades from encirclement. The Peloponnesians thereby conceded, in deed if not in word, that the Athenian fleet was far superior to their own.

The Athenian squadron in Sicily made an attack on the Aeolian Islands in the winter of 427 and ravaged them, but the islanders would not surrender and the Athenians departed for Rhegium. Elsewhere, in 426, Demosthenes, in command of a squadron of thirty ships, conducted a cruise around the Peloponnesus. Demosthenes' fleet went to Leucas and ravaged its territory. He followed this up with an attack on the Aetolians, but his troops were badly beaten. Perishing in this campaign were 120 hoplites, whom Thucydides describes as being 'in the prime of life', assuring his readers that they were 'by far the best men in the city of Athens that fell during this war'.[112]

Another mission, under the command of Nicias, comprising sixty ships embarking 2,000 hoplites, also sailed out that summer to try to compel the Sparta-friendly island of Melos to join the Athenian alliance, but they resisted him successfully. Sailing on again to Oropus, the fleet landed its hoplites, who marched for Tanagra in Boeotia.

There they linked up with the full city levy of Athens, and made camp after ravaging Tanagran land. The next day they encountered a force of Tanagrans and Thebans who had come to fight, and were victorious. Afterward, Nicias sailed off with his fleet, proceeding along the Locrian coast, which he also ravaged, and then headed back to Athens.[113]

The year 427 was notable also for the reappearance of the plague. Thucydides writes that the disease had never gone away entirely, but that there had been a diminishment in its ravages. That winter, however, it would recur with extreme ferocity. Together with the first outbreak of the plague, the historian says that nothing did more damage to the Athenians and their morale than this invisible killer.[114]

Amphibious Action at Pylos and Sphacteria

Athenian superiority at sea had scarcely been challenged in the early years of the war. Sparta, with its well-trained hoplites, enjoyed a similar reputation for invincibility on land, but a minor campaign in the western Peloponnesus would dent this reputation badly.

An Athenian fleet of twenty ships was despatched to Sicilian waters in the autumn of 427 BC, making its base at Rhegium at the toe of the Italian peninsula. Its purpose was to close the Strait of Messana, lying between Italy and Sicily, to the flow of grain to the Peloponnesus. In the next year, seeing that Syracuse was readying a powerful fleet, the Athenians prepared an additional forty ships to reinforce their Sicilian squadron. In the summer of 425, before these ships reached Sicily, a Syracusan/Locrian squadron of twenty ships arrived at Messana, which then revolted against Athens.[115]

The Athenian fleet was on its way to Sicily via Corcyra, where it was supposed to render aid to the pro-Athenian faction in that city, which was itself under attack from oligarchic exiles based at Mount Istone, prior to continuing on to Sicily. While coasting along Laconia, word came that a large Peloponnesian fleet of sixty triremes had already reached Corcyra. One of the Athenian commanders, Demosthenes, suggested that the fleet touch first at Pylos in Messenia, but the others wished to move on immediately. Nonetheless, a storm came up that carried the fleet to Pylos, and the Athenians found refuge there. Demosthenes recommended that they fortify the spot, as there was a good supply of timber and stone around to make a worthy fort and it had a good harbour near to it too. If garrisoned by the reliably anti-Spartan Messenians, Pylos would be a useful thorn in the side of the enemy.

Demosthenes was unable to persuade any of the other captains of the brilliance of his idea. Out of boredom, however, the ordinary seamen of the fleet began to improve the naturally strong position, especially at the weakest points that might potentially come under Spartan attack. The fortification work was completed in just six days, and the bulk of the fleet, thirty-five ships, moved on for Corcyra and Sicily.[116]

Demosthenes was left behind with a mere five triremes and their crews to garrison the new fortlet. The Spartan response to this construction, initially slow because they were busy celebrating a festival, and also because their army was away on an invasion of Attica, turned serious once the full import of what the Athenians had done at Pylos became apparent. The Peloponnesians left Attica quickly, having stayed there just fifteen days, and marched back to Sparta. An army was then sent to Pylos, and the sixty triremes still at Corcyra were recalled. These were hauled across the Isthmus of Leucas to slip unobserved by the Athenian squadron stationed at Zacynthus. These reached Pylos undetected, where they linked up with Spartan land troops. Just prior to their arrival, Demosthenes sent two triremes to Eurymedon and his Zacynthus squadron with word that he needed their help back at Pylos.

The Spartans began an attack on Pylos, by land and sea, thinking that the primitive fort and its small garrison would be no match for a determined assault. The geography of Pylos requires some explanation. Pylos itself sat atop a rock at the southern end of a small peninsula connected by a sandbar to the mainland, and the Spartans made their attack from this side. Just south of Pylos lay the three-mile long, heavily wooded and slender island of Sphacteria, running roughly north to south across Navarino Bay. Sphacteria thus closes off entry into the bay/harbour except for two points: in the north, the tight Sikia Channel lying between Pylos and Sphacteria, just wide enough to permit the passage of two ships at a time; and the much wider entrance to the south of Sphacteria, which Thucydides says could accommodate eight or nine ships moving through it at once.[117]

The Spartans hoped to shut these two entrances by placing their triremes in lines across them, with their prow-mounted rams facing out. They also landed a detachment of 420 hoplites, plus their Helot servants, on Sphacteria, which was otherwise uninhabited. With both entryways blocked and the island strongly held, the Spartans believed they could prevent a landing by the Athenian fleet at either Pylos or Sphacteria.

To resist the coming Spartan attack, Demosthenes took his three triremes and brought them inside a stockade. To the sailors he gave shields, but he did have enough weapons to arm all of his men. His tiny force was supplemented by forty Messenian hoplites, and the larger part of his troops were set to guard the fort. Sixty hoplites and some archers he took outside the fort down to the most probable spot on the beach where he surmised the Spartans would try and land. Demosthenes warned his men that it would be easier to defeat the Spartans before they had landed than afterward. He reminded them of just how difficult it was to make a beach landing when opposed by a resolute foe. '[S]tand fast in the present emergency,' he told them, 'beat back the enemy at the water's edge, and save yourselves and the place.'[118]

The Spartans came up in a combined attack across the slender neck connecting Pylos to the mainland and by sea with their forty-three triremes under the command of Thrasymelidas. The Spartan seaborne assault hit precisely where Demosthenes had predicted it would, and it ran into fierce Athenian opposition on the beach. Spartan ships would mount attacks in small groups, probing for a place to land, and when repulsed, each was replaced by a new detachment.[119] One of the trireme captains present was Brasidas, the same officer who had been a fleet commissioner involved in the battle off Naupactus in 429. At Pylos he displayed extraordinary courage in attempting to force a landing. Other captains had refrained from getting too close, afraid of wrecking their ships, but Brasidas impetuously drove on, insisting that his helmsman beach his ship. Once ashore, he rushed down the gangway, but was struck by the Athenian hoplites waiting for him and fell unconscious. The other ships in the fleet tried their best to emulate his brave example, but they too were driven off by the Athenians. For two days this situation persisted, the Spartans trying to make a landing and the Athenians repeatedly driving them away. Seeing that they were getting nowhere, and that taking the fort would be a more difficult endeavour than they had anticipated, the Spartans sent ships away to Asine to collect timber to build siege engines for use against the wall opposite the harbour.[120]

Fifty Athenian ships appeared during this lull, comprising the ships from Zacynthus, the Naupactus squadron and four triremes from Chios. With no place to anchor, they moved off and spent the night on the small island of Prote nearby. The next morning, the Athenians sailed out, ready for battle, and moved against the enemy ships in the bay. The Peloponnesians were slow to get off the beach of Sphacteria, and the Athenians, swooping in, were able to pass through the northern and southern entrances into Navarino Bay, which the Spartans had neglected to close. The Peloponnesians formed a line of battle but the Athenians dispersed them easily, disabling some fleeing ships and capturing five others, including one trireme with its crew still aboard it.[121] They next attacked some other Spartan ships that had failed to put out soon enough to take part in the initial battle and seized several. The Spartans troops on Sphacteria, seeing the Athenians begin to take the ships under tow, raced down to the beach and battled in the surf for their possession. The Spartans fought like madmen, grabbing the ships and pulling them back to land. After a ferocious struggle, they managed to save all of their triremes except for the five taken at the beginning of the fight.[122]

The Athenians had won a clear victory, set up a trophy to commemorate this and handed over the Spartan dead. With the Spartan fleet nullified, the Athenians established a blockade around Sphacteria, with ships on constant patrol. At Sparta, word of the defeat caused great distress, and commissioners were sent to the Spartan camp to make a decision about what to do next. The plight of the men on the island was severe. Cut off by Athenian ships from resupply, they would eventually either starve to death or be crushed by the more numerous enemy. The Spartan commissioners opened up talks with the Athenian commanders. They agreed to an armistice that brought the fighting at Pylos to a temporary halt. A Spartan delegation would go to Athens to discuss the situation at Pylos, and the armistice would remain in effect until they returned. Athens' terms were that the Spartans' ships, some sixty in number, would be interned by the Athenians until the mission of the delegates had been completed, at which time they would be given back to the Spartans. The Spartans, for their part, would be allowed to send minimal quantities of food to their trapped men on Sphacteria. Even a small infraction of the rules of the armistice, which of course forbade further attacks by either side while it was in effect, would negate the entire agreement.[123]

It is not clear why the Spartans would agree to such a draconian infraction provision that was so obviously open to abuse. In fact, it seems unforgivably naive, even moronic, particularly since they delivered up their triremes to the enemy. It is difficult to see why the Spartans would have ever believed that they would receive their ships back, since these weapons were the only things that could have genuinely threatened the ultimate basis of Athenian power, which was control of the sea. It is likely that their desperation at having their citizen hoplites, of which there were so few, trapped on Sphacteria, made this terrible provision acceptable. It seems that they assumed it would only be for the time being, before a comprehensive peace could be reached, and then the impounded ships would be rendered irrelevant.

The Spartan envoys in Athens made a strong case for a general peace. Ill fortune had struck the Spartans at Sphacteria, they acknowledged, but Athens might well suffer setbacks one day too, and it would be wise for them to make peace while things were going their way. The Athenians, however, seeing that they were in the superior position, having blockaded the Spartan hoplites on the island, increased their demands. The Spartan troops would have to surrender and go to Athens, and furthermore, Sparta must give back several places that had been lost by Athens in 446 under the Thirty Years' Peace Treaty, these being Nisaea, Pegae, Troezen and Achaea. The Spartans asked to confer privately among themselves, understandably because they did not want whatever concessions that they might be willing to make to become public knowledge that would inevitably find its way to the ears of their allies, especially since the negotiations they were contemplating could very well fail, leaving the Spartans looking bad in front of them. Further, the Spartans had lost faith that the Athenians would ever make a peace upon acceptable terms, and left Athens without an agreement of any kind.[124]

The Athenians, unsurprisingly, refused to return the interned ships to the Spartans, claiming without merit that the Spartans had made an assault on the fort during the armistice, along with a number of other trivial infractions, and so they held that the whole armistice agreement was voided. The Spartans renewed their attacks on Pylos while the Athenians continued the blockade with two cruising triremes moving in opposite directions from one another by day and night. The Athenian fleet now numbered seventy, with twenty ships having arrived from Athens while the armistice had been in effect. But despite the strength of the blockade, the Athenians found keeping it up to be draining. Food and water were in very short supply, and with scant room to beach their ships the crews had to take their meals ashore in relays. The Spartans had themselves done better in supplying their army, which was camped on the mainland. High fees were paid to any who would volunteer to run food to Sphacteria past the blockade, and even Helots were promised their freedom if they did the same. This resulted in a lively traffic to the island, with the Helots being the most enthusiastic blockade-runners. Their efforts were supplemented by divers who swam past the patrolling Athenian warships with food.

With the siege of Sphacteria taking far longer than had been expected, the Athenians began to worry that the blockade might continue without resolution into the winter months, a time in which the delivery of supplies by sea by sailing around the Peloponnesus would no longer be possible. There were insufficient supplies to be had locally, and even in the summertime their ships were unable to ferry all that was needed by their forces. The blockade of a harbourless island would then be unsustainable, and the Spartans would eventually make their escape, either because the Athenians would have given up the siege or by stealing away in bad weather.[125] They were also unhappy that they had allowed the Spartan peace offer to slip away, and sent an expeditionary force under the demagogue Cleon to bring the campaign to a close. Taking a mixed force of hoplites, archers and peltasts, with Demosthenes as his lieutenant, Cleon boldly promised to kill or capture the Spartans on Sphacteria within twenty days.[126]

Cleon's mission was aided greatly by Demosthenes' intelligent tactics. After landing an army on the island, the Athenians did not engage the Spartan hoplites directly, but stood off at a distance, with detachments of troops taking up positions on all sides of the Spartan force. When the Spartan hoplites moved to do battle with the Athenian hoplites, the Athenian light troops – archers and the javelin-throwing peltasts – kept up a steady bombardment of missiles that prevented their progress. The Spartan hoplites, heavily equipped with armour and a big shield, were not quick enough to catch the skirmishers, who would flee when chased and then return once the Spartans had rejoined their formation. The Spartans were driven back to their fort, and a small force of Athenian troops found a way to occupy some high ground to their rear. Facing certain destruction, the Spartans, their number reduced to 292 by the end of the seventy-two-day blockade, surrendered to the Athenians.[127]

The surrender of the Spartan hoplites was earthshaking news all over Greece. Thucydides wrote, without exaggeration: 'Nothing that happened in the war surprised the Hellenes so much as this. It was the general consensus that no force or famine could make the Spartans give up their arms, but that they would fight on as they could, and die with them in their hand: indeed people could scarcely believe that those who had surrendered were of the same stuff as the fallen; and an Athenian ally, who some time after insultingly asked one of the prisoners from the island if those that had fallen were noble and good men, received for an answer that the *atraktos* – that is, the arrow – would be worth a great deal if it could pick out noble and good men from the rest; an allusion to the fact that the killed were those whom the stones and arrows happened to hit.'[128]

The Spartan prisoners were taken to Athens, where the Athenians were of a mind to keep them as hostages and execute them all if the enemy should invade Attica once more. The fort at Pylos was strengthened with a garrison drawn from amongst the Messenians settled at Naupactus. These men subsequently began to make raids into Spartan territory, with the dialect they shared with the inhabitants being a big advantage. They made inroads among the Helots, and the Spartans, unused to this kind of guerrilla warfare on their own lands, became extremely anxious to put an end to the fighting. They again sent peace envoys to Athens, but their overtures were rebuffed, with Thucydides remarking that the Athenians 'kept grasping at more, and dismissed envoy after envoy without their having effected anything'.[129]

The shock of the defeat at Sphacteria and the threat of a mass Helot uprising had been enough to get the Spartans to practically beg for peace. As sieges went, Sphacteria had been a minor affair, with very few troops involved on the Spartan side. But their loss had an effect out of all proportion to the size of the force they comprised. Though the 420 Spartan hoplites were only one-twentieth of all of Sparta's hoplites, their surrender dispelled the aura of invincibility that they had long possessed. With the warriors of Sparta now looking *human*, just like all the other Greeks, the previously accepted psychological understanding of the war had been thrown off kilter. Reacting out of fear as to what fate might befall the prisoners, the Spartans ceased their invasions of Attica. By fortifying a tiny speck of land on the far side of the Peloponnesus and then taking a mere handful of Spartans prisoner after a brief blockade, the Athenians had ended those massive and damaging raids into their territory. Such was the fragility of the Spartan hold over their Helots, resting as it did on their assumed unchallengeable superiority, that they worried they were about to face a worrying period of internal insurrection as news of the defeat spread far and wide.[130]

Naval Engagements at the Strait of Messana

In the summer of 425 BC, while the Pylos-Spacteria campaign was occupying the attention of the Athenians and Spartans, Syracuse moved against Rhegium. With the bulk of the Athenian navy preoccupied at Pylos, the Athenian squadron in Italian waters was very small, just sixteen triremes. The Syracusans had occupied Messana that summer, and brought ten triremes there, along with ten allied triremes from Locri. This flotilla was soon supplemented by other ships, a little more than ten, and this combined fleet, now numbering above thirty, tried its luck against the allied Athenian-Rhegian fleet of twenty-four triremes. The Syracusan intent was to drive off the Athenians and mount a blockade of Rhegium by land and sea. With possession of Rhegium, Syracuse would hold both sides of the Strait of Messana and be able to shut it to all enemy traffic.

The Syracusans and Athenians began their battle, and once engaged, the fighting mostly favoured the Athenians, who sank one Syracusan ship. Both sides retired, the Syracusans back to Messana and the Athenians to Rhegium. The Syracusans moved on to Cape Pelorus, where they anchored their ships and linked up with their land troops. The Athenians and Rhegians attacked them there, while the Syracusan crews were still ashore, but the Athenian attack on these ships was foiled. Instead of towing away several as prizes, the Athenians themselves lost one trireme when it was caught by a grappling hook, though the crewmen of this unlucky ship escaped by swimming away. The Syracusans had by now recovered from their surprise and had regained their ships, which they towed along the coast to Messana. The Athenians struck once more at the Syracusans, but the Syracusans went immediately on the attack, sinking an Athenian trireme before reaching Messana.[131]

Naval Expeditions to Corinth and Corcyra

Soon after the capitulation of Sphacteria, an Athenian expedition, including Milesians, Andrians and Carystians, composed of eighty ships, 2,000 hoplites and 200 cavalry aboard horse transports under the command of Nicias, made landfall in Corinthian territory between Chersonese and Rheitus. The landing spot was close to the village of Solygia just 7 miles from Corinth, and the Corinthians, having learned that the Athenian expedition was being fitted out, marched to meet the Athenians. But the Athenians evaded them by making their landing in the darkness, and the Corinthians hurried to Solygia to find them. In the ensuing battle, the Athenian right wing was driven upon their ships, but the Athenians and Carystians together pushed the Corinthians back. On the other side of the field, the Corinthian right wing had the better of the fighting. The struggle continued for a long time, with each side refusing to quit. The difference was made by the Athenian cavalry (the Corinthians had brought no cavalry of their own to the battle), which helped their hoplites to drive the Corinthians from the beach.[132] The Athenians set up a trophy to commemorate their victory, but hastened to board their warships upon the approach of what they took to be Peloponnesian reinforcements.[133]

The Athenian fleet made another landing at Cromyon in Corinthian territory and laid waste to the surrounding lands. On the following day, they sailed to Methana which lay between Epidaurus and Troezen. Here the Athenians erected a wall across the narrow isthmus of the peninsula on which Methana sat, and would use the site as a base from which to launch future raids into the territories of Troezen, Halieis and Epidaurus.[134]

Yet another naval expedition was made to Sicily in 425 BC under the command of Eurymedon and Sophocles, with a planned stopover at Corcyra along the way before the fleet crossed to Italian waters. Once at Corcyra, the Athenians joined the Corcyran democrats in an attack on the conservative exiles holding out on Mount Istone. The exiles agreed to surrender under terms, including the condition that their ultimate fate should be decided by the Athenian people in Athens. Before being moved to Athens, they were first placed on the nearby island of Ptychia for safekeeping. Their democratic Corcyran opponents feared that the Athenians might spare the lives of the exiles, and plotted to bring about their demise before that could happen. The placement of the exiles on Ptychia had been done on the understanding that they would stay put until their transport to Athens was arranged. Should even one try to escape, they were warned, all of the exiles would lose the protection afforded them under the truce. Knowing of this harsh term, the Corcyran democrats secretly sent over friends of a few of the exiles on Ptychia to tell them that they must get away, and save themselves, because the Athenians were, so they claimed, about to hand them over to the commoners. To facilitate their escape, these agents provided a boat. Predictably, the Athenians were alerted by the democrats to the exiles' sailing, and they were captured before they could escape. The Athenians, ignorant of the plot, considered the treaty of surrender with the exiles to have been voided and handed them over to the vengeful democrats, who immediately imprisoned them.

Sixty of the exiles were thereafter led out of the building in which they were being jailed and made to walk between two lines of hoplites, who beat and stabbed them to death. The surviving exiles understood the fact that their compatriots were not merely being moved elsewhere, but were being murdered, and refused to leave the building, knowing what was in store for them if they too emerged. The democrats, unwilling to make a frontal assault on the doors, went up to the roof, broke through, and let loose with tiles and arrows on the remaining prisoners. Some of these men fought back, but most preferred to take their own lives, using either the arrows launched at them from above or by hanging themselves. The massacre, which took place overnight, saw all of the men within slain, and the female exiles were sold into slavery. Party strife was now at an end, Thucydides wrote acidly, 'for of one party there was practically nothing left'.[135]

The Athenians held no one among the Corcyrans to account for the murders, and departed for Sicily. Thucydides blames the commanders of the Athenian expedition, Eurymedon and Sophocles, for the gross injustice, noting that it was evident in their behaviour that they had not wanted to continue on to Sicily, the original destination of their mission, if it meant leaving the honour of conveying the exiles to Athens to other men. Their needless delay gave the popular party in Corcyra much time in which to hatch their plot, and in itself seemed to support the democrats' allegations that they were going to be handed back.[136]

More Money

The sizeable financial reserves that Athens could draw upon at the beginning of the war in 431 BC had been drawn down, and it needed more money to fund its war machine. The Athenians, optimistic in the post-Sphacteria phase of the war, hugely increased the demands that they made on the allies for money. In ordinary times raising the tribute would have been done reluctantly, since doing so might have prompted a rebellion. But in the heady atmosphere that prevailed after the Spartan surrender, no ally would have judged a revolt against the everywhere-successful Athenians to be a wise move.[137] In a major new assessment made in 425, the tribute-payers were grouped into broad geographical districts, with the assessment for the Thracian region rising from about 120 talents to somewhere between 530–550; the Aegean islands assessment more than doubled from a pre-war sixty-three talents to around 150; the Hellespont surged from a before-the-war assessment of eighty-five talents to between 250–300; and the Ionian-Carina district's, which had been not much above 110 talents, now soared to about 500. This revenue was enlarged not only by raising the assessments on the allies, but by bringing new payors into the tributary system. Prior to the war, paying cities never numbered more than 180; in 425, there were at least 380, and perhaps over 400.[138]

The overall haul that was expected to be brought in under the 425 assessment stood at about 1,500 talents. Precisely how much of an increase this was over the earlier assessment made in 428 is difficult to say, but a credible figure for that year is 800 talents, so the new assessment might have represented an approximate doubling of revenue.[139] This additional money may well have been desired not merely to cover the costs of the war, which were substantial, but also by some whose grand ambitions were conceived when it seemed that everything they did in that golden period of 425 was crowned with success.[140] The heavy demands made on the allies could not have won the Athenians much in the way of good will. Under the prevailing rules of the empire, the allies were allowed to send delegations to plead their cases if they considered their assessments to be excessive, but the final say on whether the tribute was to be paid or reduced lay with a special Athenian law court of 1,000 jurors convened for the specific purpose of hearing such matters.[141]

Ships were sent out to all parts of the empire to collect the tribute due. One commander named Aristides came across a Persian diplomat at Eion on the Strymon River and arrested him. The Persian, Artaphernes, had been despatched to Sparta by the Great King of Persia before being apprehended by Aristides, who instead sent him to Athens. He was found to be carrying papers, and these were translated from the cuneiform script then in use in Persia. The Great King Artaxerxes in his letters complained that the Spartans who had previously come to him 'did not know what they wanted, as of the many ambassadors they had sent him no two had ever told the same story'. If the Spartans genuinely desired something from the Great King, and 'were prepared to speak plainly', then they should send envoys to him in the company of Artaphernes. Instead, the Athenians delivered Artaphernes by sea to Ephesus in Asia Minor in the company of a few of their own diplomats. Upon arrival, however, they learned that Artaxerxes had recently died, and they went back to Athens.[142]

In 424, Mytilenians and other exiles from Lesbos formed a plan. After hiring mercenaries in the Peloponnesus and levying other troops in Asia Minor, they captured the city of Rhoeteum and then ransomed it back for 2,000 Phocaean staters, the equivalent of about eight talents. Their next move was made against the city of Antandrus, and they captured that as well. Their idea was to eject the Athenians from this and the other Actaean cities, which had once been held by Mytilene. With Antandrus as a base, they would draw upon the plentiful local timber to build ships with which to mount raids on Lesbos and gain control of the Aeolian cities of Asia.[143]

Cythera

In the summer of 424 BC, an Athenian naval expedition under the command of Nicias comprising sixty triremes, 2,000 hoplites, some cavalry and allied troops from Miletus and elsewhere struck at Cythera, an island lying south of Laconia, just opposite from Cape Malea. The people of Cythera were deemed *perioikoi* by the Spartans. The island was strategically important, being a stopping point for merchant ships coming north from Egypt and Libya, and was also a vital part of the defence of Laconia from naval attack, as it guarded the only stretch of coastline where it was vulnerable. The coasts facing the Cretan and Sicilian seas to either side rose sharply, making seaborne attacks there impossible.[144] The Athenians diverted ten triremes and 2,000 hoplites to the city of Scandea, which was captured, while the rest of the expeditionary force concentrated around the lower city of Cythera. The Cytherans fought but were forced to take refuge in the upper city of Cythera, and soon surrendered under terms.

The *perioikoi* of the island, not full Spartans but nonetheless a subject class, were content to cut a deal with Nicias that left them in possession of their lands as tribute-paying members of the Athenian alliance. This was a far better outcome than the alternative of being ejected entirely from the island as an enemy population. The Athenians installed a garrison there, and immediately began to raid the southern Peloponnesus. The Spartans were caught flat-footed by the Athenian move against Cythera, and seeing that their lands were being raided at will, they sent garrisons to defend the countryside. Sparta was, by this point, in an entirely defensive posture now that both Pylos and Cythera were in enemy hands. The Spartans 'became more timid than ever in military matters, finding themselves involved in a maritime struggle, which their organization had never contemplated'.[145] The Spartans were intellectually out of their depth, befuddled by 'the apparition on every side of a war whose rapidity defied precaution'.[146]

The Success of Athens' Naval Strategy

Repeated losses during wartime will naturally produce in the losing side a sense of dejection, and perhaps even hopelessness. But the Spartans had been outthought, if not outfought, by the Athenians, and they had no one to blame for their strategic reverses they had suffered but themselves. Cythera had been left almost undefended and under the control of a population of uncertain loyalty.

Why would the Spartans be so lax in protecting the island? Its importance should have been obvious, but its seizure was a stunning blow to Sparta. Thucydides notes that the Spartans had previously paid 'great attention' to Cythera, and had also sent garrisons to it on a regular basis.[147] There was, however, no garrison of Spartan troops present to defend it in 424 BC when the Athenians landed. The Spartans would easily have recalled the naval attack during the First Peloponnesian War of Tolnides, who in a single expedition in 457 had burnt the Spartan naval arsenal at Gythion, captured Chalcis and then defeated the Sicyonians in battle.[148] The threat of an amphibious war to a land power that lacked sufficient means to overcome, or at least deter, the movement of the Athenian fleet had been amply demonstrated in the years before 431. Athenian seapower had succeeded, despite repeated invasions of Attica and a debilitating plague that took the lives of tens of thousands of Athenians, in planting or preserving a ring of fortified bases along the periphery of the Peloponnesus. These were at Aegina, Cephallenia, Methana, Naupactus, Pylos, Zacynthus and, latterly, Cythera. They were, taken together, well placed to sever Sparta's maritime trading links with Italy, Sicily, Egypt and Libya; incite revolts among the Helots; and cause dissension among the members of the Peloponnesian League by means of repeated naval raids.[149]

The Spartans were aware of the threat posed by such bases, and indeed they tried but failed to take away Zacynthus in 430 and Naupactus in 429, so it was not entirely due to a lack of understanding or effort. The fall of Cythera seems, however, to have been due to a failure of imagination, and the Spartans should never have allowed that prize to be plucked away so easily. Thucydides mentions that they were disconcerted by the nature of the maritime warfare that Athens practised. Naval power gave the Athenians a matchless mobility. An amphibious force might be landed anywhere along the coast to ravage or raid further inland. This was nothing like the massed phalanx battle for which the Spartans were psychologically prepared and best equipped to handle. The Athenians had not obliged them by fighting the kind of battle that suited the Spartans, and had remained behind the safety of their Long Walls, even as Attica burned. So the Spartans began to fall apart as the war turned against them and lasted for far longer than they had ever guessed. Their offensive spirit was sapped as their hoplites were distributed in small groups around the Peloponnesus. 'Accordingly, they now allowed the Athenians to ravage their seaboard, without making any movement, the garrisons in whose neighbourhood the descents were made always thinking their numbers insufficient.'[150]

This uncharacteristic diffidence played right into the hands of the Athenians, who raided wherever they chose. In one instance, some Athenian light troops were landed near Cortyrta and Aphrodisia, and the Spartan garrison found the courage to drive them away. But as soon as the Spartans encountered Athenian hoplites a little further on, they pulled back after losing just a few of their number. The Athenians claimed the minor scuffle as a victory and set up a trophy. They then sailed away to Cythera. From there they set out again, to ravage Epidaurus Limera, and then reached Thyrea. Thyrea, it may be recalled, had been settled by the Spartans with Aeginetan refugees who had been cast out of their island in 431, when the Athenians had decided that they needed to control the island with their own loyal colonists.[151] The Aeginetans of Thyrea were in the midst of building a coastal fort, but abandoned their work while the Athenians were still at sea, and sought out the safety of Thyrea's upper city, which lay more than a mile inland. There was a Spartan garrison present, and these troops had been helping the Thyreans to construct the fort. They were unwilling to become trapped in a city that might soon come under siege. They took up a position on some high ground nearby and refused to engage what they believed to be a superior enemy. The Athenians made landfall and quickly captured Thyrea, burned and pillaged it, killed many, and took the survivors back to Athens as captives, where they were all put to death.[152] Athenian aggression in prosecuting their maritime strategy was fired by the corresponding fecklessness of the Spartans, who shrank from battle. The attack on Thyrea may have even been occasioned by knowledge that the fort was rising, spurring the desire to destroy it before it was completed.[153]

It would seem then that Pericles' bedrock belief in the value of Athenian seapower was on the mark, albeit more time would be needed than he may have anticipated for its full weight to be felt. The Peloponnesian League was a tough opponent; Athens would find itself badly wounded by the unforeseen arrival of the plague; and the naval strategy itself could only work once Athens had succeeded in encircling the Peloponnesus with a string of forts and naval bases such as those found at Pylos, Naupactus and Cythera. Once the latter had been achieved, Sparta was placed on the strategic defensive, wrong-footed at almost every turn, and constantly fearful of a Helot uprising that their own harsh regime made likely.

Congress of Gela

Athenian ambitions in Sicily received a check in 424 BC when Camarina and Gela agreed to an armistice, and a congress of all the cities of Sicily was held at Gela to work out a general peace. Athens was the bogeyman in the speech given by Hermocrates, the Syracusan delegate. 'Sicily,' he warned, was 'menaced by Athenian ambition.' Athens was 'watching our mistakes with the few ships that she has at present in our waters [in fact, the fleet then numbered an impressive sixty triremes] and under the fair name of alliance speciously seeking to exploit the natural hostility that exists between us. If we go to war, and call in to help us a people that are ready enough to carry their arms even where they are not invited, and if we injure ourselves at our own expense, and at the same time serve as the pioneers of their dominion, we may expect when they see us worn out, that they will one day come with a larger armament, and seek to bring all of us into subjection.'[154]

Hermocrates' plea was heeded, and the Sicilian states agreed to a peace at the Congress of Gela in which each kept what it currently held. Athens' allies summoned her generals and informed them that they were going to be included as parties in the treaty. To this the generals in the theatre – Pythodorus, Sophocles and Eurymedon – consented, and the peace was formalized. The Athenians withdrew their ships from Sicilian waters and returned to Athens, but their homecoming was unpleasant. Understanding nothing of the realities of the war in Sicily, the Athenian Assembly simply assumed that its generals had been bribed to leave instead of conquering the island. Pythodorus and Sophocles were both banished, and Eurymedon was hit with a fine. 'So thoroughly had the present prosperity persuaded the Athenians that nothing could withstand them, and that they could achieve what was possible and what was impracticable alike, with means ample or inadequate it mattered not,' Thucydides said. 'The reason for this was their general extraordinary success, which made them confuse their strength with their hopes.'[155]

Attack on Nisaea

A plot unfolded in Megara in the summer of 424 BC in which the popular party sought to betray their city to the Athenians. The territory of Megara had been subjected to semi-annual invasions by the Athenians, and was also suffering from attacks made by Megarian exiles based at Pegae who had been driven out by the democrats controlling the city. The Megarians at large came to think that if the exiles were allowed to return, then one of the two major dangers facing the city would be ended. Seeing that the resolve of the populace had eroded after years of war, the democrats opened talks with the Athenians to forestall a reconciliation with the exiles. Their plan called for the Athenians to initially take the long walls that ran for almost one mile from the port of Nisaea to Megara. By seizing the walls, the Peloponnesian garrison in Nisaea would be prevented from sending any help to Megara. Once the long walls were in hand, the Athenians would next move against Megara.[156]

During the night, the Athenians under Hippocrates sailed with 600 hoplites to Minoa, a small island lying off Megara, and these took up a position in a ditch on the mainland, while Demosthenes took a force of light troops and hid these in ambush not far from the gates of Nisaea. The democratic conspirators inside had arranged to alert the Athenians outside when the gate was open. The Megarian democrats had been undertaking, so they claimed, privateering raids against the Athenian ships conducting the blockade out of Minoa. Each night they would take a rowboat out of the gates atop a cart via a ditch and sail it out to sea. The Athenians, so their story went, would have no idea how this little craft was evading them since no boat could be seen leaving the harbour, which was under their observation. The conspirators would then return, rolling the rowboat along the same ditch on the cart and back through the gate. This was a clever and simple way to ensure that the gate would be routinely opened for them on their return. On this night, with the gate open, the waiting Athenians made a dash for it. Demosthenes' men were the first in, and they held the gate long enough so that the Athenian hoplites could make their way inside too.[157]

The Athenians fended off a counter-attack by the Peloponnesian garrison in Nisaea, and soon were in possession not only of the gates but of the wall as well. When morning came, an Athenian force of 4,000 hoplites and 600 cavalry approached after a night march. The conspirators inside Megara tried to persuade the rest that they must open their own gates and march to do battle with the Athenians. What they actually intended was that the Athenians nearby would surge in once the gates opened, and they had prepared a means to differentiate themselves from the multitude by anointing themselves with oil, and the forewarned Athenians would not harm them if they were so marked. But one of the conspirators had a change of heart and informed the other Megarians about the plan. The gates of Megara remained closed, and the Athenians, becoming aware that the plot had been foiled, began a siege of Nisaea.[158]

The Athenians erected a wall between the sea on either side of Nisaea, shutting it off from Megara. They ransacked the buildings of the suburbs of Nisaea for stones and bricks, and chopped down trees to form a palisade. By the next afternoon, the Athenians had finished their improvised siege wall. The garrison holding out in Nisea was not self-sufficient. Shortsightedly, the troops had been made to rely on the flow of provisions from Megara to sustain it. Thinking that Megara was itself held by the enemy, and not expecting help from outside to arrive any time soon, they agreed to surrender terms under which they would relinquish their weapons and each man would be ransomed for a fixed amount of money. The fate of the Spartans present, including the commander of the garrison, were to be left to the 'discretion' of their Athenian captors.[159]

With the Athenians now in possession of Nisaea, the siege wall was torn down. The indomitable Spartan Brasidas, who had performed so fearlessly at Pylos in 425, soon arrived at Megara with a small force of picked troops detached from his larger army of some 4,000 Peloponnesian hoplites. The Athenians were busy elsewhere, and he was able to get close to the walls of Megara, where he implored the citizens to let him inside, saying that he would also try to recapture Nisaea. But the same factionalism that had riven the city and caused the fall of Nisaea prevented either the party friendly to the exiles or the democrats from allowing him in. He rejoined his army, was soon reinforced by 2,200 hoplites and 600 cavalry from Boeotia, and advanced against the Athenians. The Athenian light troops were completely unprepared for his assault, as no relief had before come to Megara, and they were spread out all over the plain. The Boeotian cavalry hurled them into the sea, and were themselves then charged by the Athenian cavalry. The clash lasted a long while, but the result was indecisive. The Boeotian horsemen went back to their army, and the Athenians returned to Nisaea.

Brasidas came up with his full army, numbering over 6,000 hoplites, and arrayed it for battle. He refused, however, to order an attack on the Athenians, who were also forming up outside the long walls. Brasidas' thinking was that there was no need for him to go on the attack, as merely by forming up he was showing his readiness to fight without risking a battle whose outcome was uncertain. His intended audience for this display was the civilian spectators in Megara, whom he wanted to impress. Had he refused to come out to fight, the Megarians would have judged him as good as beaten. On the other side of the field, the Athenians were even more reluctant to fight, since they already held

Nisaea, and a battle with the Peloponnesians entailed serious danger to their valuable hoplites. Even if they won, they would only take Megara, an insufficient reward for the risk to be run. After standing around staring at each other, the Athenians blinked first and withdrew to Nisaea. Seeing that the Spartans had stood firm, and had not retreated until after the Athenians were gone, the Megarian faction tied to the city's exiles opened the gates to Brasidas.[160]

After speaking with the exile faction inside the city, Brasidas sent the allied troops home, and went off to Corinth to get ready for an expedition to Thrace, while the Athenian army outside Nisaea went home too. Thucydides presents this episode as a highlight of Brasidas' cleverness and fortitude, and the Spartan may certainly be commended for his shrewdness. But the overall strategic outcome of the attack on Megara was that the Athenians now held yet another base, Nisaea, from which to conduct raids on the Peloponnesus, that had been obtained at little cost to themselves. Sparta's position had worsened, even if the fall of Megara itself had been prevented by Brasidas' show of strength.

The Athenians that summer had also learned of the Mytilenian intention to fortify Antandrus as a base from which to raid against Lesbos. An Athenian fleet under the command of Demodocus and Aristides were on a mission to collect tribute from the allies in the Hellespont, and became worried that with Antandrus taken by hostile forces it would become a problem just as Anaia currently was for Samos, held as it then was by Samian exiles who harassed it and sent experienced helmsmen to serve with the Peloponnesian fleet. Demodocus and Lamachus collected troops from the allies in the area and sailed to Antandrus, where they defeated the exiles in battle and recaptured the city.[161]

Delium

Again, in the summer of 424 BC, the Athenians under Demosthenes sailed with forty ships to their base in the Gulf of Corinth at Naupactus with the intention of conducting raids against Boeotia. The Athenians had been in contact with parties in the Boeotian cities who were interested in changing their governments and introducing democracy, and the port city of Siphae and Chaeronea were to be betrayed to the Athenians by friendly factions in each. Another, simultaneous operation under Hippocrates was planned in which troops operating out of Athenian territory were to strike out and capture the sanctuary of Apollo at Delium. All of these moves were scheduled to take place on the same day to prevent the Boeotians from mounting an effective resistance at Delium, as they would be preoccupied elsewhere by Demosthenes' concurrent moves.[162]

Demosthenes took his forty ships to raise troops among the Acarnanians and other allies, and then sailed for Siphae. Upon arrival in the area, he discovered that the Oeniadae had been forced to join the Athenian alliance. He raised yet more troops, took the city of Salynthia and subdued the Agraeans. After this he busied himself in preparation for the assault on Siphae to take place on the prearranged day.[163]

Winter had by now arrived, and his colleague, Hippocrates, who had with him an army recruited at Athens, was biding his time, waiting to strike at Delium on the same day that Demosthenes made his own move against Siphae. But the Siphae operation was betrayed to the Spartans, who in turn alerted the Boeotians to the impending threat. The Boeotians promptly secured both Siphae and Chaeronea, and Demosthenes could achieve nothing. There was also a mistake made as to the precise date when the combined operations were to take place. Demosthenes seems to have acted too early, and when Hippocrates marched against Delium it was too late to prevent any of the Boeotian troops from going to the aid of Siphae and Chaeronea. With the failure of his operation on Siphae, Demosthenes contented himself with taking what troops he had on hand, 400 Athenian hoplites and some Acarnanians and Agraeans, and made a descent against the coast of Sicyon. The Sicyonians reacted to his landing before all of his men could disembark, slaying many of the ones who had already gone ashore and taking the rest prisoner.[164]

Hippocrates did manage to take the sanctuary of Apollo as planned, and fortified the temple area with a trench, a wall and some towers. Once this work was completed and a garrison had been installed, the bulk of the Athenian army began its homeward march. They were intercepted by a Boeotian army just after it had crossed back into Athenian territory. The Battle of Delium, as it came to called, was undecided initially, with the Athenians winning on their right and the Boeotians having success on their own right, on the other end of the line, opposite the Athenian left, where their tough Theban hoplites were positioned. But then two squadrons of Boeotian cavalry circled around undetected to the rear of the Athenian right wing. Thinking that they had been set upon by a new army, the Athenians panicked, leading to a rout. Up and down the line the Athenians fled, with some struck down in the pursuit, while others escaped however and wherever they could.

The Boeotians erected a trophy after the victory, but refused to return the bodies of the Athenian dead unless the Athenians evacuated the fortifications at the sanctuary at Delium. The Athenians refused to do this, saying that their holding of the sanctuary was less sacrilegious than the Boeotian unwillingness to give back the bodies of the fallen Athenians. Nothing came of the parley, and the Boeotians assaulted the fort and captured it, bringing to an end the disastrous chapter on Athenian operations in Boeotia.[165]

Brasidas Goes North

Brasidas had in the meantime been busy with getting his expedition to Thrace up and running. He marched north through Thessaly to Macedonia and Chalcidice. There were cities in Chalcidice and Thrace that either wished to revolt against Athens or were already in revolt against it, and Brasidas was to bring them help in the form of 1,700 hoplites.[166] Thucydides writes that it was comparatively easy for the Chalcidians and Thracians, as well as King Perdiccas of Macedonia, who had his own problems with Athens, to convince the Spartans to send an army outside of the Peloponnesus. Harried as they were by Athenian naval raids on the Peloponnesus, and Laconia especially, for which they had developed no direct counter, the Spartans hoped that the expedition might make for a useful diversion against Athens, which would have to turn its attention elsewhere.[167]

Fear of the Helots also guided Spartan strategy, and they undertook to recruit troops from among them, enrolling 700 for service as hoplites with Brasidas. They were happy to have them out of the country. Thucydides relates a horrifying story in which the Spartans, ever anxious about a Helot uprising, called upon the Helots to nominate those of their people who were 'the most distinguished in the wars'.[168] Such men would, they promised, then be granted their freedom. But the Spartans instead were seeking to learn who were most likely to rebel. When 2,000 such men had been recruited, they were given their freedom, but the Spartans' next move was to kill them all in secret, and 'no one ever knew how each of them perished'.[169]

Brasidas arrived in Chalcidice with his troops, and the Chalcidians were pleased to have such an energetic officer on hand. His conduct toward the cities, which Thucydides calls 'just and moderate', convinced many of them to revolt against Athens. Brasidas' mission succeeded in moving the focus of the war away from the Peloponnesus, and the reputation that he won for his bravery and behaviour was so high that other Greeks came to think that all Spartans were like him.[170]

Spartan moves in Thrace caused the Athenians to declare war on Perdiccas of Macedonia, correctly seeing Perdiccas as the driving force behind the expedition. In fact, the king was paying half of the expenses of Brasidas' army, but the two soon had a falling out when Brasidas wished to arbitrate a dispute between Perdiccas and another Macedonian king, Arrhabaeus of Lyncestis. Perdiccas insisted that they march out together to subdue Arrhabaeus, not talk to him – that was why he was funding the Spartan army so heavily. But Brasidas took a broader view, seeing an opportunity to make an ally out of Arrhabaeus. He held talks with him, over Perdiccas' objections, and heard enough to dissuade him from invading Lyncestis. Perdiccas accused Brasidas of acting in bad faith, and in retaliation reduced his monetary contribution to the army from one-half to one-third.[171]

Brasidas next took his army, along with the Chalcidians, against Acanthus, an Andrian colony. The city was divided over whether to receive him, but the time of the grape harvest was near, and out of fear for their fruit the Acanthians allowed Brasidas, and him alone, to speak before them. Brasidas was not 'a bad speaker for a Spartan', Thucydides remarks.[172] He told the Acanthians that the Spartans were at 'war with the Athenians ... to free Hellas'.[173] Interestingly, Brasidas admitted to the Acanthians that it had taken the Spartans quite a long while to come to them seeking alliance. This was because, he explained, they had had 'mistaken expectations about the war in Greece' and also had sought to defeat the Athenians through their 'own unassisted efforts'.[174] Just what these mistaken assumptions had been, Brasidas did not say, but it is plain that the war had taken on a character very different from any that the Spartans had fought before or had ever contemplated fighting. It was a war in which the centre of gravity of the Athenian enemy lay not in its fields or its army, but in the network of overseas client states that contributed the money that paid for the fleet that raided the Peloponesus at will. Brasidas proved so persuasive that Acanthus agreed to revolt against Athens, but only on the condition that the independence of any allies that came over to Sparta be guaranteed. Acanthus was soon joined in revolt by the city of Stagirus, another Andrian colony.[175]

Brasidas' mission was beginning to succeed, despite its rather improvised character. That Sparta had to rely upon funding from Macedonia to pay its troops operating abroad shows that Athens' strategy of tying down Spartan resources in defending the Peloponnesus had been working. Brasidas' expedition must have only been mounted when Sparta professed a willingness to become involved in Perdiccas' private war with Arrhabaeus, a promise on which Brasidas quickly reneged because it did not suit Sparta's strategic interests to make war on behalf of Perdiccas.

Amphipolis

Brasidas' next move came in the winter of 424/3 BC, when he marched against the Athenian colony at Amphipolis. The city was girded on two sides by the Strymon River, which flowed around it, and was further protected by a long wall. Amphipolis was served by the city of Eion some 3 miles away at the mouth of the river as its commercial seaport, much as Piraeus was for Athens. His first thought was to take Amphipolis by surprise, as the weather was stormy, but he was approached by men from Argilus, a nearby city, who allowed him into it. Argilus rose in revolt against Athens, and during the night Brasidas was conducted to the bridge over the Strymon. The bridge was only lightly guarded, and was quickly taken. Brasidas took control of the buildings that lay outside Amphipolis, along with many inhabitants, and there he waited.

The Argilians had some of their own natives inside Amphipolis, and had been plotting with them since before Brasidas' timely arrival on the scene. They could not open the gates for Brasidas to enter, and the Athenian garrison commander there, Eucles, immediately sent word of the threat to Amphipolis to none other than Thucydides himself, who was at that time on the island of Thasos, which lay just a half-day's sail away. Upon receiving Eucles' plea for help, Thucydides sailed with seven triremes to save the city.[176]

Brasidas was aware of the Athenians stationed at Thasos, and further knew that Thucydides had rights to work the gold mines in that area of Thrace, and thus that he had influence with the people on the mainland. This made it necessary for him to capture Amphipolis before Thucydides could intervene effectively. He gave them good terms to secure their surrender, letting all Amphipolitans and Athenians remain as full citizens, or if they would not stay, they would be allowed five days in which to leave and take their property with them.[177]

These eminently fair terms were more than acceptable to the Amphipolitans, most of whom were not Athenian, and the gates were opened to the Spartan general. The Athenians took the opportunity to leave while they could, and Thucydides says that they had little expectation of a speedy rescue. Later that day, Thucydides sailed into the harbour of Eion, too late to help Amphipolis but in the nick of time to prevent Brasidas from capturing the port too.[178] Brasidas made a sortie against Eion down the river with some boats, but these were beaten back by Thucydides, as was the land attack he made against it.[179]

The fall of Amphipolis caused intense distress at Athens. The city had been of importance as a source of shipbuilding timber and for its contribution of tribute, and had previously blocked Spartan access to Athens' allies on the other side of the Strymon River. Now the way was open. The threat that more of her allies would revolt loomed, and Brasidas' wise policy of moderation towards the cities of the area, with him everywhere proclaiming that his mission was to free the Greeks from Athenian domination, made this possibility seem worryingly real. Several cities at this time began a correspondence with Brasidas about escaping from Athens' alliance.[180] Thucydides himself could hardly be faulted for the capture of Amphipolis. Brasidas had cleverly and quickly offered good surrender terms that were speedily accepted by the populace, who were happy to be left with their lives and property. With the city capitulating so readily, Thucydides had no time in which to react. Yet he was nonetheless made a scapegoat for the debacle, and was sent into exile.[181]

The Athenians reacted promptly by sending garrisons to the cities of the region to secure their loyalty, and Brasidas, who began to construct triremes along the Strymon, was denied the reinforcements that he requested, partly because of jealousy felt towards him in Sparta, and also because the Spartans were themselves more interested in getting back the prisoners taken at Sphacteria in 425 than in extending any of the gains Brasidas had made in Thrace.[182]

Brasidas seized Acte and then moved against Torone, which contained an Athenian garrison. Approaching without being sighted by the Athenians, a handful of partisans friendly to Brasidas opened a postern gate for him. A second gate leading to the marketplace was also thrown open, and Brasidas' troops rushed in. Brasidas was in possession of the city before the Toronaeans had a chance to recover from their surprise. A small force of Athenians and those friendly to them managed to take refuge in the fort of Lecythus, which stood in a corner of Torone on a narrow isthmus. Brasidas' offer of a truce in which to evacuate the fort was turned down, and both sides spent the next two days strengthening their defences. When Brasidas launched his attack, the Athenians held him off for a day until his assault proved overwhelming, and all but some who escaped by sea to Pallene were slain.

Armistice

Brasidas' efforts in the north were undeniably successful, and their effect on Athens was profound enough to convince them to agree to an armistice with Sparta in 423 BC. Athens hoped that she might use this time to take measures to prevent Brasidas from causing any more of their allies to revolt, while the Spartans, knowing that their strategy had caused the Athenians deep discomfort, believed that once a truce was in effect they would be more amenable to making a lasting peace and return the prisoners captured at Sphacteria.[183] Under its terms, the armistice was to last for one year; no further aggressive moves would be made by either Athens or Sparta, and both were to keep their current territorial acquisitions, if Athens should agree to conclude a peace treaty; the Spartans and their allies were to be allowed to sail upon the sea, but only in small oared ships, not in warships; deserters would not be received by either side; and delegations would be exchanged to conduct negotiations to make a general peace treaty.[184]

There was an immediate hiccough. The Chalcidian city of Scione rose against Athenian domination not long after the armistice was concluded, but before word had reached them of the truce. Brasidas, in Chalcidice, was spurred to action by the revolt, and went to the assistance of the Scionaeans. Brasidas was greeted like a hero and deposited a garrison in Scione with the intention of using it as a base to attack the cities of Mende and Potidaea before substantial Athenian forces could appear in response. When a trireme sailed to Scione with news of the armistice, informing Brasidas that he would have to evacuate the city, he refused point-blank, insisting that the revolt had been made before the armistice had come into effect, when in reality it had taken place two days afterward.

The matter was reported to Athens, which then prepared to despatch an expeditionary force to bring the Scionaeans to heel. The Spartans warned them against this, saying that it would be a breach of the truce, but the Athenians were unwilling to submit the dispute to arbitration and incensed that its allies had revolted in the hope of Spartan intervention. A decree was sponsored by Cleon, in which the Scionaeans were condemned to death, and the outfitting of an expedition continued.

Brasidas welcomed another Chalcidian city, Mende on the Pallene peninsula, into the fold despite the fact that it had incontestably revolted during the armistice period. The Mendeans were encouraged by Brasidas' energetic work in freeing the Greek cities from Athenian overlordship, and especially by his obstinate refusal to withdraw from Scione despite the pressure on him to abide by the armistice terms. The Athenians were made even angrier by this second theft of one of their allies, and readied an expedition to attack both Mende and Scione. Knowing that the blow would soon fall on them, Brasidas sent away their women and children to Olynthus for safekeeping, and in turn brought over 500 Peloponnesian hoplites and 300 Chalcidian peltasts to help defend the cities.

While the Scionaeans and Mendeans got ready for the Athenian attack, Brasidas and Perdiccas of Macedonia undertook an expedition against Arrhabaeus of Lyncestis. They defeated Arrhabaeus in battle, but waited in vain for Illyrian mercenaries to join them. When two or three days had gone by without sight of the Illyrians, Brasidas wanted to return to Mende, expecting the Athenians to show up at any moment, and refused to go any further with Perdiccas, who wished to strike deeper into Lyncestian territory. While Brasidas and Perdiccas were still at loggerheads, a panic erupted during the night that caused the Macedonians, thinking that a much larger army had appeared nearby, to flee for home. This left Brasidas and his Peloponnesian troops all alone to face an attack by Arrhabaeus and the Illyrians. The latter, it had been learned, had switched sides and gone over to Arrhabaeus. By morning, Brasidas formed his soldiers into a square to conduct a fighting retreat.

With his youngest, fittest men placed in the centre of the square, ready to race out to fight on whichever spot the enemy struck, and he himself stationed in the rearguard with 300 picked troops, Brasidas fended off repeated assaults on his square. At last, he and his men reached the safety of the city of Arnisa in Perdiccas' territory. The Peloponnesians were so filled with anger at the desertion of the Macedonians that they slaughtered all of the oxen that their allies had left behind in their pell-mell flight and took for themselves the baggage that had been left on the animals. This caused such bad blood that, from this moment forward, Perdiccas held an enormous grudge against Brasidas, and despite his longstanding antipathy towards the Athenians, he sought to make peace with them and turned against the Peloponnesians.[185]

Mende

In the meantime, the Athenians had struck at Mende. An expeditionary force under the command of Nicias had sailed with fifty triremes, including ten from Chios, with 1,000 Athenian hoplites, 600 archers, 100 Thracian mercenaries and some peltasts drawn from the allies who had arrived while Brasidas was preoccupied in Lyncestis. The Athenians made an attempt on Mende but were driven back by a force of Mendaeans supplemented by 300 Scionaean and 400 Peloponnesian hoplites in a strong position atop a hill just outside the city. The remainder of the Athenian army under Nicostratus made an assault on the hill along a different route, but these men were repelled too.[186]

The Athenians sailed away and mounted an attack on the other side of Mende. They captured the suburb and looted the countryside against no opposition, since the city was riven by factional strife that hindered effective resistance. Mende's garrison and the Peloponnesian troops were preparing to resist the Athenians when members of the democratic party took up arms and attacked them. These were smashed by the surprise assault, and the survivors found refuge in the citadel. The city now opened its gates to the Athenians, without first establishing terms, and Nicias' troops rushed in and sacked it.[187]

The Athenians next turned their attention to Scione, and were met by the garrison of Scionaeans and Peloponnesians which had taken up a position on a hill in front of the city. These were uprooted from the hill, and the Athenians began to build a wall around Scione. At this time the troops that had withdrawn into the citadel at Mende escaped and found their way over to Scione during the night.[188] Perdiccas of Macedonia reappeared, sending word to the Athenians outside Scione that he wanted to make peace with Athens. Nicias wanted some assurance that this former enemy was being sincere, and as proof of his desire to switch sides, Perdicas prevailed upon the Thessalians to prevent reinforcements from Sparta, which were even now on the march, from making their way north to join with Brasidas. The Spartans' progress was brought to a halt before they could cross Thessaly.[189] After this the two sides abided by the armistice for the rest of the year, though the ever-enterprising Brasidas launched a surprise night attack on Potidaea at the end of winter in 422. The Spartan officer managed to set a ladder against the wall, but the watchful garrison detected his move and raised the alarm, forcing Brasidas to call off the operation and speed away in the darkness.[190]

Athenian Counter-attack

The year-long armistice came to an end in 422 BC, and an expedition under the command of Cleon left Athens to reclaim the cities taken by Brasidas. Cleon, with thirty ships, 1,200 hoplites, 300 cavalry and a larger force of troops from the allies, first alighted at Scione, where the siege was ongoing. Deserters informed Cleon that Brasidas was away and that the garrison was weak. He sent ten ships to sail into Torone's harbour, and with his army marched on the city. The two-pronged attack proved too much for the Spartans to deal with all at once, and the garrison was taken prisoner before it could put up an effective resistance.[191] Brasidas was hurrying to the relief of Torone and was just 4 miles away when news of its fall reached him, and he turned his army around. The Athenians enslaved the women and children of Torone, and sent the Chalcidian and Peloponnesian prisoners back to Athens. After installing a garrison to hold Torone, Cleon set sail for Amphipolis.[192]

Cleon established a base at Eion. His attack against Stagirus was beaten back but his assault on Galepsus met with success. Cleon sent word to Perdiccas, Athens' new ally, demanding that he bring troops to aid him, and made a similar demand on Polles, the king of the Odomantians, in Thrace, to bring to Eion as many Thracian mercenaries as he could find. While Cleon waited for reinforcements to come from Perdiccas and Polles, Brasidas, on the hill of Cerdylium, kept watch on Cleon in Eion, expecting him to move against Amphipolis since the Spartans were so badly outnumbered. But Brasidas quickly built up his strength, raising 1,500 Thracian mercenaries and cavalry and peltasts from among the Edonians. He also had a 1,000 Myrcinian and Chalcidian peltasts on hand, as well as some additional peltasts in Amphipolis, plus 2,000 hoplites and 300 cavalry. On Cerdylium itself, Brasidas had some 1,500 troops all told, while the remainder were inside Amphipolis under the command of Clearidas.[193]

Cleon was forced to move against Amphipolis after his inaction had caused his men to grumble about him. He broke camp and marched on a reconnaissance mission to the city, and was not expecting to be brought to battle by Brasidas. As the Athenians departed Eion, Brasidas, seeing them leave, made his own way to Amphipolis. Cleon arrived and took up a position atop a hill to the city's fore. Seeing nobody on the walls, and with no one issuing out of the city's gates, Cleon decided to withdraw. Brasidas, with 150 picked hoplites, launched an attack on the retreating Athenians before the rest of their army could come to their aid. Cleon had initially ordered his left wing to take the lead back to Eion, but had grown impatient at the speed with which his army was conducting the retreat, and then ordered that the right wing wheel about and go first. While the Athenians were manoeuvring their army into position to complete the retreat to Eion, Brasidas' small group emerged from the city and struck at the very centre of the disordered Athenian line. At the same time, the rest of Brasidas' army in Amphipolis ran out from the city gates and attacked the Athenians. Beset on two sides, the Athenians broke and fled, but not before Brasidas suffered a wound himself and fell, being carried off the field. In the midst of the disaster, Cleon bolted from the scene, but did not escape and was slain by a Myrcinian peltast.

Brasidas lived long enough to learn of the extent of his victory, and then died of his wound. The casualties taken in the battle were vastly lopsided, with just seven of Brasidas' men perishing, while the Athenians lost some 600. But Brasidas was one of those seven, an incomparable soldier and one of the few Spartan commanders in the first half of the war who had a real grasp of the strategy needed to defeat Athens. The fallen Spartan received tremendous honours from the people of Amphipolis, who made sacrifices to him as a hero and declared him to be the founder of their city instead of the Athenian Hagnon, who had actually founded the colony there in 437/6.

What Brasidas Proved

In no small measure, Brasidas' campaigns in the north showed that the Athenian Empire was vulnerable to partial dismemberment if Sparta made the effort to convince her subject states that their revolts would succeed and that they would be shielded from Athenian vengeance. It took an imaginative and bold officer such as Brasidas to bring about the defections, which were achieved with only minimal support from the Spartan government. Most of his troops were either Helots or non-Spartan Peloponnesians, and half of his expedition's funding (at the beginning) came from Macedonia. Brasidas assiduously tried to implement the strategy of detachment that King Archidamus had considered just prior to the start of the war, but had rejected the idea on the grounds that Sparta did not have the naval power required to carry it out.[194] Brasidas, however, had shown that an energetically conducted land campaign could achieve laudable results in this sphere, despite the inferiority of Spartan naval resources.

Notwithstanding Brasidas' obvious successes, Spartan officialdom was not interested in following up on the dead commander's gains in the north, but in getting back the Spartans captured on Sphacteria. What they wanted most right then was an end to the war, and Brasidas had acquired the bargaining chips that they needed to bring Athens to the negotiating table.

The Peace of Nicias

In the winter of 422/1 BC, the Spartans again tried to send reinforcements, some 900 hoplites, northward, but they were refused passage by the Thessalians once more. With Brasidas dead and seeing little prospect of further success, they turned back. Apart from these impediments, Thucydides writes that the Spartans went home because they knew that the mood at Sparta was one that favoured the making of peace. Both sides, in fact, were looking to conclude some sort of agreement, and in the aftermath of the battle at Amphipolis and the thwarting of the reinforcement mission, both sides stopped their efforts to continue the fighting. The Spartans had seen her early war strategy of ravaging the lands of the Athenians fail completely to bring about the defeat of Athens. Instead of a victorious war that lasted just a few years, the war had now dragged on for ten, and there was no sign whatsoever that the Athenians were about to quit. They had also endured humiliations and unexpected setbacks of their own. On Sphacteria in 425, Spartan hoplites had for the first time in history been taken prisoner in battle; Pylos and Cythera were bases from which the coasts of the Peloponnesus were raided and plundered; in the wake of their defeats, the Helots were deserting them, and a terrible uprising among those left behind in the Peloponnesus seemed more likely than ever. In addition, the thirty-year peace that Sparta had made with Argos was soon set to end, with the Argives refusing to extend it unless Cynuria was handed back to them. Sparta dreaded a war now with both Athens and the powerful and wealthy city of Argos. There were also fears that some of the cities of the Peloponnesus desired to switch sides and join the Athenian alliance.[195]

For the Athenians, there were also good reasons to seek peace. They too worried that their allies might see their setbacks and decide to defect. They were no longer overwhelmingly confident in their own strength, as they had been in the glorious year of 425 when they had overcome the previously invincible Spartans at Pylos and Sphacteria. They had also suffered defeats of their own, at Delium in 424 and Amphipolis in 422. Many in Athens now rued their failure to make peace when the Spartans had offered it to them earlier in the war.

Thucydides viewed the Spartans as having been the most eager for peace, as above all, they wanted to secure the return of the men who had been taken captive at Sphacteria in 425. Their number included full citizen Spartiates who were members of Sparta's leading families and were related to its most prominent men. The Spartans had been very willing to make peace to get these men back as soon as they had been captured, but the Athenians had been so sure of themselves that they had arrogantly snubbed their offer.[196]

Thucydides also saw the deaths of both Brasidas and Cleon as having removed the two chief opponents of peace on either side of the war. Brasidas wished the war to continue because of the 'success and honour' that it had brought him, while Cleon feared that if peace came 'his crimes would be more open to detection and his slanders less credited'.[197] Their departures left behind less belligerent prominent men such as King Pleistoanax in Sparta and Nicias, the Athenian general, who both desired peace. Nicias had enjoyed real success in the war to date, having led victorious missions against Minoa in 427, Tanagra in 426, Solygia and Methana in 425, Cythera in 424, and Mende and Scione in 423. He understandably wanted to end the conflict as an undefeated commander. Pleistoanax, on the other hand, had been restored from exile, some said unjustly, and the wartime setbacks that Sparta suffered caused many to blame them on the king. Thinking that an end to the fighting would bring an end to these setbacks, and that this would mean an end to the stinging attacks made on him, he sought peace.[198] Over the winter of 422/1, negotiations took place. The Spartans were also considering conducting a fortified occupation of Attica, and told her allies to be ready to carry out the plan. This threat was made to get the Athenians to take their peace offers seriously, and in due course a peace was made, with the agreement being named the 'Peace of Nicias', after the foremost Athenian who negotiated it. Plutarch writes that Nicias was 'praised as a man especially favoured by the gods, and one who as a reward for his piety had been chosen to give his name' to the peace, 'the greatest and fairest of all human blessings'.[199]

Regret weighed heavily on the Athenians. They saw Nicias as being the author of the peace, just as they also blamed Pericles for the war. The cause for Pericles taking the city to war had been too slight, they now felt, and Nicias was praised for convincing them to put the past behind them and make peace with the Spartans. The desire for peace was very real among the people, especially among those who were older and wealthier, and in particular owned some land, which would no longer be subject to the depredations of the enemy.[200]

The agreed peace was to last for fifty years, and was to bind Athens and its allies with Sparta and its allies. In the main, apart from bringing hostilities to a halt, the treaty provided for the exchange of cities captured by either power over the previous ten years. The Spartans returned Amphipolis and several other cities that Brasidas had won during his campaigns in Thrace. Of these latter cities, the inhabitants of Argilus, Stagirus, Acathus, Scolus, Olynthus and Spartolus would be free to depart if they so chose, and the tribute that Athens could demand from them would be that which had been originally assessed by Aristides back in 478/7 when the Delian League had first been formed. The Athenians pledged not to undertake any wars against these cities so long as they paid the tribute due to Athens. Further, they were to be neutral, allied to neither Athens nor Sparta, but would be entitled to become allies of Athens if the cities desired to do so. In turn, the Athenians gave back Coryphasium, Cythera, Methana, Pteleum and Atalanta to Sparta. Of foremost interest to the Spartans were the prisoners taken at Sphacteria, and these were to be repatriated, as were any Athenian prisoners held by the Spartans or their allies. Any Peloponnesians who were still holding out in besieged Scione were to be allowed to leave, as well as any friends of Sparta who wanted to depart.[201]

The implementation of the treaty was not at all smooth, since some of the allies refused to go along with its terms. The Amphipolitans would not hear of being returned to Athens, and Clearidas, the Spartan officer holding the city, would not give it up against the will of its inhabitants. He journeyed to Sparta seeking an alteration of the terms but when this could not be done he was sent back to Amphipolis to turn it over or at least to evacuate all the Peloponnesians still there.[202] Sparta next sought an alliance with Athens, believing that Argos, which had resisted overtures to extend the truce between it and Sparta, would not be so threatening an opponent if Athens was not on friendly terms with it. So the Spartans and Athenians entered into an alliance of fifty years' duration, in which both pledged to come to one another's aid if attacked. Despite the loyal service that had been given to them by the freed Messenian Helots at Pylos and Naupactus, the Athenians also specifically agreed to aid the Spartans in the event of a Helot uprising.[203]

The peace and the ensuing alliance between Athens and Sparta were to endure for about seven years, but the treaty had serious flaws from the outset. For one, it was not a general peace, as it did not include all of the combatants. Corinth was not party to the treaty, and neither were Megara, Elea or Boeotia, which like Corinth did not approve of the peace; there were other cities in the Peloponnesus that were also against it.[204] Thucydides was adamant in seeing the treaty years as being a mere pause in the fighting, and that the twenty-seven years extending from the war's eruption in 431 to when the Long Walls and Piraeus were captured represented just a single long war. If the word 'peace' means anything, it must mean an absence of war, and the period after the Peace of Nicias was made was far from peaceful, supporting Thucydides' thesis that it was not a true peace at all. Neither Athens nor Sparta fully abided by the terms to which they had agreed, there were several violations of the treaty and their allies were soon to be at war in Thrace.[205] Athens, for example, did not relinquish Pylos, and Sparta did not give back Amphipolis. Tensions between them mounted over disputed lands, whether claimed by themselves or by Argos, which wanted Cynuria back from Sparta.

Sparta's perennial manpower problems had by now worsened to the point where they granted freedom to the Helot soldiers who had fought beside Brasidas in the north. These were settled at Lepreum, together with a new group of Spartans called the *Neodamodeis*, who were free, and could bear arms, but were not full citizens. The Spartans themselves in this regard were bowing to military reality, acknowledging that their country was simply not capable of producing enough full Spartiate citizen-soldiers for her armies.[206] The Spartan prisoners taken at Sphacteria who had been returned as part of the Peace of Nicias were at first deprived of some of their rights, on the grounds that they might attempt a revolution if they felt that they were to be degraded at home. They were consequently barred from holding offices or buying or selling things. Eventually, though, they had their rights restored, as the Spartans saw that their numbers were necessary to preserving Sparta's fighting strength.[207] Sparta's inability to produce more full-citizen Spartans was creating a powerful drag on its military power, and the problem would only worsen as the years wore on.

During this period of diplomatic flux, a young Athenian rose to prominence in his city, Alcibiades, who would go on to play an outsized role in the politics of his country. Alcibiades' pride had been wounded by the Spartans' failure to negotiate the peace treaty through him, since his family had once acted as *proxeni*, or native representatives who acted on behalf of a foreign power in their own city, for the Spartans. Instead, they had chosen to hold their talks, very sensibly, with the older Nicias and Laches, another Athenian who had previously commanded triremes in Sicilian waters in 427/6. In 420, Alcibiades engineered an alliance between Argos and Athens, which came to include Mantinea and Elea. Despite its pre-existing alliance with Argos, Corinth refused to join the new alliance, and Athens and Sparta themselves did not formally end their own alliance with one another. The end result of the twists and turns of the formation and reformation of alliances was to bring Sparta and Argos to loggerheads in 418 over Epidaurus. The Argives had as a grievance the failure of the Epidaurians to send sacrifices to the temple of Apollo Pythaeus, but they and Alcibiades had the strategic goal of seizing Epidaurus so as to keep Corinth neutral and ensure a shorter passage of their reinforcements from the island of Aegina, which currently had to sail the longer route around Scyllaeum.[208]

An Argive army marched out and plundered Epidaurian lands. Sparta responded by sending its own army under the command of King Agis to the aid of its ally, and after some manoeuvring agreed to a truce of four months. This caused distress for both Agis and the Argive commanders who agreed to it, with both sides thinking that each had been in the perfect position to inflict a serious defeat on the enemy. In their next encounter outside Mantinea, they got the battle they wanted. The Spartans were surprised by the sudden appearance of the Argive-allied army in full battle array, but their training and discipline allowed them to form up for battle very rapidly. The Spartans had the better of the day. Argive-allied losses in this fiercely fought battle were much heavier, as was usual among defeated armies in the ancient world, but the Spartans, Thucydides speculates, may have lost some 300 men.[209]

In Argos in 418/7, an anti-democratic, oligarchic faction had gained the upper hand over the popular party, and they were the driving force between a peace treaty with Sparta as well as an alliance with it. Once the alliance had been made, they brought in Perdiccas of Macedonia and the Chalcidian cities.[210] But very soon, in 417, the popular party in Argos overthrew the oligarchic faction, banishing those who were not slain.[211] The Spartans were slow to respond, but the Argives, knowing that an attack would come eventually, began to construct with Athenian help long walls to the sea of her own, hoping that she too could import what she needed by sea if she were to be blockaded by land. But the Spartans at last moved, arriving at Argos in the winter of 417/6 with an army under King Agis, and they razed the long walls. Perdiccas in Macedonia was blockaded by the Athenians as a retaliatory measure for his earlier alliance with Argos and Sparta.[212]

Despite the participation of the Athenian contingent on the side of the Argives in the Battle of Mantinea, the war did not yet resume formally between Athens and Sparta, though it was obvious to all that the peace treaty was a 'dead letter'. The peace between Athens and Sparta had begun to sputter almost as soon as it had been made, and its basic terms had never been completely fulfilled. The confusion of this interwar period, if such a term may be used for one in which so much fighting occurred, shows that the underlying conflicts that had brought about the war had not been resolved, and that it was in fact more of a time in which the various combatants could recuperate from their struggles.

The Fate of Melos

One incident, perhaps above all others, shows the ruthless nature of Athenian imperialism at this stage. Though the conquest of the island of Melos was a relatively small event in a large war, it is worth a closer look to get a sense of the underlying rationale the Athenians used to justify and maintain their brutal hold over their seaborne empire. Thucydides, fully aware of the horror that was about to be perpetrated on the overmatched Melians, records the negotiations between the Athenians and the islanders in the form of a dialogue, almost as if he were writing a play, a tragedy in fact, something he does nowhere else in his history.

In the summer of 416 BC, Athens sent to Melos a fleet of thirty Athenian triremes, six Chian warships and two other ships from Lesbos, with 1,600 hoplites, 300 archers and twenty mounted archers from Athens, together with around 1,500 additional hoplites from her allies. Melos was a Spartan colony that had refused to join the Athenian alliance. It had stayed out of the war for a long time, maintaining its neutrality, but Athenian aggression had seen its territory raided and plundered. When the Athenian naval expedition appeared offshore, the leading Melians denied the Athenians the chance to speak before the general public. The two sides then engaged in a discussion of the nature of power.

The Athenians were blunt: 'We will not trouble you with specious pretences – either how we have a right to our empire because we overthrew the Mede [Persian], or are now attacking you because of wrong that you have done us – and make a long speech which would not be believed; and in return we hope that you instead of thinking to influence us by saying that you did not join the Spartans, although their colonists, or that you have done us no wrong, will aim at what is feasible ... since you know as well as we do that right, as the word goes, is only in question between equals in power, while the strong do what they can and the weak suffer what they must.'[213]

The Melians responded by saying that arguments based upon morals would be useful to Athens if and when her own empire fell. Should that ever happen, Athens would find itself subject to the 'heaviest vengeance'. But the Athenians answered them that the 'end of our empire, if it should end, does not frighten us: a rival empire like Sparta ... is not so terrible to the vanquished as subjects who by themselves attack and overpower their rulers'. The Athenians declared to them that they had come to Melos in the 'interest of our empire', and that they desired to 'exercise that empire over you without trouble, and see you preserved for the good of us both'.[214]

The Melians naturally asked how being compelled to serve Athens would be as good for them as the Athenians to rule over them. The Athenians replied that by submitting they would be spared the worst, and 'we should gain by not destroying you'. When the Melians asked whether the Athenians would allow them to remain neutral, not an enemy, and not become an ally of either side, the Athenians said that 'your hostility cannot hurt us so much as your friendship', because if Athens let them stay neutral, and thus outside the alliance, it would seem that Athens was somehow weak, while even if Athens incurred the enmity of Melos, it would make Athens seem strong.[215] Melos would have to be made subject to Athens in order to preserve the respect that her allies felt towards her. Athenian security would be enhanced if the empire were enlarged. 'The fact that you are islanders and weaker than others', they said, made it 'all the more important that you should not succeed in thwarting the masters of the sea'.[216]

The Melians pointed out that by conquering her they would be engaging in a policy bound to frighten all other neutral states, and make enemies of them out of fear of Athenian power. These would determine 'that one day or another' they would be attacked by Athens. The enemies that Athens already had would become even more staunchly opposed to her, and other neutral states that had not contemplated becoming her enemy would become so because of Athenian aggression.[217]

Of the mainlanders, there was little to worry about, the Athenians responded. It was the islanders 'outside our empire, and subjects smarting under the yoke, who would be the most likely to take a rash step and lead themselves and us into obvious danger'.[218] The Melians then observed that it would behove them to resist becoming subjects of Athens, considering the lengths to which the Athenians would go to preserve the empire and her unhappy subjects to escape from it, or else they would be cowards. To this the Athenians said that they were wrong, and that the struggle between them and the Melians was not an equal one, and that their surrender was truly a matter of self-preservation, not honour.[219]

The Melians replied that 'the fortune of war is sometimes more impartial than the disproportion of numbers might lead one to suppose'. There might yet be a chance that they could fight back and succeed. The Athenians thought little of this argument. 'Hope, danger's comforter, may be indulged in by those who have abundant resources' who could absorb severe losses and not be destroyed by them. But the Melians were 'weak and hang on every turn of the scale'. False hope for survival would only lead them to destruction.[220]

The Melians then said that they were fighting in a just cause, and that aid could be expected to come from Sparta, so their hopes of resistance were not so irrational as the Athenians thought. The Athenians warned against anticipating help from Sparta. 'The Spartans, when their own interests or their country's laws are in question, are the worthiest men alive; but of their conduct toward others much might be said, but no clearer idea of it be given by shortly saying that of all the men we know they are most conspicuous in considering what is agreeable honourable, and what is expedient just. Such a way of thinking does not promise much for the safety which you now unreasonably count upon.'[221] The Melians insisted that being so close to the Peloponnesus, and sharing blood in common, that the Spartans would be more likely to come to their assistance than for others. But the Athenians pointed out that the Spartans were having problems simply mounting attacks on other land powers, and could do this only in conjunction with its allies. She would be far less willing to take chances to send help to an island people with Athens being 'masters of the sea'.[222]

Sparta could send others to help them, the Melians countered, and the Cretan Sea, in which Melos sat, was 'a wide one, and it is more difficult for those who command it to intercept others, than for those who wish to elude them to do so safely'. Further, if the Spartans failed to help them, there was still the possibility of the Spartans reigniting the strategy employed by Brasidas, in which they would strike at Athenian holdings elsewhere, in which they would be compelled to fight.[223]

The Athenians assured the Melians that 'some diversion of the kind you speak of you may one day experience, only to learn, as others have done, that the Athenians never once yet withdrew from a siege for fear of any'. The Melians had advanced arguments against submitting to Athens based upon hope or some future events. It would be better for them to 'not think it dishonourable to submit to the greatest city in Hellas, when it makes you the moderate offer of becoming its tributary ally, without ceasing to enjoy the country that belongs to you'.[224]

The Athenians retired and the Melians discussed their options. After deliberating, they declined Athens' offer. They would not submit to becoming a subject of Athens, they said, and would put 'their trust in the fortune by which the gods have preserved' their city's freedom.[225] The Athenians, rebuffed, built a wall around Melos, and left a force behind to carry on the siege. The Melians fought on fiercely, and were successful in two separate attacks on the Athenian siege lines, but Athens sent reinforcements for their army already in place during the winter of 416/5, and the siege was conducted with greater energy. The Melians were soon driven to surrender, at Athenian discretion. The Melian men were put to death, and the women and children were sold into slavery. Five hundred colonists were later despatched to resettle the emptied island on behalf of Athens.[226]

The Athenian Condundrum

In subsequent history, despite the sincere admiration granted to Sparta for the bravery of its people, Athens won the war for public perception. Athens is remembered as the fountainhead of Western civilization. It is recalled as the source of its philosophy; the originator of its unique artistic tradition; it is the wellspring of democracy. Sparta is remembered for its soldiers. Thucydides' theatrical presentation of the conversation between the Athenians and valiant but doomed Melians is something of a morality play intended to highlight the harshness of Athenian imperial rule. It might seem that Athens would have been clearly preferable as an imperial master (if one had to have one at all) to that of Sparta if we judge such matters with the values of modern times. It seems confusing at times that so many states would wish to escape from Athens to ally themselves with a retrograde and reactionary military regime. The ancient Greeks were different from us. Not only were there still-relevant cultural cleavages based upon archaic tribal origins, i.e., the Ionians, the Dorians, etc.; there was also the matter of the relative weight of the rival power's overlordship. The Athenians demanded tribute, whereas the Spartans did not. Sparta's coalition was less demanding, while the yoke of Athens was noticeably heavier. The success of Brasidas in peeling away states from the Athenian Empire is proof of this. The desire on the part of subject states to be free of Athenian rule was very real, and a continuing vulnerability for Athens as the war dragged on.

PART FOUR

THE SICILIAN EXPEDITION

Thucydides opens Book Six of his narrative with an exploration of the history of Sicily. He does this because the Athenians had decided to undertake against the island an expedition much larger than the one they had sent to Sicily that had been commanded by Laches and Eurymedon between 427–426 BC. The stated reason for their campaign against Sicily was to bring aid to kindred peoples and allies there, but their actual aim, if possible, was to conquer the island, though most Athenians, Thucydides writes, were 'ignorant of its size and the number of its inhabitants'.[1] Envoys from Segesta had come to Athens in 416/5 to plead for help against Selinus, which, allied with the powerful city of Syracuse, had put Segesta on the defensive. Athens had years before sent ships to bolster Segesta in the Leontine War of 427–426. In 424, peace had been made at the Congress of Gela between the various powers of Sicily. This saw the Athenians leave Sicily, but factional conflict in Leontini emerged over the democratic party's plan of land redistribution. This worried the wealthy very much, and in 422 they had sought help from Syracuse. As their Athenian allies had departed, this left the popular faction vulnerable. The Syracusans came and drove out the common folk, and the rich, after laying waste to the city, went to Syracuse, where they were made citizens. But a few were not happy with their stay in Syracuse, and these established themselves at Phocaeae, a city quarter of Leontini, and also fortified Bricinniae, which lay in Leontine territory. An Athenian delegation under Phaeax had sounded out the Sicilians about forming an alliance against Syracuse, but though Camarina and Agrigentum were willing, Gela was adamantly opposed, and Phaeax decided not to continue with his mission since he saw no chance of success without Gela onboard.[2]

The Segestans wanted the Athenians to help them, and warned that if they did not, and the Syracusans were not punished for their actions at Leontini, and were allowed to bring ruin to the other allies of Athens on the island, then there was the possibility that Syracuse would in the future make an expedition to Greece of the Dorian peoples of Sicily to help the Dorian Peloponnesians. The Segestans said that they should act quickly to form a coalition that could resist the Syracusans, and promised that they had money sufficient to pay for Athens' war expenses. The Athenians first voted to send envoys to Segesta on a fact-finding mission to learn the truth about the claimed wealth and the conflict with Selinus. The envoys returned to Athens in the summer of 415 with their ships loaded with sixty talents of uncoined silver – enough money to cover a month's pay of sixty trireme crews. The Segestans and the envoys spoke before the Athenian Assembly, and Thucydides says their report on Sicilian affairs and the amount of wealth there in the treasury and temples was as 'attractive as it was untrue'.[3] The Assembly voted in favour of sending sixty triremes to Sicily, with the command of the fleet to be shared by Alcibiades, Nicias and Lamachus. Their remit from the Assembly was to help Segesta against Selinus, restore Leontini if they should gain any advantage in the war and to do whatever else was needed to be done in the best interests of Athens.[4]

Five days after this initial vote, the Assembly came together to discuss the fastest way to equip the expedition. Nicias, as one of the generals, was under no illusion that the expeditionary force had as its true goal the conquest of Sicily, and that this was a terrible idea. Command of the fleet alongside Alcibiades and Lamachus had been forced upon him by the Assembly, and he tried to dissuade them from what he saw as a reckless course of action.[5]

That Nicias should have been selected as a general, despite his unhappiness with the appointment, is not altogether surprising. As a politician, he enjoyed the broad support of the people. He owed much of his political advancement to the backing of the wealthy, who saw him as a counterweight to the obnoxious demagogue Cleon, and many of the common people too preferred the polite and nervous Nicias to Cleon, whom they thought greedy.[6] In the military sphere, he had held several significant commands before, having led the naval force that captured Minoa in 427 and an expedition of sixty ships whose hoplites had won a battle on land at Tanagra in 426. Next, in command of a fleet of eighty ships, he had won another victory on land at Solgyia in 425, and had captured Methana during the same voyage. In 424, he had also pulled off a great coup when he seized Cythera from the Spartans, this time sailing with another fleet of sixty ships. His experience at sea was unquestionable, and the fleets he had previously directed had been substantial in size. In Nicias, the Athenian Assembly was entrusting the expedition to what they believed was a safe pair of hands.

But Nicias was not the right man for this forbidding mission, which required daring and a firm belief in its potential success, two things that Nicias lacked almost entirely. Though he had achieved laudable results as a general of Athens during the Archidamian War, Plutarch attributed his success more to caution than to capability: '[Nicias] was by nature timid and inclined to defeatism, his good fortune enabled him to conceal his lack of resolution.'[7] He had also been very careful in avoiding risky military commands. 'Nicias ... did his best to evade any difficult or lengthy enterprise; whenever he served as general he played for safety, if he was successful, as he naturally often was under these conditions, he never claimed any credit for foresight, or energy, or courage on his part, but thanked his good fortune for everything and gave the glory to the gods.'[8]

Nicias reminded the Assembly that the treaty with Sparta (it was still in effect in spite of all that had happened since it had been concluded) should not be counted upon to preserve the peace. A setback might see the war suddenly heat up again and Athens would find herself under attack by her enemies in Greece. Some states had never accepted the treaty, many parts of the treaty were in dispute and the Spartans had only entered into a peace because they had suffered disaster (at Sphacteria), and so it was not for them an honourable peace. Athens should not send so much of her strength to Sicily, said Nicias. Her enemies in Greece, learning of this division, would attack her. There was no need to run such risks, with Athens in such a precarious situation, and they should not 'grasp at another empire before we have secured the one we have already'.[9] The revolt of the Chalcidians in Thrace had yet to be put down, and the loyalty of other mainland allies was uncertain. There was work to do in putting down rebels in Greece, and that should take priority over going to the aid of the Segestans, he urged.

Sicily was too distant a land to be ruled effectively by Athens even if it were to be conquered, Nicias continued. The threat from a Sicily dominated by Syracuse was overblown, and indeed would be less threatening than the present in which individual states might come to the aid of Sparta. This would not occur if Syracuse gained control of Sicily, because she would see that even if she should tear down the empire of Athens in concert with the Peloponnesians, her own empire would then be overthrown in the same manner by the Spartans.[10] This was perhaps not the best of arguments, as it does not contemplate a likely reaching of a *modus vivendi* between a Spartan-dominated Greece and a Syracusan-dominated Sicily as two widely separated imperial powers. Yet Nicias' effort should be seen as a last-ditch attempt to avoid what he believed would be an error of vast proportions. Nicias had always been a man of immense caution,

Plutarch says.¹¹ Now this man was being presented, against his will, with a share in the command of one of the most chancy enterprises in the history of warfare. He struggled to dissuade his countrymen from the great mistake that they were about to make, but he was perhaps so inherently cautious that he could not deliver the blunt and forceful argument against the expedition that was required to have it called off. Had he been able to make his case more effectively, he might have spared his city what was to come.

Nicias further argued before the Assembly that it was too dangerous to risk the reputation of Athens in a war in Sicily. As things stood now, the prestige of Athens was very high, and this reputation was as high as it was because it had not been put to the test. But if Athens should suffer 'the least reverse … they would at once begin to look down upon us, and would join our enemies here against us'.¹² This would place Athens in the same position that Sparta currently had. Before the war the Spartans had been figures of dread, but they had been so hurt during the war that the Athenians had become contemptuous of them, so much so that the Assembly was now considering the conquest of Sicily. The Spartans, he reminded them, would be looking to get revenge for the humiliation they had endured, and they should be a threat to be guarded against. Athens was also at long last experiencing relief from war, in which she had suffered from the plague, and should take this time to rebuild her strength, not dissipate it on behalf of the Segestans. He also attacked the main proponent of the expedition, Alcibiades, who was some twenty years his junior, whom he claimed desired it because he hoped to 'profit from his appointment' as a general and thereby pay off his 'heavy expenses' (Alcibiades, it was known, was especially fond of horses).¹³

Alcibiades was next given the opportunity to speak before the Assembly, and he, Thucydides says, held hopes of not merely subduing Sicily, but Carthage as well. Plutarch mentions that Pericles had in his day resisted talk of ventures against Carthage and other distant places, but it is clear that such ideas, while perhaps submerged by emergencies during the Archidamian War, had not been forgotten by the more aggressive and ambitious of Athens' political class.¹⁴ Alcibiades argued that his military instincts were sound. By bringing together the most powerful Greek states, he had forced the Battle of Mantinea on the Spartans in 418, and though they had nevertheless won, the Spartans had yet to regain their confidence. The Sicilian cities were just 'motley rabbles' and their inhabitants were without any feeling of patriotism.¹⁵ They also lacked the numbers of hoplites claimed, and Athens would have the benefit of non-Greek allies in Sicily to attack Syracuse. In Greece, the Peloponnesian fleet would not be a threat because Athens would be retaining one at least as strong at home after the expedition sailed.[16]

Alcibiades argued that Athens was bound to go to the aid of her allies, and that the assistance given to all other states that requested it was how she had expanded her empire in the past. For Alcibiades, imperial expansion was predicated upon sending help to other states and incorporating them into the empire's tributary structure. If Athens became too picky in choosing whom to support, then she would find herself making few new additions to the empire. He insisted that Athens must either continue to expand her empire or see it taken from her: '[W]e have reached a position in which we must not be content with retaining what we have but must scheme to extend it for, if we cease to rule others, we shall be in danger of being ruled ourselves.' [17]

The Athenian fleet, Alcibiades said, was more powerful than all the fleets of Sicily taken together, and this would guarantee their ability to remain in Sicily if they were victorious, or to return home if they were not. Athens must not remain passive, as Nicias wished: 'By sinking into inaction, the city ... will wear itself out, and its skill in everything decay; while each fresh struggle will give it fresh experience, and make it more used to defend itself not in word but in deed.'[18]

The Assembly was swayed by Alcibiades to favour the expedition even more, and Nicias, seeing that his outright opposition to the mission was getting him nowhere, tried again to dissuade the Assembly by frightening its members with the enormity of the cost of the undertaking. He pointed out that their main enemies, Selinus and Syracuse, were 'full of hoplites, archers, and dart throwers, have triremes in abundance and multitudes to man them; they also have money'. Besides these, the Sicilians also had many more horses than the Athenians, and grew their own grain on their own lands instead of having to import it, as Athens did.[19]

To fight the Sicilian enemies, Athens would need not just a navy, but a powerful land army too to accompany it. The expedition would have to embark a large number of hoplites from Athens and the allies, together with light troops such as archers and slingers. Logistics would also be an issue. Nicias said: 'Meanwhile we must have an overwhelming superiority at sea to enable us the more easily to carry in what we want; and we must take our own grain in merchant vessels ... wheat and roasted barley, and bakers from the mills compelled to serve for pay in the proper proportion; so that if we become weather-bound the armament may not lack provisions ... above all we must take with us from home as much money as possible, as the sums talked of as ready at Segesta are readier, you may be sure, in talk than in any other way.'[20]

Nicias compared the object of the expedition to founding a city in a hostile land, and warned that it was necessary for them to be ready to dominate the country as soon as they landed. The expeditionary force must be as strong as possible if it was to conquer Sicily or to be capable of escaping the island if it failed.[21] If the expedition were to be made at all, it was paramount that it be capable of operating totally independently of the land in which it operated.[22] Such a thing would have been a tall order for modern armies equipped with extensive motorized logistics trains. For an ancient army, this would have been next to impossible, and we have seen how fleets, with their thousands of oarsmen, were heavily dependent upon local markets in which their crewmen could purchase their food. Nicias' desire for a self-sufficient expeditionary force not reliant on Sicilian supplies was logical and desirable, but unrealistic.

Nicias ended his speech, thinking that he might have talked some sense into the Assembly by showing it just how dicey an enterprise it had approved, or if the Athenians had not been completely put off by the costs and attendant risks, that they might outfit the expedition in such strength that it would stand a better chance of success. The Athenians were even more entranced by the prospect of the attack on Sicily, despite Nicias' words, and they judged that he had given them sound advice. '[T]he Athenians had already come to regard Sicily not as a prize which would end this war,' Plutarch says, 'but as the springboard for another, the advanced base from which they could embark on a struggle with Carthage and make themselves masters of Libya and the whole Mediterranean up to the Pillars of Hercules.'[23] Some thought that by making such a strong armament as Nicias had set forth would make them either victorious or at least immune to disaster; others were enchanted by the lure of a foreign adventure; 'while the idea of the common people and the soldiery was to earn wages at the moment, and make conquests that would supply a never-ending fund to pay for the future'.[24] Support for military action was perennially stronger among the lower classes of Athens, who provided the bulk of the oarsmen for the fleet, and thereby earned some money by their service, whereas the well-off, whose lands in Attica had been burned, and who did not profit from fighting, broadly desired an end to conflict. They did not, though, seem to have made much of a stand against the

Sicilian venture. Plutarch writes that some of the wealthy, would-be opponents of the project held their tongues out of fear. 'The rich were afraid of being accused of evading their contribution to the cost of the expedition and the provision of ships, and so kept silent against their better judgment.'[25]

Nicias was next asked point-blank by one of the members of the Assembly who demanded to know what forces they should vote for him. He responded, not enthusiastically, that he would need at minimum 100 triremes, as many transport ships as could be mustered and at least 5,000 hoplites from Athens and the allies, together with light troops such as archers from Crete and slingers.[26] The Assembly cast an immediate vote that gave full powers to the generals of the expedition to do as they saw fit. Preparations began right afterward, with enlistment rolls drawn up in Athens and summonses sent to the allies to provide troops. Thucydides writes that Athens was able to provide for the expedition because it had by now recovered from the effects of the plague. A generation of young men had grown to manhood, and there had been an accumulation of money in the city since the Peace of Nicias had been made that was not going out immediately to pay for war.[27]

Sacrilege

Then something very strange happened. The doorways of private homes and temples in Athens typically had small square stone *Hermae* in them, and the faces were discovered to have been mutilated by persons unknown. Rewards were offered to induce someone to come forward and say who had performed the sacrilege. The Assembly voted that anyone with information about any other religious sacrilege should come forward without fear of any consequences or reprisals. The defacement was thought to constitute an ill omen for the fate of the expedition, and a component of a plot to disturb the democracy of Athens.[28] Other disturbing material soon surfaced, not about the mutilation of the *Hermae* but about similar disfigurements of images by drunk young men performing mock celebrations of the Eleusinian Mysteries. These sacrilegious acts were said to have occurred in private homes inside Athens.[29]

Alcibiades was named as having taken part in the latter mutilations, and his political opponents immediately saw a chance to be rid of him and take the lead in Athenian politics. They put forward the notion that the mutilations of both the *Hermae* and in the Mysteries had been part of the same plot to overthrow the democracy of Athens. As evidence, they proffered the undemocratic, licentious nature of Alcibiades' notoriously lavish lifestyle.[30] Alcibiades insisted on his innocence of the charges. He was so eager to go to Sicily that, with the outfitting of the expedition finished, he requested that he be put on trial before he left to get the matter out of the way. If he were to be found guilty, he would accept his punishment, but if he were to be judged not guilty, he would still be able to take his place as one of the expedition's generals. So much did Alcibiades wish to avoid going off on such an important mission with this dire charge hanging over his head that he insisted that he be executed immediately if he should be found guilty. His opponents, however, refused a quick trial, thinking that the army, which was still present in the city, might be with him, and that the Assembly might be swayed in his favour. Alcibiades' offer of an immediate, definitive trial was rejected at their urging, and he was made to sail with the expeditionary fleet and then return within a set number of days to stand trial. The plan of his enemies was that in Alcibiades' absence they would concoct some more serious charge against him and then try him on that upon his return to Athens.[31]

The Expedition Sails

It was midsummer 415 BC when the fleet sailed for Sicily from Piraeus. The allies and the grain transports had gone ahead and were to rendezvous at Corcyra before they crossed the Ionian Sea to Italy. The Athenians and what allies who were there with them climbed aboard their ships at dawn, while the populace of Athens gathered to watch them go. The soldiers and sailors said goodbye to their loved ones, and it was now that the full danger of the project upon which they were embarking sank in. They took some solace, though, in the scale of the expedition and all of its obvious power and provisions. Thucydides says that this armament was 'by far the most costly and splendid Hellenic force that had ever been sent out by a single city up to that time'.[32] What made the current fleet different was not so much the number of ships, which had been exceeded in earlier times by fleets commanded by Pericles when he sailed to Epidaurus or by Hagnon when he had gone to Potidaea, but by the great distance which the fleet would travel. Those previous fleets had gone to sea with 'scanty equipment', while the current one had been lavishly equipped at great expense to the ship captains and the Athenian state. The state treasury was paying one drachma per day to every seaman, and the trierarchs had added a bounty to this to attract the best crews to their personal ships. In this way, sixty triremes and forty transports were crewed. Money was also spent on ship decorations, such as figureheads, and every effort was made to ensure that the ships would be fast sailers.[33]

The land forces were not neglected either; the men selected to go were drawn from the best enlistment rolls, and these competed amongst themselves to display the finest arms and equipment. Thucydides saw the entire expedition as being an immensely costly enterprise, not only in terms of the money that the state paid out, but also in the money that private individuals spent on their gear or the trierarchs on their ships. We have seen that paying the crew of a single trireme for one month was said to cost one talent, and with so many ships being outfitted – sixty triremes and the forty transports – plus the pay for the thousands of hoplites and other soldiers, the cost of the Sicilian armament would have had to far exceed one hundred talents over the course of its first month of operation alone, not including all of the other sums paid to get the triremes in shape for the voyage and the private expenses of the crewmen and hoplites. The expedition would be burning through money at a furious rate once it left Piraeus.

With the crews and soldiers aboard the ships, ready to depart, a trumpet sounded, commanding silence. It was the custom of the Athenians to say prayers before the fleet sailed, and these were spoken on behalf of all the ships taken together by a herald. Bowls of wine were distributed among the ships of the fleet, and libations were made by the soldiers and officers with gold and silver goblets. The people waiting ashore took part in the prayers, and when the libations were completed, and the hymn had been sung, the ships put out in line of column, making first for the island of Aegina, and thence to Corcyra for the passage to Italy.[34]

There was no way to disguise the outfitting of such a massive fleet and army. In Syracuse, word of the expedition had been arriving from many sources, but the Syracusans themselves could scarcely countenance the reports of the tremendous armament. Hermocrates, who had been instrumental in brokering peace among the Sicilians at the Congress of Gela, addressed them. He warned that the Athenians were truly getting ready to mount an attack of great size against Syracuse. Though the professed goal of the expedition was to help Segesta and restore Leontini, he said, their true purpose was to conquer Sicily, and Syracuse in particular.[35]

The sheer size of the armament that the Athenians had made would work to Syracuse's advantage, Hermocrates said: '[T]he greater is the better, with regard to the rest of the Sicilians, whom dismay will make more ready to join us.' The Athenians were bound to fail, he argued. 'Few indeed have been the large armaments, either Hellenic or barbarian, that have gone far from home and been successful.' Athens would experience operational problems so far from their own lands. They would never outnumber the inhabitants of the country they invaded, who would unite against them out of fear, and obtaining supplies would be difficult too. Hermocrates noted that Athens had survived the invasions of the Persians, who were themselves operating in a foreign land far from home, and rose to power in the wake of the Persian defeat, which was in larger part the result of accidents, not Athenian actions. Syracuse could itself do the same.[36]

Hermocrates urged the Syracusans to gather together allies from the rest of Sicily, Italy and Carthage too, because she had the 'most gold and silver, by which war, like everything else, flourishes'.[37] He even suggested that they mount a counter-expedition of their own, and meet the Athenian fleet at Tarentum and the Iapygian promontory (Cape Iapygium) to show the Athenians that the crossing from Italy would itself be contested. With Tarentum as a base, they could harry the strung-out Athenian fleet as it made the difficult crossing over to Italy from Corcyra. If they made their triremes lighter and drew their fastest ones together and attacked, the Syracusans could wait until they had exhausted themselves with rowing and then counter-attack. Even if the Syracusans did not bring them to battle, these stripped-down Athenian warships would find themselves stranded in Italy with few provisions, to either stay behind and be blockaded, or if they should attempt to sail down the coast, they would be of no further use to the rest of the Athenian fleet.[38]

Hermocrates' words did not sway many to this way of thinking. There were those who disbelieved that the Athenians were sailing at all, while others thought that if they did they would suffer grievously in attacking. The popular party at Syracuse was led by Athenagoras, and he spoke against Hermocrates, accusing him of causing fear among the public in the city for his own reasons. The Athenians were not coming, he said, because they were experienced and shrewd, and would never leave the Peloponnesians unguarded in Greece to undertake a foolhardy war in Sicily.[39] Syracuse was 'more than a match for this alleged army of invasion', if it did come, even if it was twice the size as reported.[40] He criticized Hermocrates, and others like him, for their alarmism, and saw his talk of an Athenian attack, which he discounted, as a means to scare the people and take control of the government of Syracuse.[41]

An unnamed Syracusan general then came forward and brought the discussion to a halt. He reminded the Assembly that personal attacks on each other were of no benefit to Syracuse, and that they had best look to the defence of their city, even if it should turn out that there was no need for them to do so. He told them that horses, arms and other equipment should be gathered, and the other cities of Syracuse be alerted to the possible threat. Once they were finished, he and the other generals would deliver a report to the Assembly concerning what they had learned.[42]

While the Syracusans were busy debating whether an Athenian invasion was likely, the Athenians themselves had made their way to Corcyra. The commanders of the expedition made a review of the fleet, dividing the ships into three divisions in which they were to sail, with one general per division. The ships were also given instructions as to where they would anchor and make their shore camps so that their men would not exhaust the locally available water and provisions.[43]

Three ships were sent ahead to Italy and Sicily to find out which of the cities would welcome the Athenian fleet, and were told to report back as to where they could make landfall. Sailing from Corcyra, the Athenians crossed to Sicily with a fleet that numbered 134 triremes and two smaller pentecontors from Rhodes. Of the triremes, 100 were Athenian hulls – sixty triremes and forty troopships – with the remaining thirty-four drawn from Chios and other allied cities. The ships carried a total of 5,100 hoplites, of which 1,500 were Athenian citizens. Seven hundred *thetes*, Athens' poorest folk, served as marines. Of the rest, some were Athenian subjects, while 500 Argive and 250 Mantinean mercenaries had been recruited too. In addition, there were 480 archers aboard the ships – which include eighty men from Crete – 700 Rhodian slingers, 120 light troops composed of exiled Megarians and a single horse transport with thirty horses.[44]

Accompanying the military fleet were thirty merchant freighters loaded with grain for the troops and crews. These ships also carried in them bakers, stonemasons and carpenters, and tools for building fortifications. There were 100 other boats that had been taken into service for moving supplies, and apart from these there were many other private boats and merchantmen that tagged alongside the fleet, hoping to trade with the great Athenian armament.[45]

First landfall took place at the Iapygian promontory and Tarentum, but as they sailed along the coast of southern Italy they found that many cities refused to allow them access to their markets, and held their gates closed against them, giving them just water and permission to anchor. Tarentum and Locri would not even allow them that minimal accommodation. They were permitted to make camp only when they had arrived at Rhegium at the toe of Italy, but they were kept out of the city, and a market for them was set up outside the walls. Their appeal to the Rhegians to get them to join in the assault on Syracuse came to nothing, with the Rhegians, who were usually well-disposed to Athens, saying that they would prefer to remain neutral, waiting to see what the other Italians did first before they committed themselves.[46]

It was at this point that the reality of the massive Athenian expedition became undeniable to the Syracusans, who began their work of readying their defences in earnest. The three ships despatched by the Athenians to confirm Segesta's money came back and met the Athenians, and their report was disappointing. Instead of the promised abundance of money, Segesta could only produce thirty talents. This would only be enough to pay the crews of the sixty triremes for half a month. All three of the generals were taken aback by the news. Nicias bore the news well compared to the other two men, who were deeply shocked. The Segestans were summoned, and their deception uncovered. The envoys who had been sent to Segesta, and should have known better, were themselves deceived by the apparent value of the treasure heaped inside the temple of Aphrodite at Eryx. Though the bowls, ladles and other objects were made of silver, their real value was insignificant compared to the impression of wealth they made on the envoys. The Segestans had also feted the Athenian common seamen extravagantly, using all of the gold and silver cups they could scrounge in Segesta or borrow from other cities, giving an unwarranted impression of great wealth, as in each of several banquets the same cups were reused as if they were the property of the specific banquet's host. Altogether, these ploys had the effect of convincing the visiting Athenians that there was much more wealth in Segesta than there actually was.[47]

Doubt has been cast on the reality of this alleged deception, it would have been unreasonable for the Segestans to undertake such a fraud when their deceit would surely be discovered once the Athenians arrived in force in Sicily. Further, Nicias seems to have been not at all surprised by the actual fiscal situation of the Segestans, once the truth was made known. He seems to have even expected it. He had previously intimated in his speech before the Assembly that the supposed great wealth of the Segestans was more of a fiction than a reality. He had from the start been opposed to the expedition. If he had genuine information on the matter of Segestan finances, then why did he not deploy it to prevent the armament from sailing at all? Contrary to Thucydides' report, the story of Segestan deception may itself have been a falsehood, perhaps concocted by Alcibiades and transmitted by him directly to Thucydides. Alcibiades' motive in putting out this story of Segestan double-dealing would have been to relieve Athens of any requirement to assist them in their own conflict with Selinus. Alcibiades had much more important goals in Sicily, and once the expedition had sailed out, he no longer had any need of the excuse that Segesta had originally provided for mounting it. As it turned out, the Athenians did very little to aid the Segestans.[48]

Whatever the case, now that the Segestans had been found out, and the true state of their finances made known, the Athenian generals held a council to talk over what to do next. Nicias wanted to go on to Selinus, which was their primary objective. The Segestans would have to put up the money for the expeditionary force, he said, but if they could not, then they should still have to supply the sixty triremes that they had requested with provisions. The Athenians would then bring about a resolution to their dispute with Selinus either by military means or by a negotiated settlement. Once this was accomplished, the fleet would sail along the coast of Sicily, demonstrating the power of Athens to the Sicilian cities, and go back home unless some unforeseen opportunity presented itself to help the Leontines or some other cities might be brought into alliance. Otherwise, the fleet would return to Piraeus, there being no reason to risk so much of Athens' might in Sicily.[49] Since little money would in fact be forthcoming from the Segestans, and the expeditionary force would need large amounts of it to sustain its operations, this would seem to have been the most sensible course of action, and was fully in keeping with Nicias' cautious temper.

Alcibiades, unsurprisingly, was of a very different mind. It would be a 'disgrace' for the expedition to go back home without achieving anything. They should try to gain as many allies as they could from the cities of Sicily, and attempt to foment a rebellion among the Sicels against Syracuse. Messana especially would be a useful ally to have on their side; her harbour was wonderful and the city would be a good base for the army. Once this grand Sicilian coalition had been prepared, they could turn their attention to fighting Syracuse and Selinus.[50]

The last of the three, Lamachus, wanted to sail immediately to Syracuse, before its inhabitants could complete their preparations and while its people were still in a panic. A sudden attack would be the most effective means of securing a quick victory. Even if the Athenians did not carry the city then and there, they would probably catch by surprise many who were still outside the walls, and they might also lay their hands on the property that they were bringing into the city for safekeeping. The Athenians would have all this booty to themselves if they had to settle into a siege, the Sicilians would think twice about forming an alliance with the Syracusans once an Athenian army was parked outside its gates, and would instead become allies of Athens. Megara Hyblaea, lying to the north of Syracuse, would make for a fine naval base from which to launch their strike and also a place to retreat to.[51] A quick, immediate assault at Syracuse at least promised the chance of taking the city before the inhabitants could ready themselves to resist it.

Lamachus was still willing to support Alcibiades' strategy, and Alcibiades took a ship to Messana to make an alliance. He was turned down, with the Messanans refusing to let him inside, though they would provide a market for the Athenians. Back at Rhegium, the three generals provisioned sixty ships of the fleet and coasted with them southward, first to Naxos, where they were received. They then coasted on to Catana, where they were denied admission. Their next stop was the Terias River, where they camped for the night. On the next day, the Athenians sailed in single file with fifty of their ships to Syracuse behind a vanguard force of ten that was sent ahead to see if a Syracusan fleet might issue forth to challenge them. Once there, the vanguard entered the city's Great Harbour and by herald proclaimed the reason for the coming of the Athenians, that they were in Sicily to restore the Leontines to their country. Having done this, the ships made a reconnaissance of Syracuse's features and the harbour, and then departed for Catana.[52]

The Catanans were not willing to receive the fleet in their city, but they did permit the three generals to come inside and make a presentation to the Assembly. While Alcibiades was speaking to the people, some of the Athenian soldiers stuck outside forced their way through a poorly walled-up postern gate, and these men made their way to the marketplace. The pro-Syracusan faction, which was not very large, hid itself away, and the Assembly, despite the incursion, voted to join Athens in an alliance and permitted the generals to call in the remainder of the armament still waiting at Rhegium.[53]

News came to the Athenians at Catana that Camarina was willing to go over to them if they sailed there, and also that the Syracusans were manning their fleet for a sortie. The Athenians sailed by Syracuse, where they found no evidence of this, and when they reached Camarina, they were rebuffed by its citizens. On the way back to Catana, they descended on the coast of Syracusan territory and plundered what they could before being forced to leave by the appearance of cavalry from Syracuse.[54]

Alcibiades Recalled

While at Catana, they saw that one of Athens' state galleys, the *Salaminia*, had come to ferry Alcibiades back to Athens relating to the charges brought against him concerning the Mysteries and the disfigured *Hermae*. The investigations into these matters had not stopped with the departure of the fleet, but had gone on, with the multitude accepting all manner of accusations levelled against Alcibiades without discrimination, since they feared above all the reimposition of tyranny at Athens, and this made them extremely fearful and suspicious of everyone.[55]

The Athenian people were worried that the earlier sacrilege of the Mysteries had been part of an oligarchic and monarchical plot to impose a tyranny on them. A sort of 'witch hunt' hysteria ensued, during which numerous citizens were charged and executed on baseless grounds.[56] It was in this atmosphere of terror that the *Salaminia* came for Alcibiades, and if Thucydides' appraisal is to be believed, and there is no reason to doubt him, the result of his trial in Athens was a foregone conclusion, and he would be sailing home to his death. Alcibiades did not board the *Salaminia*, but departed for Athens in his own galley, and this ship stayed close to *Salaminia* until they reached Thurii, where they lost sight of her.[57]

Alcibiades had prudently ditched his ship at Thurii, and crossed in another vessel to the Peloponnesus. In Athens, a sentence of death was pronounced on him and the others who had failed to return.

Nicias and Lamachus divided the Athenian force into two and sailed for Segesta and Selinus. At Segesta, they wanted to find out if the Segestans would deliver the money they had promised. Along the way, they assaulted and captured the small seaport town of Hycara, where they enslaved the inhabitants. Continuing on to Segesta, the Athenians were given thirty talents, and then they sold the Hyccarans as slaves for some 120 talents.[58]

Though the finances of the expedition had been improved greatly by the money obtained by the sale of the slaves and delivery of the money by the Segestans, these 150 talents, it should be remembered, would be enough to pay the sixty triremes' crews for just two-and-a-half months, and did not begin to cover the expenses of the land forces and sundry others in the armament. The Athenians were still not financially ready for a long war in Sicily.

The Athenians sent half of their force to Hybla at this time, but were repelled. With the dreaded attack on their city failing again and again to materialize, and the failure of the assault on Hybla, the Syracusans began to grow more eager to go on the offensive against the Athenians, whom they suspected were not as powerful as they had first thought. They demanded that their generals move against the Athenian base at Catana, but when they arrived outside the city, they learned that the Athenians had sailed off during the night to Syracuse. The Syracusans hurried back home, and found the Athenians had occupied a good position that limited their use of cavalry, an arm in which the Syracusans were much superior to the Athenians. In the ensuing battle, the Syracusans were taken by surprise by the suddenness of Nicias' attack, and some of their troops were not in their proper places in the battle line.[59] The fighting was hard, and neither side was willing to retreat. Thunder and lightning then erupted over the battlefield, and it began to rain heavily, which disheartened the Syracusans, who were much less experienced in war than their opponents. The Athenians and their allies drove them back, but were unable to pursue for very long because of the presence of the Syracusan cavalry.[60] Without a sizeable cavalry arm of their own, the Athenians were prevented from turning their victory over the Syracusans into a rout.

The Athenians retired to Naxos and Catana, where they would pass the winter. Shortly afterward, the Athenians at Catana sailed to Messana, thinking that friendly parties in the city would betray it to them, but the plot had been spoiled by Alcibiades, who had sent word of it to the Syracusan party in Messana. Thus alerted, they executed the traitors before they could put their plan into action, fell upon the pro-Athenian faction and succeeded in keeping the Athenians out. The Athenians, rebuffed after waiting outside Messana for thirteen days, then went to Naxos, where they built slips for their ships and threw up a palisade around their encampment. A single trireme was despatched to Athens to request that money and cavalry be delivered to them in the spring.[61]

Both sides made an effort to sway Camarina to their side. The Camarinans were already allies of Syracuse, but their loyalty was doubtful. On learning that the Athenians had sent envoys to Camarina, the Syracusans did likewise, sending Hermocrates and others to convince them of the danger posed by Athens to all of Sicily. Hermocrates addressed the Camarinans, saying that the Athenians were attempting to do in Sicily exactly what they had done in Greece. The Athenians, he said, had been chosen to lead the Ionian alliance against the Persians, but then had begun to accuse 'some allies of failure in military service, some of fighting against each other, and others, as the case might be, upon any specious pretext that could be found, until they thus subdued them all'. The Athenians were not fighting for the liberty of the Greeks, Hermocrates explained, but to make the Greeks their servants.[62]

The Athenian envoy, Euphemus, was given his turn to speak, and admitted that yes, Athens had an empire, and had every right to it too. The purpose of the empire was to defend against the more powerful Dorian alliance. The Ionian states and the islanders had been subjected, but that had just been because their ancestors had joined the Persians in the invasions of Greece years before. 'They, our kinsfolk, came against their mother country ... together with the [Persians], and instead of having the courage to revolt and sacrifice their property as we did when we abandoned our city, chose to be slaves themselves, and to try to make us slaves too.'[63] Athens deserved to rule them because it had deployed both the biggest fleet and the patriotism of its citizens on behalf of the Greeks. The subject states had hurt Athens by going over to the Persians, and further, the empire was needed to keep the Peloponnesians at bay. But it was also necessary for the Athenians to come to Sicily to enhance her own security, Euphemus continued, not to become masters of Sicily themselves but to prevent the island from falling under Syracusan domination.[64]

Euphemus was frank concerning Athenian *realpolitik*. As for the seeming contradiction as to why the Athenians should desire freedom for the Sicilians while they had subjected the Chalcidians, Euphemus said that the Chalcidians were most useful to them by paying money and not bearing arms, while cities such as Leontini and other friends of Athens 'cannot be too independent'.[65] Athens' goal in Sicily was to strengthen her friends and weaken her enemies. Back in Greece, it was Athenian policy to 'treat our allies as we find them useful. The Chians and Methymnians govern themselves and furnish ships; most of the rest have harder terms and pay tribute in money.' Yet other states had been left free because they occupied strategic positions around the Peloponnesus.[66]

The Camarinans, after hearing out both sides, declined to join either, and remained neutral in the war. In truth, they wished to supply very limited support to Syracuse, even though they feared Syracuse more than they did the Athenians, as they worried that Syracuse would win and be displeased with her otherwise. The Athenians also tried to win over the Sicels, and had some success in bringing them over to their side. After moving their winter quarters from Naxos to Catana, the Athenians despatched a trireme to Carthage to make an appeal for friendship, in the hope that aid might be forthcoming, and another ship was sent to the Etruscans, where several cities had already expressed interest in joining the war in Sicily.[67] The Syracusans made their own efforts to improve their position, and envoys arrived in the Italian cities to ask them to help them against the Athenians, whom they claimed were just as much a threat to them as they were to Syracuse. After Italy, the envoys travelled on to Corinth, and made an appeal for aid. The Corinthians were eager to provide it, and quickly voted their approval. The Syracusan ambassadors next went to Sparta, in the company of envoys from Corinth, to make their request of the Spartans. There they encountered Alcibiades, only recently one of the top-ranking officers of the expedition that had made war on Syracuse. After having eluded *Salaminia* near Thurii, Alcibiades and his fellows had boarded a merchant ship out of Thurii, crossing to Cyllene in Elis, and thence to Sparta, where the Spartans had given him a pledge of safe conduct.[68]

The Spartans generally approved of the appeals made by the Syracusans, the Corinthians and Alcibiades himself, but the ephors, the kings and the elders were reluctant to do more than send envoys to encourage the Syracusans not to surrender. Actual military assistance would not be forthcoming. Alcibiades did his best to change their minds. He now disclosed the inside information that he possessed as one of the three generals who had led the Athenians to Sicily. The Sicilians, he said, were only the first target of the expedition. After conquering them, the plan was to overcome the Italians and move on to conquer the Carthaginian empire too. If these actions panned out, Athens' next move was to launch an offensive against the Peloponnesus, bringing with them the vast collection of Greeks they had subdued in Sicily and Italy, together with non-Greek mercenaries. They would also build large numbers of triremes with timber from Italy, and with her fleet thus augmented, they would blockade the Peloponnesus by sea and attack it with her land forces. All of this was to be made possible with the money and grain that they acquired from the newly conquered territories, which would be in addition to the income that Athens received in Greece. The overarching goal of this extensive plan of conquest, Alcibiades said, was the eventual and total subjection of Greece to Athens.[69]

Alcibiades warned that the Athenians would eventually subdue Sicily: '[I]f Syracuse falls, all Sicily falls also, and Italy immediately afterwards ... none need therefore imagine that only Sicily is in question; the Peloponnesus will be so also, unless you speedily do as I tell you, and send on board ship to Syracuse troops that shall be able to row their ships themselves, and serve as hoplites the moment that they land; and what I consider even more important than the troops, a Spartiate as commanding officer to discipline the forces already on foot and to compel shirkers to serve.'[70]

His words were effective. Convinced now of the need for some action, the Spartans appointed Gylippus as commanding officer for the Syracusans, ordering him to make preparations in concert with the Corinthians to send support to Sicily as soon as possible, and a fort was to be erected in Attic territory at Decelea.[71]

It was now the summer of 414 BC, and the Athenians conducted raids around Sicily. They descended on the coast of Megara, laid waste to the countryside and made an attack on a Syracusan fort, which failed. The fleet then moved on to the Terias River, and moving inland the troops despoiled the countryside. Back on their ships, the Athenians sailed to Catana, reprovisioned and made an attack with their entire force against Centoripa, a Sicelian city, which surrendered to them. They then set afire the grain of the Inessaeans and the Hybleans before going back to Catana, where they were met by a reinforcement sent from Athens of 250 horsemen (but no horses), thirty mounted archers and a much-needed delivery of 350 talents of silver.[72]

Having learned that the Athenians had formed a small cavalry arm, the Syracusans also discovered the strategic importance of Epipolae, a piece of high ground overlooking the city that, if kept out of Athenians hands, would prevent them from easily besieging it. They took a force under Hermocrates and other generals to the heights, marching along the Anapus River.[73] The same day, the Athenians sailed from Catana with their whole force to Leon, around a half mile from Epipiolae, where they landed and disembarked their troops. After this, the fleet moved off and anchored at the Thapsus peninsula, and there they erected a stockade across the isthmus. The Athenian army made a dash for Epipolae. The Syracusans were still at some distance, and when they intercepted the Athenians they were in disarray and were defeated. The Athenians occupied Epipolae, and built a fort upon it at Labdalum to be a depository for their baggage and money.[74]

The Athenians then began to apply themselves to investing Syracuse. They started a circumvallation wall to seal off Syracuse from landward reinforcement, while the Syracusans frantically responded by building counterwalls perpendicular to the expected direction of the construction of the Athenian wall. The first counterwall was attacked and wrecked by the Athenians, and a second counterwall begun soon after was also smashed. The Syracusans counter-attacked, and in the battle for the stockade Lamachus was slain. A subsequent attack on the Circle, the primary Athenian fort along the circumvallation wall, was beaten off by the Athenians when Nicias, who had been left behind in the Circle because of illness, ordered that his siege machines and timber be set alight. The blaze kept the Syracusans at bay, and they withdrew.[75] The Athenians pressed on with their building, and completed a double wall that reached southward down to the Great Harbour. Their prospects seemed to brighten. Provisions began to flow in from the Italian cities and many others joined the cause, Sicels, believing that the Athenians were going to win, as well as three Etruscan pentecontors.[76]

The Syracusans, after having experienced these setbacks, were wavering. Some were considering surrender, seeing that the Peloponnesians had failed to send any help and their own efforts had proved insufficient to drive off the Athenians. Talks were opened with Nicias, the only Athenian commander now that Lamachus had perished.[77] But help was on the way. Gylippus and some Corinthian ships had reached Leucas and were poised to make a speedy run to Sicily. While there, erroneous reports came in that the siege line had been completed around Syracuse, and Gylippus gave up on his hopes of saving the situation in Sicily, instead thinking that he would preserve the cities of Italy from Athenian conquest. Gylippus and his Corinthian colleague, Pythen, sailed across the Ionian Sea to Tarentum with two Laconian ships and two more from Corinth. Other Corinthians were to follow with ten more of their ships, plus two Leucadian ships and two from Ambracia once they had been crewed. From Tarentum, he sailed to Thurii, where his appeal for aid against Athens fell on deaf ears, particularly in light of the mere handful of triremes he had brought with him. He sailed away, but a storm arose that caused his ships considerable damage, and he was forced to put into Tarentum for repairs. Nicias knew of his mission, but thought little of it on account of its insignificant size, and judged that Gylippus had come merely to engage in piratical raids.[78]

In Greece, the Spartans launched an invasion of Argive territory, and most of the country was laid waste. The Athenians sent support in the form of thirty triremes to Argos, and this was the most definite breach of their treaty with the Spartans. While the Athenians had been conducting raids out of Pylos and making landings along the coast of the Peloponnesus, they had avoided direct strikes upon the coasts of Laconia, and thus their military cooperation with Argos and Mantinea had been limited, despite the appeals of the Argives for a naval descent with a force of hoplites somewhere against Laconia. The Athenians had not been willing to take such steps, but this time, in the summer of 414, they relented and made landings at Epidaurus Limera, Prasiae and a few other spots, and they plundered what they could. These actions gave the Spartans the justification they needed to resume open hostilities with Athens.[79]

Gylippus Arrives

Gylippus finished repairing his ships, and left Tarentum for Locri. While there, the actual extent of Athenian siege works outside Syracuse were made known to him, and thus that it was still possible to do something to forestall the capitulation of Syracuse. Gylippus was presented with two ways to get past the Athenians and into the city. He might go by way of Epipolae with an army, or he might sail to Himera and then march on Syracuse with any Himerans or others who were willing to go with him. Gylippus settled upon Himera, departed Locri, and after crossing from Rhegium to Messana, made his way to Himera. He was successful in convincing the Himerans to take part in the war, and support was forthcoming from Gela and Selinus, as well as some of the Sicels. Gylippus' force in Sicily now numbered 700 armed sailors and marines, 1,000 Himeran hoplites and light troops, 100 Himeran cavalry, some light troops and cavalry from Selinus, a smattering of Gelans and approximately 1,000 Sicels. With these men, he began his march to relieve Syracuse.[80]

Back in Leucas, the Corinthians had completed their preparations and set sail for Syracuse. One of the commanders of this flotilla was Gongylus, who sped ahead in his trireme, reaching the besieged city before all the other ships despite having left last. There he found that the Syracusans were in the midst of an assembly to discuss capitulation. Gongylus put a stop to this defeatist talk, telling them that more ships were on the way, and that Sparta had sent Gylippus to take command of Syracuse's defence. Gylippus arrived not long after, having captured Ietae, a Sicelian fort along his route, and was met by the whole army of the Syracusans, so eager were they to greet him. Gylippus quickly got his army in marching order, set off for Epipolae and advanced against the Athenian siege lines. To the west and south of the city, the Athenians had all but completed a double wall of about a mile in length, which reached almost to the Great Harbour. On the other side, the wall they were building towards Trogilus was largely unfinished, with some sections complete and others only half-finished. Gylippus had arrived in the nick of time, not long before Syracuse would have been shut up totally by Athenian walls.[81]

Seeing Gyllipus and his troops on the march, the surprised Athenians recovered their balance and formed their own men into battle array. They were met by a herald sent ahead by Gylippus, who promised that he would make a truce with them if they would agree to evacuate Sicily within five days. The Athenians scoffed at this offer and sent the herald away without a reply. Nicias would not lead his men out far from his wall, and Gylippus retired for the night. On the next morning, he led his soldiers out once more, stationing them directly in front of the Athenian walls. Having hemmed in the Athenians, he sent another force against the fort at Labdalum, which was captured.[82]

The Syracusans, energized by the appearance of Gylippus, and given fresh hope, began the construction of a new counterwall, this time extending to the north and east so as to cut off the Athenian wall that was still being built towards Trogilus. Gylippus led an attack against a weak spot of the wall at the Epipolae heights, but the Athenians were aware of his coming and drew up their troops outside the wall to meet him. Gylippus, seeing them ready, withdrew. At this time, Nicias decided to fortify Plemmyrium, a promontory lying to the south of the city, across the mouth of the Great Harbour. He did this to have a secure place in which to land supplies, and it was also a better location in which to base his triremes so that he could have them at the ready should the Syracusan fleet ever sortie from the harbour. Nicias was already aware that with Gylippus' arrival the complexion of the war had changed, and that his chances of winning a victory over Syracuse by land had decreased. He now began to think more of winning by sea. Bringing over ships and soldiers, he erected three forts to house the bulk of his baggage, and anchored there his triremes and larger vessels.[83]

The move to Plemmyrium was not without its risks. The crews of the Athenian fleet suffered heavily from attacks by Syracusan cavalry. A body of enemy horse had been based at the nearby town of

Olympieum to counter plundering raids by the men at Plemmyrium. But Plemmyrium itself had insufficient sources of water, there was little wood to be had for cooking fires and the crewmen had to go out long distances to find both. This left them very vulnerable to the Syracusan cavalry, which mercilessly cut them down.[84]

The counterwall across Epipolae was still being constructed, with Gylippus making use of stones that had first been laid by the Athenians for their own siege wall. The Athenians came out to fight, and in the ensuing battle amidst the siege works the Syracusan cavalry was ineffective because of the confined space in which they fought. Gylippus and the Syracusans were defeated, but Gylippus manfully addressed his troops afterward and took the blame for the loss upon himself, saying that because he had kept them too much inside their own works the cavalry could not have been of much help. The next time, he assured them, would turn out better.[85] It is a testament to Gylippus' confidence in himself and his leadership ability that he was able to admit his own mistakes to his troops, thereby showing that he was indeed a capable leader and the right man for Sparta to have given the job of saving Syracuse.

With their confidence restored, Gylippus led his hoplites again in an attack and did battle with the Athenians, who had themselves come to the conclusion that stopping the Syracusan counterwall was of paramount importance. Should the counterwall be permitted to intersect and pass their own siege wall, their chances of taking Syracuse would be nil. Gylippus came on, taking his troops further from his works than he had done on the prior occasion, where his cavalry would have more space in which to operate. The horsemen smashed the Athenian left wing, while the Athenian right was defeated and pushed back into their own lines. With the Athenians huddling behind their own works, the Syracusans on the next night continued their own counterwall to the Athenian wall, and then kept going. With the Athenians now prevented from building their own siege wall any further, there was no possibility now of them instituting a full siege of the city.[86]

Further improving the Syracusan position was the arrival in the Great Harbour of the twelve Corinthian, Leucadian and Ambraciot triremes under the command of Erasinides of Corinth. With Athens preparing to send more troops to Sicily, Corinthian and Syracusan envoys were sent to Sparta and Corinth to drum up reinforcements for the siege. Gylippus took this time to travel in Sicily to recruit land and naval forces and to bring over to his side any cities that had been until then hesitant to join in the war, and with great import for the future, the Syracusans applied themselves training crews for a sturdy fleet of their own.[87]

Nicias Writes Home

Nicias observed the growing strength of the enemy with alarm. His own troubles were increasing, and he begged Athens for more help. He had been duly sending reports of the situation in Sicily back home for some time, to keep the people there informed as to what was transpiring on the island. He believed that his current position was a poor one, and that the Athenian force outside Syracuse had come to a strategic crossroads of a sort. Athens must either call the expedition back from Sicily right away, or if the war was to continue, then it must send large numbers of reinforcements. If neither was done, then the safety of the expedition would be in jeopardy. It seems that at least some of his earlier reports had been made orally by his messengers, and he worried that the seriousness of the situation would not be made clear to his audience in Athens if he had to rely upon their possibly faulty memories or indifferent speaking skills. He also feared that their desire to 'please the multitude' might keep them from delivering the true facts to the Assembly. So on this occasion, Nicias chose to write a letter so that his exact thoughts would be made plain. When he was done, he gave it to his emissaries, with instructions, and these men took it to Athens for delivery. While he waited for a response from home, Nicias, ever cautious, went over to the defensive, running no risks and intending to preserve his force from harm.[88]

These messengers made their way to Athens at the end of 414 BC. The letter was read aloud to the Assembly, and the picture painted by Nicias was very gloomy. The Athenians had been largely successful against the Syracusans, but the arrival of Gylippus to direct the defence of Syracuse had changed the war's tenor, and the circumvallation wall could not now be completed. The Athenians were on the defensive mainly, with many of their troops occupied by protecting their own lines, and unable to prosecute the siege effectively. Nicias wrote: '[T]he besieger in name has become, at least from the land side, the besieged in reality; as we are prevented by their cavalry from even going any distance into the country.'[89]

Syracuse had made requests that it be reinforced by troops drawn from the Peloponnesus, and Gylippus was seeking aid from the Sicilian cities at the same time. An attack on the Athenian position at Syracuse by land and sea was under consideration by the enemy, Nicias warned, and no one should be surprised that an attack from the sea was a possibility. Ancient galleys were extremely vulnerable to deterioration if they were not properly maintained, and this had been lacking in the time that the fleet had sat outside the city. The Syracusans were aware 'that the length of time we have now been in commission has rotted our ships and wasted our crews, and that with the completeness of our crews and the soundness of our ships the pristine efficiency of our navy has departed'. The triremes could not be pulled out of the water to allow them to dry out, since they had to be perpetually ready for a sortie by the much more numerous Syracusan fleet. The Syracusans, on account of their larger numbers, held the initiative at sea, were busy training their crews and, without the need to keep up a blockade, could haul their ships out of the water to let them dry.[90]

The supply situation was also problematic. If the Athenian fleet were to be hauled ashore for drying out, then getting supplies in would be impossible. The ships' crews had taken a beating too, and Nicias enumerated the causes of their high losses. There was the dangerous task of obtaining water, forage and wood, which made them easy prey for the lurking Syracusan cavalry; slaves were deserting because of the diminishment of the Athenian position. So too were impressed foreign sailors. Seeing that the enemy now had a navy and that the city's resistance was strong and continuing, many of them had left for their home cities as soon as they were able. Other seamen, those who had joined willingly, had been lured into Athenian service by the prospect of high pay and low risk, thinking that they might make money easily. Now that the situation had worsened dramatically, they were either deserting over to the Syracusans or disappearing into the vastness of Sicily. Some foreign sailors had even taken to trading on their own account, and had persuaded their ship captains to take aboard slaves from Hyccara in their stead, and this had 'ruined the efficiency of our navy'.[91]

The period of peak efficiency, Nicias explained, though it is probable that few in the Assembly would not have known this already, was a short one, and the oarsmen who could get a ship moving and row in time with their fellows were few in number. Nicias complained that he was hampered in holding his position at Syracuse by the 'natural indiscipline of the Athenian seaman'. He could not recruit new crewmen, being able to draw on only those men whom they had brought with them on the expedition, as Athens' allies in Sicily, Naxos and Catana, were not up to the task of providing them. The enemy, in contrast, could find fresh rowers in many places. The Athenian expeditionary force possessed only one advantage that the enemy did not, and that was access to the markets of Italy from which to obtain supplies. Yet even this was precarious. Should Athens fail to send help, the Italians might switch sides and refuse to furnish any more provisions. 'Famine would compel us to evacuate, and Syracuse would finish the war without a blow.' Nicias acknowledged that he had sent tidings that were unpleasant to hear, but it was best that the Assembly know the truth of the situation in Sicily, and make their decisions according to the actual state of affairs.[92]

Athens' forces had once been a match for those of the enemy that they faced, but a coalition of hostile Sicilian powers had taken shape against them, and new troops from the Peloponnesus were on their way. The choice that Nicias presented was that Athens must either order a recall of the armament or act quickly to send out another fleet and army of the same size that had been despatched back in 415, along with a large amount of money. He also requested that the Assembly send a new general to replace him, as he was troubled by an ailment of the kidneys and thought himself unfit to remain in command.[93]

If Nicias had hoped that the dire report that he had written would have prompted the Assembly to rethink its strategy and bring the troops back home, he was to be disappointed. The Athenians would not give up on Sicily, and decided to despatch a new fleet and army to the island. They would also not allow Nicias to resign, making him remain in command, a serious mistake, considering that the general was both ill and obviously severely depressed. They voted that two officers present in Sicily right then, Menander and Euthydemus, should join him as his temporary colleagues until two other men, Demosthenes and Eurymedon, could make their way to Sicily. Eurymedon departed immediately with ten triremes, 120 talents of silver and instructions to reassure the army at Syracuse that reinforcements were on the way. Thucydides places Eurymedon's mission to the time of the winter solstice of 414.[94]

The bulk of the second expeditionary force was being organized by Demosthenes, with a departure set for the spring. While the Athenians busied themselves with summoning troops from her allies and rounding up ships, money and hoplites of her own, they mounted a naval expedition around the Peloponnesus with twenty triremes to intercept any Corinthian or Peloponnesian ships that might try to cross to Sicily. The Corinthians had themselves put together a force of hoplites to send in merchant ships to Sicily, and the Spartans were doing likewise elsewhere in the Peloponnesus. A Corinthian fleet of twenty-five was also readied with an eye toward doing battle with the Athenian squadron at Naupactus and to prevent it from interfering with the troop-carrying merchant ships bound for Sicily.[95]

Spartan Confidence

Spartan confidence had also increased. They decided upon another invasion of Attica, which was intended to tie down Athenian troops who might otherwise be sent to reinforce those at Syracuse. Alcibiades, who was still in Sparta, advised them to construct a fortification at Decelea, and that war should be conducted with energy. Sparta was especially encouraged by the strategic predicament in which Athens found herself. She was fighting a war on two fronts, in Greece and Sicily, and with her forces thus divided she would be less formidable. There was also a moral dimension to Sparta's renewed confidence. Reflecting on the disasters that they had suffered in the Archidamian War, they had concluded that there had been more wrong done by their side, namely the peacetime attack by the Thebans on Plataea and their own unwillingness to agree to the Athenian offer of arbitration, despite arbitration being called for by the treaty that brought about the Thirty Years' Peace Treaty of 446 BC. Thucydides writes that they came to believe that their setbacks in the early war years, such as the Pylos catastrophe, had been deserved. However, raids were still being launched out of Pylos and a fleet of thirty Athenian ships operating from Argos had descended on Epidaurus and Prasiae, and ravaged them. With regard to disputes emanating from the treaty of 421, of which there were many, the Athenians had shown themselves to be quite willing to reject Spartan offers of arbitration when it suited them as well. To the Spartan mind, this meant that the Athenians were guilty of the same kind of offence that they had committed, and had thereby become the guilty ones at present. This perception of moral superiority instilled enthusiasm for war in the Spartans. The winter of 414/3 was used to collect iron and tools for building the planned fort at Decelea, and troops were raised at home and around the Peloponnesus to sail in merchant ships to Sicily.[96]

When spring arrived, the Spartans made an invasion of Attica, together with their allies. This campaign was different, however, in that instead of just devastating the land around and then heading back home, the Spartans began to fortify Decelea, which lay about 14 miles from Athens. With Decelea, the Spartans would have a permanent base in Attica from which to conduct raids and deny the Athenians use of their lands outside the city. Around the same time, the hoplites left for Sicily in the merchant ships, with the 600-strong Spartan contingent consisting of a picked force of Helots and Neodamodeis under Eccritus, a Spartiate, which was accompanied on the voyage by 300 Boeotian hoplites. Corinth despatched 500 hoplites comprised of Corinthians and Arcadian mercenaries, under the command of the Corinthian Alexarchus, while Sicyon contributed 200 hoplites to the effort. Twenty-five Corinthian triremes and their crews were readied over the winter to keep the Athenian squadron of twenty ships at Naupactus occupied while the merchant ships carrying troops to Sicily had transited to the island in safety.[97]

While the Spartans were busying themselves at Decelea, the Athenians sailed a thirty-ship fleet around the Peloponnesus in the early spring. This fleet, under Charicles, put in at Argos to demand that the Argives provide hoplites for the fleet in accord with the terms of their alliances with Athens. Demosthenes had by now completed his preparations for the second fleet that had been organized over the winter, and sailed with sixty Athenian triremes and five Chian warships for Sicily, stopping first at Aegina to wait for the arrival of the Argive and allied soldiery and to join in raids upon the Laconian coast with Charicles.[98]

Gylippus had spent his time raising troops in other parts of Sicily, and he brought these to Syracuse. To the Syracusans themselves he insisted that they must crew as many triremes as possible, and be ready for a naval battle. The Athenian hope of taking the city by a landward investment had been dashed when he had cut off the construction of the wall any further toward Trogilus to the north of Syracuse, and any chance that the Athenians had of success rested with their fleet. He found in Hermocrates a staunch supporter, who told his fellow Syracusans that taking the fight to the Athenians at sea was the proper move. The Athenians had not been great naval fighters of old, he said, but had only become a major power on the waves in response to the Persian invasions. They had been landlubbers once, just as the Syracusans were now, and could be successfully fought. A daring enemy, he said, would paralyze the Athenians by the boldness of his attack, just as the Athenians were prone to do to their enemies. The Athenians would never expect the Syracusans to go on the attack, and would be terrified by them when they did. Any advantage that the Athenians had in their nautical skills would be overcome, and make up for the Syracusans' own lack of experience.[99]

Plemmyrium

Thus counselled, the Syracusans resolved to try their luck against the Athenians in a naval fight. With their crews placed aboard, Gylippus took out the entire army at night in an attack on the Plemmyrium forts, while at the same time thirty-five Syracusan triremes sailed to attack the Athenian ships lying in the Great Harbour. Forty-five other triremes were to sail out of the Lesser Harbour, with the intent that they would meet up with the thirty-five inside and together make an attack against Plemmyrium in conjunction with Gylippus' land forces. The Athenians boarded their own ships, sending twenty-five against the thirty-five Syracusan ships inside the Great Harbour, while the remainder moved to block the enemy ships coming round from the Lesser Harbour from entering via the Great Harbour's mouth.[100]

Gylippus' men succeeded in taking the biggest of the Plemmyrium forts in the early morning, and the Athenian troops in the other two abandoned their posts upon seeing how quickly the larger fort had succumbed. The naval battle inside the Great Harbour at first went in favour of the Syracusans, but then turned against them. At the harbour's entrance, access was hotly contested. The Syracusan ships managed to push their way through the Athenian blocking force, but then, rowing onward out of formation, became fouled with their fellows, and they were easy prey. The Athenians were also victorious in the fight deeper inside the Great Harbour, and all told, they sank eleven Syracusan triremes and killed the greater part of their crews, except for those of three triremes that they took captive. Athenian losses were very light, being just three triremes.[101]

Though the naval engagements had gone against them, the Syracusans succeeded in taking the Plemmyrium forts. One of the smaller forts was demolished, while the biggest and the other lesser fort were restored and garrisoned. This was of great significance, and Thucydides considered their capture to be 'the first and foremost cause of the ruin of the Athenian army'. The Athenians had used the forts to warehouse much of their supplies. Naval equipment sufficient for forty triremes, including masts, was captured, as well as three complete triremes that had been brought ashore. Apart from the immediate material and moral effect of the loss of these valuable stores, the fall of the forts at Plemmyrium meant that any new provisions being brought in would have to be run past a Syracusan gauntlet to reach the Athenians. There was a Syracusan blockading force positioned now at the entrance to the Great Harbour, and these ships would be doing their utmost to prevent any Athenian resupply efforts.[102]

After the battle, the Syracusans undertook naval missions further afield. One of their own, Agatharchus, took eleven ships on a raid in Italy against supply ships that were bound for the Athenians. Most of these ships were destroyed, and in Caulonian territory on the southern coast of the toe of Italy, they descended and burned shipbuilding timber that had been stockpiled by the Athenians. From there the Syracusans went to Locri, where they anchored. There was a merchant ship there bearing Thespian hoplites, and the Syracusans took these men aboard their own ships and set sail for home. An Athenian squadron of twenty ships had been stationed at Megara Hyblaea to watch for their return, and they spotted them, but all but one ship slipped by and back to Syracuse.[103]

In Syracuse's harbour itself there was some limited action. The Syracusans had driven piles deep into the sea in front of their docks to keep the Athenians from getting close to them. Using a merchant freighter, fitted with turrets and screens, the Athenians came up to the piles and tried to pull them up with ropes. Divers were also sent down to try to saw them apart. Some of the piles were especially perilous, as their tops did not rise above the surface of the water, but remained hidden below. The Athenians offered bounties to divers willing to cut them down, while the Syracusans continued to erect more. This period was one in which 'there was no end of contrivances to which they resorted against each other' as each side sought an advantage over the other.[104]

Why did Nicias delay so long in attempting to destroy the Syracusan fleet while he possessed clear naval superiority in the Great Harbour? One answer is that Nicias was expecting that the Syracusans would be surrendering relatively shortly, and so there would have been no compelling reason for him to rush to destroy ships that would then become useful to Athens. Nicias had been in contact with sympathizers inside the city, and these men fed him a steady diet of intelligence that seemed to promise a capitulation, thus encouraging Nicias to hold off.[105] But Nicias had also shown himself to be a lethargic general during his time in command, and a lack of drive may have been just as much the cause for his delay, with Plutarch writing that he was typically 'slow and timid in forming' his plans.[106]

The effect of the Spartan fortification at Decelea over the summer of 413 BC was profound. Unlike earlier invasions of Attica that had been more akin to major raids, the Spartans and their allies were now there to stay. From a secure base, the Spartans under King Agis were able to ravage the surrounding countryside as they liked. It had been bad enough when the Athenians had been told by Pericles to wait out the Peloponnesian intrusions at the beginning of the war, but those had come to an end relatively swiftly. With Decelea now in enemy hands, Attica was constantly under attack. Slaves deserted in large numbers. Thucydides says that over 20,000 departed, many of them skilled artisans, and they took their livestock with them too. The need to be always on guard in Attica overtaxed the cavalry, with many of their mounts pulling up lame after being ridden on the stony ground or in combat with the Peloponnesians.[107]

Money Troubles

The body blows suffered by Athens so far in the war, not least of which were the enormous expenses incurred as a result of having so many ships at sea and the ongoing operations at Syracuse, caused it to change the manner in which the city paid for war. In place of the customary tribute due from Athens' subjects, the Athenians now levied a 5 per cent tax on all imports and exports, seeing this as a more efficient means of raising funds. Athens' tribute system had clearly been found insufficient to produce the money needed after some eighteen years of warfare. Thucydides had earlier noted that even in the fourth year of the war, 428 BC, Athens was sustaining heavy financial costs in keeping large numbers of triremes at sea as well as undertaking simultaneous land operations. Matters had not improved since then, and Athens was exceeding the limits of her resources in sustaining operations in Greece and Sicily.[108] The money troubles that Athens was experiencing had also caused her to expand the number of tributary states sending money to her as well as greatly raise her assessments on the allies in 425. But the search for money was never-ending.

A desire to pinch pennies saw the Athenians dismiss at this time a group of 1,300 Thracians recruited to join the fight at Syracuse but who had arrived too late at Athens to make the voyage. These Thracians were used on their way back to their homeland to make a handful of landings where they might do some harm to the enemy. But the Thracians were savage in the extreme, and at Mycalessus in Boeotia they massacred the pitiful inhabitants, including the women and children. Even the animals were killed. Thucydides, himself inured to realities of war, described the barbaric slaughter as being 'unsurpassed in magnitude, and unapproached by any in suddenness and in horror'.[109]

Demosthenes, in the summer of 413, was himself on his way to Corcyra, and on the way in Acarnania met up with Eurymedon, who was heading back to Athens after having delivered money to the forces in Sicily. From Eurymedon he learned of the state of affairs at Syracuse and the fall of the Plemmyrium forts. The squadron commander at Naupactus, Conon, also arrived in Acarnania, and asked that they give him some ships to take back with him to Naupactus, as he was currently outnumbered in the Gulf of Corinth by the Corinthians, having just eighteen triremes to the enemy's twenty-five. Demosthenes and Eurymedon detached ten of their swiftest triremes to go back with Conon to Naupactus. Eurymedon then sailed for Corcyra, to command the Corcyrans to man fifteen triremes and to enlist hoplites, while Demosthenes recruited light troops in Acarnania. These troops, when ready, were put aboard ships and Demosthenes and Eurymedon sailed across to Italy, arriving first at the Iapygium promontory at the extreme southern tip of the heel of the Italian boot. They recruited 150 javelineers from among the Iapygians and sailed on to the allied city of Metapontum, which contributed 300 javelineers and two triremes. From there, the Athenian fleet moved on again to Thurii, where the anti-Athenian party had only recently been expelled. The Thurians were, in the new political climate that prevailed, willing to send 700 hoplites along with the expedition.[110]

The Battle of Erineus

In the Gulf of Corinth, battle was joined off Erineus in Achaea between the Athenian Naupactus squadron under Diphilus, now numbering thirty-three triremes, and the Corinthian fleet, which numbered just slightly fewer ships, under the command of Polyanthes. The Corinthians remembered well the virtuoso performance of the Athenian fleet at Chalcis and Naupactus in 429 BC, and knew that it was a losing proposition to try to match them in a battle of manoeuvre. They had prepared a surprise for the Athenians that would enable them to make up for their comparative lack of rowing skill. At the prows of their ships, Polyanthes had strengthened and widened the *epotides*, or catheads, so that when they crashed into the enemy triremes prow-to-prow, the outriggers of the swifter but more lightly built Athenian ships would be shorn away.[111] Though the numerical result of the battle favoured the Athenians in terms of ships lost, with the Athenians losing no ships to the Corinthians' three, the Corinthians did succeed in disabling seven Athenian triremes through the use of their tactical innovation. Thucydides writes that the Corinthians saw this outcome as a victory, and set up a trophy for it, while the Athenians, who had expected to win, saw their failure to gain a clear-cut triumph as a defeat.[112]

The two-fold innovation of strengthened catheads and prow-to-prow ramming was to be of enormous importance for the war at Syracuse. Athens had always maintained its edge at sea by having the finest oarsmen. The complicated manoeuvring that had been displayed at Chalcis and Naupactus in 429 by heavily outnumbered Athenian fleets was made possible by supremely skilled rowers. There was nothing fundamentally different about an Athenian seaman and one drawn from any other city. His training, however, was from the start of the war much more rigorous and intensive than that found anywhere else, and this allowed the Athenians to turn in the performance at Chalcis in 429, and to recover from an initial setback at Naupactus and snatch a victory from the jaws of defeat later that year. These Corinthian innovations would soon go a long way to diminish any lingering Athenian superiority.

Demosthenes and Eurymedon, with their land forces collected, held a review of the troops along the Sybaris River in southern Italy before they made the final voyage to Sicily. After this they sailed to Locri, and then stopped at Petra, which lay in Rhegian territory. In Syracuse, word of the approach of the new armament had come, and the Syracusans wanted to take the offensive one more time on land and sea before it arrived. In light of the experience they had gained in the naval battle in and around the Great Harbour during the attack on Plemmyrium, the Syracusans made alterations to their naval equipment. They also had learned of the Corinthian success at the Battle of Erineus, and set about changing the prows of their triremes to make better use of the tactics employed by Polyanthes there against the Athenians. The modifications included cutting down the prows to a smaller compass to make them more solid. The *epotides* were strengthened, and to these they also installed support beams that extended outward from both sides of their triremes. The Syracusan changes were acknowledgements that the Athenians had the edge in manoeuvring skill, but that the Corinthians had pointed the way to defeating them without the need to match them in rowing technique. The Athenians were used to employing the *diekplous* and *periplous* manoeuvres as the tactical occasion required. Space in which to adopt such tactics was critical to their effective employment. At Chalcis, Phormio had caught the Peloponnesian fleet in the middle of the Gulf of Corinth, where he had room in which manoeuvre. So much room did he have that he was able to encircle the entirety of the enemy fleet.

The situation that prevailed inside the Great Harbour, which was itself about 2 miles north to south and a mile and a quarter from the Anapus to the harbour mouth, was vastly different from the earlier battle in the Gulf. The Athenians had cornered themselves inside the harbour, and had relinquished one of the prime necessities of their preferred style of naval fighting, which was ample space in which to manoeuvre. In the constricted waters of the Great Harbour, lightly built ships would prove detrimental. The lightness of the Athenian prows should not be mistaken for a defect or an oversight. This was fully in keeping with their manoeuvre tactics. Athenian triremes had been built with the intention that they be aimed for ramming strikes against the weaker sides of an enemy trireme, or stern, after an *anastrophe*, not its stronger prow.[113] The Syracusan ships, with the reinforced prows, would have an advantage in the confined harbour. Their planned tactic was brutally simple, which was to aim straight for the prow of the Athenian trireme and ram it head-on. Head-on collisions were easy enough to accomplish, especially in the trireme-choked waters of the Great Harbour, and did not make much of a demand upon the crew or helmsman. When used against the lighter prows of the Athenian triremes, such straightforward, if unelegant, tactics seemed to augur success without the need to painstakingly develop the formidable rowing skills that the Athenians had spent decades mastering.[114]

Thucydides writes that the prow-to-prow ship collision had previously been judged to signify a 'lack of skill in a helmsman', but such a thing was an irrelevance in the environment in which both fleets would be operating. Successful manoeuvring tactics required that the ramming trireme be able to back water, or move backward, to disengage from its target, so that it could then seek out a new victim. In the Great Harbour, though, there was no room for the Athenians to do this, with the exception of the direction of the shore heading towards their camp, and there was scarcely any of that. All of the rest of the interior shoreline of the harbour area was in the hands of the Syracusans, who would be able to fall back in almost any direction if the fighting turned against them. The Athenians would have much preferred to fight a sea battle in open water, outside the harbour, but the narrow entrance was controlled by the Syracusans too, and there would be no egress for them, particularly with Plemmyrium occupied by the Syracusans.[115]

Their ships thus modified, the Syracusans attacked the Athenians by sea and land. Gylippus led his troops against the wall of the Athenian encampment that faced the city, while the Syracusan troops in Olympieum moved against the wall on the opposite side of the camp. Then the Syracusan and allied ships came up, eighty in number, and the Athenians scurried to man their own ships, putting to sea with seventy-five. At the outset, each side's ships advanced and then backed off, with just minor skirmishing taking place on the first day resulting in the sinking of two Athenian triremes. The following day, Nicias made his captains repair their ships, and moored merchant vessels in front of the stockade they had embedded in the water in front of their ships. This created an enclosure in which any Athenian trireme could find safety if the fight turned against it.[116]

On the third day, combat resumed an hour earlier than was the norm, with the Syracusans again making attacks by both land and sea. There was skirmishing between the naval forces, similar to what had taken place on the first day. Then a Corinthian by the name of Ariston, said to be the best helmsman in Syracusan service, had an idea. He convinced the Syracusan officials to set up a marketplace for the fleet's crews to go and get their food close to their ships, saving them the time of having to go deeper into the city to obtain their meals. This, he said, would let them eat and go back aboard their ships so that they could make another attack on the Athenians, who would not be expecting another assault so soon.[117]

The Athenians, seeing the Syracusans retreat, thought that this was because the enemy thought themselves defeated, and they disembarked from their own ships to take their own meals, assuming that the fighting for the day was finished. They were thus in no hurry to eat when they discovered that the Syracusans had climbed back aboard their triremes and put out to sea. The Athenians did the same, but fighting did not commence at once, with both sides watching and waiting for the other to move. The Athenians blinked first and went on the attack. In the ensuing clash, the heavier, reinforced prows of the Syracusan triremes smashed the weaker prows of the Athenian ships, ripping away their outriggers and disabling them. The Syracusans had also carried with them light troops serving as marines on their ships, and these javelineers took a fearful toll on the Athenians, but even more hurt was done by the Syracusans who sailed among the wounded Athenian triremes in small boats. These tiny craft would impudently sail up close to the enemy ships and hurl their javelins directly at the unprotected oarsmen inside.[118]

The fight was a hard one, but the tactics developed at Erineus worked even more successfully inside the Great Harbour, with the Syracusans sinking seven Athenian triremes and crippling many more.

The Athenians retreated within the safety of their improvised harbour works, with the pursuing Syracusans kept out by the presence of 'dolphins' hung above the passageway. These were heavy metal objects suspended from wooden beams hung from the merchant ships moored just outside the enclosure. When two Syracusan ships came close, the dolphins were dropped down on them, and these were substantial enough to penetrate their hulls and destroy them. The clear-cut victory engendered an enormous sense of confidence in the Syracusans in their naval edge over the Athenians, and they even began to believe that they might be successful on land too.[119]

It was only after the battle had been fought that the second expedition under Demosthenes and Eurymedon arrived. With them they brought seventy-three triremes, a total which included allied ships, along with close to 5,000 hoplites and a substantial number of light troops – javelineers, archers and slingers. On seeing the new fleet, the hearts of the Syracusans sank. Just when it looked like they were making progress, another expedition, this as large as the first that had come in 415, appeared offshore. This new force had been despatched even though Sparta had fortified Decelea, a move that was supposed to have tied down Athenian troops and resources in defending the Attic homeland. The Syracusans had just spied light at the end of the tunnel, and then Demosthenes and company turned up. The dejected Athenians, in contrast, took some heart at the coming of reinforcements from home. Demosthenes took stock of the situation and came to the conclusion that he must strike hard, at once. Nicias had blundered badly when he had decided to spend the winter of 415/4 at Catana, giving the Syracusans time to recover from the shock of his arrival in massive force. Such hesitation had also given the Spartans time to send Gylippus with a force of men to the rescue of a city that was on the verge of surrendering when he arrived. Demosthenes decided that he would attack straight away, and take the city. If he failed, he would not remain in Sicily and waste Athenian lives and resources but take the expeditionary force back home.[120]

This was sensible plan, and had such sense been displayed earlier in the campaign, the Athenians might have spared themselves much loss and heartbreak. Demosthenes attacked Syracusan lands around the Anapus River by land and sea, and the Syracusans refused to meet him on either, though they did harass his troops with javelineers and cavalry operating out of Olympieum. Demosthenes also assaulted the Syracusan counterwall with his siege machines. These were put to the torch by the Syracusan defenders, and his attacks elsewhere along the wall were turned back.[121] He abandoned this effort, and moved against Epipolae as he had first intended. This attack, made by night, succeeded at first, but the Athenians became overconfident as they surged over Epipolae, their lines becoming disordered as they advanced. A force of Boeotians made a stand and hurled them back. The Athenians found themselves in disarray, and as it was still nighttime it was difficult for them to gain an understanding of just what was going on. The moon cast some light, but this was not enough to see anything clearly, and it was impossible to tell if a figure was that of a friend or an enemy. In the confusion that prevailed, the Athenians heard the singing of the *paean* in a Dorian dialect, and became terrified. They assumed that the singers were their enemies, but in truth it was their allies, the Argives, Corcyrans and other Dorian peoples. They fought with friendly forces in the dark, and many fell to their deaths as they scurried down the narrow tracks from the Epipolae heights.[122]

Demosthenes and the other generals took stock of the situation in the wake of the failure of the attack on Epipolae. Demosthenes thought that the siege should be abandoned then and there, and that the entire armament should head home. The sea was still open to them, and their overall superiority in ships was far greater now that the second expedition had brought ships to supplement those of the first. There would be more to gain by making war in Attica against the Peloponnesians than in continuing to make war against Syracuse, which had proved to be very difficult to capture. There was no point in spending so much money on the siege of a city that promised little chance of success.[123]

Nicias agreed that the situation was poor, but did not want word that the generals had voted for a retreat to reach the Syracusans, since this would give warning to them of what the Athenians planned and give them the opportunity to hinder their departure. Apart from this, he said that he had information that the Syracusans were running out of money. The Syracusans were burning through their money more quickly now that they had outfitted such a powerful fleet; these ships required crews, and crewmen needed to be paid.[124] There was also, he said, a faction within Syracuse that was willing to betray the city, and they had been pleading with him not to give up on the siege. Thucydides saw Nicias' caution arising more from his inability to choose between giving up on the siege or staying put, and wishing to wait until he could 'see his way more clearly', said in his public address to the troops that he would not abandon the siege, believing that the Athenian Assembly would not approve of such a move unless it had voted him permission to do so. Nicias warned that the Assembly could not be trusted to make a decision based on the facts, but would listen instead to 'hostile critics' and 'be guided by the calumnies of the first clever speaker'. Nicias even showed his distrust of the soldiers under his command, saying that though most of the soldiers present were loudly complaining of the danger of their position, once they were safely back at Athens they would say the opposite, and accuse the generals of having been bribed to lift the siege and return home.[125]

Nicias said that he preferred to remain in Sicily and take his chances with continuing the siege than go back to Athens to die under a dishonourable charge. The Syracusans, he said, were in dire financial straits. They were spending so much money on mercenaries, manning fortified posts and maintaining a large navy that their money was about to run out. Nicias, having information from the friendly faction in the city, claimed that the Syracusans had so far spent 2,000 talents on the war and were deeply in debt. They were spending more money on mercenaries than they were on their own soldiers, and if they failed to pay just a small part of their force it would be their downfall. In terms of money, the Athenians were much better off, and should not give up on the siege.[126]

To this, Demosthenes demurred. If it were true, as Nicias said, that they could not leave Sicily without the permission of Athens, then they should at least go off to Thapsus or Catana. Operating out of either of those locations there would be ample territory to plunder, which would be harmful to the enemy, and the fleet would be fighting in the open sea, as opposed to being cooped up inside the harbour, where the Syracusans, with their stoutly prowed ships, had the advantage. In open water, the Athenians could find the space in which to employ their manoeuvre tactics, advancing and retreating as they wished, and going wherever they chose. With this, the other general, Eurymedon, agreed, but Nicias rejected this course of action, and the three generals were unable to agree to any plan, with some suspicion arising that Nicias was privy to additional information that he did not disclose to the others that made him believe that it was worth continuing with the siege.[127] The Athenian impasse at Syracuse, yet another example of Nicias' indecisiveness, kept them rooted in place while an escape was still at least theoretically possible.

While the Athenians dithered, Gylippus, who had gone off on a recruiting mission elsewhere in Sicily, returned with more troops, including some hoplites raised in the Peloponnesus. The Syracusans decided to attack again on land and sea. Many Athenians, living as they were in unsanitary and unhealthy conditions in their encampment, had fallen sick, and with the arrival of a new army at Syracuse, they began to rue their failure to clear out when they had the chance. Nicias too was not so opposed to leaving, though he insisted that no open voting be allowed for the retreat, and that the orders to sail out of the camp be issued in secret. When the men were aboard, and the fleet just about to set sail, there occurred a lunar eclipse. The Athenians saw this as a bad omen, and insisted that the generals should wait. Nicias himself responded very differently from Pericles when an eclipse had occurred right before his fleet was to depart in 430. Nicias, Thucydides writes, was 'somewhat overaddicted to divination and practices of that kind' and thereafter would not consider leaving until the waiting period of 'thrice nine days' as prescribed by the soothsayers had passed.[128] Plutarch notes that the eclipse need not have been interpreted as an ill omen at all, since the darkness that it provided would have acted to hide the Athenian escape preparations.[129] Nicias, of course did not see it that way. In the aftermath of the eclipse, Nicias would become 'more and more oblivious of his other duties and completely absorbed in sacrifice and divination'.[130] The Athenian commander was suffering from nervous exhaustion, not at all helped by his superstitious and anxiety-ridden nature.

The occurrence of the eclipse was enough to strand the Athenians in Sicily, and the element of surprise needed to effect a clean escape was lost forever. Syracusan confidence surged once they knew that the Athenians themselves did not think that they held the advantage on either land or sea, as evidenced by their desire to leave, and they wished to go back on the offensive. The Syracusans were reluctant to see them depart only to relocate to some other part of Sicily, where they would be better positioned to resist attack, and so they sought to engage then at sea as soon as they could. They boarded their triremes, and after a period of intensive training of several days' duration they sailed against the Athenians with seventy-six ships. The Athenians met them with eighty-six triremes and in the ensuing fight the Syracusans defeated the Athenian centre. Eurymedon, commanding the Athenian right wing nearer to the shore, tried to envelop the Syracusans in a *periplous* manoeuvre, but his movement was countered, his ships were sunk and he was slain. Following this, the remainder of the Athenian fleet was chased back to the shore.[131]

Gylippus, ever alert, and seeing that many of the Athenian ships had grounded themselves outside the protection of their encampment, attacked them to secure the area to make it possible for the Syrcusans to tow off the enemy ships. The Athenians and their Etruscan allies fought back desperately, and recovered most of their triremes, but not before eighteen ships were hauled away by the Syracusans and their crews killed. The Syracusans sent a fireship against the surviving Athenian ships, an old freighter filled with brush and pinewood that they set alight. The Athenians took hold of the drifting ship and stopped its progress, and extinguished the fire on it before it could do any damage.[132]

The Syracusans had won a clear victory over the Athenian fleet, and this had been done even though the enemy had only recently been substantially reinforced with many ships by Demosthenes. Up until then, they had been worried by the presence of so many more ships, but these extra warships had not fundamentally altered the balance of power at sea in the Athenians' favour. It might have been expected that Demosthenes' new triremes, together with those already at Syracuse, would have so outnumbered those of Syracuse that victory would have been assured, but this was not the case. Demosthenes had brought seventy-three ships with him in the second expedition, and these would have been added to the sixty-eight that remained to the Athenians after subtracting the seven destroyed by the Syracusans in the battle fought just before Demosthenes appeared, in which the Syracusans had employed their reinforced catheads and prow-to-prow ramming tactics for the first time. This would have given the Athenians a total of 141 triremes. Yet in this latest engagement, the Athenians put just eighty-six ships to sea. It should be remembered that apart from the seven ships lost in the earlier fight, Thucydides reports that many others had been disabled, and so it is likely that a number of these were either left unrepaired or judged not worth the effort of repairing. Also, on the basis of the report made by Nicias to Athens, the ships that the Athenians had on hand since the arrival of the first expedition in Sicilian waters in 415 had been subject to overuse, and their hulls had not been given sufficient time to dry out because of the need to be constantly on guard for an enemy attack. In addition, Nicias complained of a deterioration in the number and quality of the crews, for a variety of reasons, and so it may be presumed that the Athenians could not find enough oarsmen for all of the ships they had on hand. It stands to reason that many of the older ships would have been worn out and unsuitable for further service, and that the bulk of the ships fighting in the most recent battle would have been newer vessels brought from Athens in 413, and that given the lack of trained rowers, the Athenians would have preferred to put full crews into a more limited number of triremes.

This more streamlined and theoretically capable fleet still suffered defeat in battle against a smaller Syracusan fleet. This had less to do with Athenian deficiencies than the effective tactics that the Syracusans had adopted from the Corinthians. It might seem to have been an elementary innovation to strengthen a prow to make it more durable in a head-on collision, but it took the enemies of Athens until the Battle of Erineus in 413 to put it into practice. In the tight confines of the Great Harbour, such tactics worked even better than they had in the Gulf of Corinth.

The Athenians were disheartened by their defeat, and finally realized that they had bitten off more than they could chew by attacking Syracuse. The city was big, populous and wealthy, and far beyond their means to defeat. Had the Athenians recalled the offer of Syracuse to lead the defence of Greece against the Persians, they would have remembered the great strength that had been offered by the city. Until then, Athens had bullied and beaten much smaller and less formidable states, and compelled them to join her alliance. Syracuse could not be overcome, and could not be made to become an ally. To make matters worse, the Athenians, self-styled lords of the sea, had been defeated in a naval engagement. The Athenians found themselves in a predicament similar to that of the doomed German Sixth Army trapped at Stalingrad in the winter of 1942–3. They lacked the power to overcome their enemy, and at the same time lacked the ability to flee from the enemy that surrounded them.

Such was the extent of their success and manifest edge that the Syracusans broadened the scope of what they hoped to achieve against the Athenians. Securing the enemy's departure, which would have been more than welcome not too long ago, was no longer enough. Now the Syracusans wished to hold the Athenians in place and crush them completely. This would garner them renown in Greece, and in so doing, the Greeks would be freed either from Athens' control or the threat of her attack. Syracuse would thereby be seen as the restorer of the freedom of the Greeks. Their ships began to patrol unhindered along the harbour, and they decided to shut its mouth, to prevent the Athenians from escaping.[133] This grand enlargement of Syracuse's strategic aims was startling and unprecedented. The defeated Persians, for example, had been permitted to depart for home after the battles of Salamis and Plataea, but such was the confidence that the Syracusans felt after their long resistance of Athenian arms that their ambition grew to encompass a much grander design of routing the Athenians.[134]

The Syracusans began work on blocking the harbour entrance, which was almost a mile in width, to the Athenians with boats, merchant freighters and triremes anchored bow to stern. The Athenians held a war council to consider their response. Their supply situation was dire. They had only recently sent most of their provisions on to Catana, thinking that they would soon be leaving too, so there would be no new supplies unless they could achieve dominance at sea. The plan they devised called for a withdrawal from their upper lines, and defending a much smaller space around their ships. They would then put all of the men they could aboard their triremes, even if some of these were not in a seaworthy condition, and fight at sea. Should they earn the victory, they would then proceed to Catana. If the battle went against them, they would burn their ships and retreat overland to the closest friendly city they could find.[135]

The plan, once it was decided on, was carried out immediately, with the Athenians evacuating their upper lines and climbing aboard their ships. Everyone who was old enough to be of use was made to take his place on a trireme, and by this insistence the Athenians were able to find crews sufficient for 110 triremes. As marines, they put on deck archers and javelineers.[136] Despite the great size of the fleet, the despair of the Athenians was palpable. Nicias, seeing that they were downcast by their most recent loss, spoke to them about the impending engagement. All that would be useful in a closely packed battle, he told them, had been taken into consideration. There would be archers and javelineers aboard, as well as additional soldiers whom they would not ordinarily have embarked 'in an action in the open sea, where our science would be crippled by weight of the vessels'. The fight in the harbour would be more akin to a fight on land, and so marines would be useful. The Athenian ships had also been modified to make them survivable in collisions with the reinforced prows of the Syracusan ships. 'Against the thickness of their cheeks, which did us the greatest mischief,' he said, 'we have provided grappling irons, which will prevent an assailant backing water after charging, if the marines on deck here do their duty.'[137]

There could be no thought of holding back in the coming fight, and they could not allow themselves to be driven ashore. Once they had come alongside an enemy ship, they could not let it go until its marines had been cleared from its deck.[138] He warned the Athenians that there was no alternative to victory. Should they lose, there were no other ships left behind in Athens to meet their enemies when they sailed against her. There were no more 'hoplites in their flower' in the homeland to stand against them. Their own present, personal survival as well as that of Athens were at stake, and 'if any man has any advantage in skill and courage, now is the time for him to show it, and thus serve himself and save all'.[139] With that, Nicias ordered his men to board their ships on what would be the most fateful day of the war in Sicily.

On the other side of the Great Harbour, Gylippus and the Syracusans were watching. There could be no mistaking the Athenians' intentions, and they knew about the grappling irons that they had put aboard their ships. To counter these, the Syracusans had erected stretched hides over the prows of their own ships so that the irons, when cast, would bounce off and not find any purchase.[140]

Gylippus and the other generals spoke to their men, just as Nicias had done with his. The Athenians, he told them, already masters of the greatest of empires, had come to Sicily seeking to conquer it, and then Greece. But at Syracuse they had encountered men able to resist them at sea. Though their navy had made them masters everywhere else, at Syracuse the Athenians had been defeated. This setback would likely be all the worse for them because it came in a sphere, naval warfare, in which they considered themselves to be the best.[141] Of the Syracusans and their allies it was the opposite. Their achievement in overcoming the finest mariners had made them much more confident in their abilities. The alterations that the Athenians had made to their ships were known, and Gylippus promised that counters had already been devised. With regard to their newly adopted tactics, they would never be able to use them effectively. Their javelineers and archers would not be able to keep still enough to shoot from the decks of their triremes without unbalancing them. Confusion would reign amongst the enemy as they tried to employ unfamiliar tactics. True, they had many more ships, but this would be of no use to them. The Great Harbour was so confined that a larger quantity of ships would just make their movements more ponderous and their ships more vulnerable to Syracusan attack. Gylippus also claimed that their intelligence had told them that it was desperation that had led the Athenians to attempt this breakout, their sufferings being so extensive that they would either sail out by way of the harbour mouth or, if defeated, try to escape by land, since either alternative was better than staying put.[142]

'Let us engage in anger,' he said, 'convinced that nothing is more legitimate between adversaries than to claim to satisfy the whole wrath of one's soul in punishing the aggressor, and nothing more sweet ...

than the vengeance upon an enemy which it will now be ours to take.' The Athenians had come to Sicily to enslave the Syracusans; they should not be allowed to depart without a fight. If the Athenians were beaten right then and now, Sicily would be given back her freedom, and Syracuse win an extraordinary victory.[143]

The Athenians could be seen manning their ships, and the Syracusans did likewise. It was at this moment that Nicias became extremely anxious, recognizing as he did the apocalyptic nature of the battle about to be fought. He called again on the captains to do their duty and reminded them of the liberty they enjoyed. Nicias himself remained ashore with the army, to lend encouragement to the seamen, while Demosthenes, Menander and Euthydemus took out the fleet. Their aim was to break through the harbour entrance that was guarded by the Syracusans. The Syracusan and allied fleet of seventy-six ships was deployed partly inside the harbour, with others stationed at the outlet left open in the harbour mouth. Their plan was to keep the Athenians inside the harbour, and attack them from all sides as they sought to break out. Their land troops had been brought down to the shore in support at points where it was anticipated that ships might beach themselves. In command of the Syracusan fleet were Sicanus and Agatharchus, each leading a wing, while in the centre were placed the Corinthian ships, under Pythen, the Corinthian officer who had originally accompanied Gylippus to Syracuse.[144]

The assault of the Athenians on the barrier at the entrance smashed through the ships on guard there, and they tried to cut the fastenings binding the ships together. The Athenian plan was transparent, it could be nothing else other than a breakout attempt, and the Syracusans chose this moment to swoop down upon the Athenians fleet from all sides. The battle would be fought all across the Great Harbour, and it was the bitterest one yet, since the stakes were so high. Whether rower, helmsman or marine, 'every man strove to prove himself the first in his particular department', Thucydides writes.[145]

The restricted space inside the harbour worked to Syracusan advantage, as expected. There were almost 200 triremes doing battle, with Thucydides reckoning that, in this instance, they were the largest fleets ever to fight in such a small space, and ramming attacks were consequently few in number. There was simply no room to manoeuvre, or back water once a ship had rammed. There was no space in which to attempt a *diekplous* breakthrough, and the collisions that did occur were more typically caused by ships running afoul of each other. The fight inside the Great Harbour was a land battle fought at sea, and the very antithesis of the sophisticated tactics that the Athenian navy had worked so long and hard to develop. The ship-to-ship fights were boarding actions, with mastery of a vessel resolved by marines. Some ships attacked and then were attacked by other ships coming against them while they were busy with another opponent, and the impression that Thucydides gives of the battle is of a free-for-all, with tactical direction non-existent because the noise from the clashing ships was so great as to make hearing orders impossible.[146]

The desperation of the men crammed inside the triremes was palpable. The Athenians especially were in a do-or-die moment, with a return homeward possible if they could force the passage through the harbour mouth, while the Syracusans hungered to utterly annihilate the Athenians. When a trireme captain tried to back away from the fight, the fleet admirals would call to each by name and order them back into the melee.[147] On the shore, the spectators to the carnage, whether Athenian or Syracusan, watched anxiously as the battle progressed, the hearts of the Athenians especially rising and sinking as it seemed the fighting went in their favour or against it.[148]

Then, after a long and pitiless battle, the Athenian triremes turned and fled for shore, pursued by the exultant Syracusans. The Athenian seamen bolted from their ships and made for the safety of their camp, while the land troops came down to the beach to the aid of the stricken triremes, and others took up positions guarding the camp wall. Panic surged through the Athenian ranks as the realization settled in that they were stranded in Sicily, with no immediate way home. Thucydides likened the loss to the catastrophe that they had once inflicted at Pylos, which had left the Spartans on Sphacteria in 425 stranded when the Peloponnesian fleet had been defeated.[149]

The losses to both sides had been terrible, with the Athenians having some sixty seaworthy triremes left to them as opposed to fewer than fifty for the Syracusans. Athenian morale had been so shattered by defeat in the battle that when Demosthenes and Nicias decided that they should make another attempt at forcing the harbour passage the next morning, as they retained a slight advantage in numbers, nothing that they could say or do would persuade the seamen to go back aboard their ships.[150]

The only option left open to the Athenians was to escape by land. Two days after the final battle in the Great Harbour, what was left of their once mighty host departed from its camp, in desperation leaving behind the sick and wounded who begged them not to abandon them to the Syracusans. Thucydides likened the enormous rabble that set out, some 40,000-strong, to the escape of a 'starved-out city'.[151] The pitiful remnant of the expeditionary forces so proudly despatched from Athens would fare no better on land than they had at sea. The Syracusans mercilessly harassed the retreating Athenians, pelting them with missiles from a distance and refusing to do battle hand-to-hand. Demosthenes' rearmost division was the first to surrender after suffering from a hail of darts throughout an entire day. Nicias, in the lead with his own division, plunged on, deprived of food and hope. The Syracusans kept up a rain of missiles on them just as they had done to Desmosthenes' men. Trapped along the banks of the Assinarus River, with the Syracusans both ahead of them and behind, Nicias surrendered his command.

Of the survivors, these would be housed in wretched conditions inside quarries, and would be sold as slaves, not including the Athenians, Sicilians and Italians, a fate to which the Athenians had consigned so many other conquered peoples. Nicias and Demosthenes, however, were executed, much to the dismay of Gylippus, who hoped to take the enemy generals home with him to Sparta. It was said by Thucydides that some of the Syracusans feared that if Nicias were to be tortured, he might reveal much about his contacts with them inside the city, and in so doing spoil what was now a great victory, while the Corinthians worried that he, a rich man, might bribe his way to freedom, and be a menace to them in the future, and so both parties had cause to see him dead. '[O]f all the Hellenes in my time,' Thucydides wrote, Nicias 'least deserved such a fate, seeing that the whole course of his life had been regulated with strict attention to virtue.'[152]

Of the failure of the disaster-fraught expedition to Sicily, Thucydides gave his assessment, writing that it 'was the greatest Hellenic achievement of any in this war, or in my opinion, in Hellenic history: at once most glorious to the victors, and most calamitous to the conquered. They were beaten at all points and altogether; all that they suffered was great; they were destroyed as the saying is, with a total destruction, their fleet, their army – everything was destroyed, and few out of many returned home.'[153]

What if?

We have seen the many defects, some avoidable, some not, in Athenian operations at Syracuse, as so carefully laid out by Thucydides.

The Sicilian Expedition 171

An insufficiently large expeditionary force was unable to overwhelm the defenses of Syracuse in a timely manner, and this allowed the siege of the city to drag on. Athenian triremes deteriorated by being kept in the water for too long, and Athenian crews declined in quality as oarsmen deserted and replacements could not be found for them. All the while, Gylippus of Sparta gallantly rallied the city's defense, and the Syracusan navy began its rapid ascent as it acquired tactical acumen, confidence and incorporated technical improvements into its ships. The Athenian expedition to Sicily would appear to have been doomed from the start.

That has been the assessment, for the most part, of history, and 'Sicilian Expedition' has become something of a byword for hubristic disaster. Was there any chance of success for the expedition? If so, what would success have looked like? What benefits, if any, might it have brought?

The expedition might have succeeded if the Athenians had followed Lamachus' proposal and made an immediate attack on Syracuse. They had with them sixty triremes in excellent condition and were able to sail unchecked straight into the Great Harbour and then depart without interference. A rapid strike at Syracuse, it has to be allowed, had at the very least some chance of success, which in this case would have meant capturing the city. From later events of the two-year siege it is almost certainly true that the Athenians never had a better opportunity to deliver a knockout blow than they did in the earliest days of the campaign.[154]

Had they succeeded in seizing Syracuse, Athens would have altered the balance of power in Sicily at a stroke. Yet what then? They would still have found themselves at war with the Peloponnesians in Greece, and it is unclear just how big a benefit Syracuse would have been to Athens within the larger strategic context of the war there.

Further, it is not altogether certain that the Athenians, who had undertaken such a risky venture, would not have continued on with ever more reckless projects. Conquests in Etruria and Carthage had been bruited about in the heady years of Athenian ascendancy, and Pericles had openly worried about and warned against such ill-advised adventurism. Carthage held a strong position in the Sicilian west. Isn't it reasonable to assume that an Athenian presence in Syracuse would have sparked conflict with the Carthaginians? Isn't it also reasonable to assume that a direct attack on Carthage would have been considered, and maybe launched, had Syracuse fallen quickly and easily? Perhaps Athens would have avoided the disaster that befell it in Sicily only to meet with catastrophe some time later in Africa. Whether the expedition against Syracuse succeeded or failed, it was a poorly-conceived decision to go there at all, and it diverted strength from the main theatre of the war, Greece itself. This was Athens' great blunder. The risks were great, while the benefits were vastly uncertain, and most likely minimal.

PART FIVE

THE IONIAN WAR

Athenian Distress and Recovery

Such was the scale of the catastrophe in Sicily that the Athenians, when news of it arrived in Piraeus, would not believe it. They could not give credence to any tale which claimed that the entire expeditionary force had been wiped out. Once they could no longer deny the extent of the defeat, the people turned against those who had spoken in favour of it, not acknowledging that they themselves had voted for sending the expedition too. Athens' strategic outlook in the war had not been good, with enemies massing everywhere and Attica harried from fortified Decelea. When word came of the calamity in Sicily, they began to experience dread of unprecedented proportions. To lose so many thousands of hoplites was terrible enough, but the sinking or capture of the navy's triremes could potentially be fatal. There were few ships left in their harbours, money was scant in the treasury and crews were few – most of the men who might have pulled an oar on behalf of Athens were now dead in Sicily. The Athenians feared that the enemy fleet in Sicily would shortly make a descent on Piraeus, which was practically undefended, while on land they would be subject to attacks by land and sea while their allies revolted. Athens had been weakened drastically by the events at Syracuse, and the empire was ripe for rebellion.[1]

Yet the Athenians, in the midst of this crisis, pulled themselves together and began to think more rationally than they had when deciding to send out the expedition. Thucydides noted that 'as is the way of a democracy, in the panic of the moment they were ready to be as prudent as possible'. Using what resources were left to them, they voted money to buy timber for new ships, and to fit out a new fleet as well as they could. They would also move to lock down their allies, especially Euboea, which was of enormous economic importance to Athens.[2]

The winter of 413/2 BC also saw the empire begin to grumble loudly against its tottering overlord, and with such a dramatic defeat inflicted on Athens' navy, her enemies saw the opportunity to challenge them for control of the sea. Prior to Sicily, the Athenians had been invincible. Now they looked vulnerable. Even hitherto neutral states considered taking up arms against Athens, while the Spartans, expecting the arrival of naval help from her victorious allies in Sicily, saw the chance to bring the war to a conclusion and become the masters of Greece.[3] Their Peloponnesian League allies were ordered to produce 100 triremes for the war effort. The Spartans were to build twenty-five of these themselves, while the Boeotians were to construct another twenty-five, the Phocians and Locrians were to make fifteen ships, the Corinthians fifteen, the Arcadians, Pellenians and Sicyonians ten, and ten further ships were to be built by the Megarians, Troezenians, Epidaurians and Hermionians.[4]

The Athenians were busy with their own preparations, and new ships began to take shape in their yards. Cape Sunium was fortified to protect the transit route of grain ships coming round, and economizing measures were taken to reduce state expenditures. There was still the ominpresent fear of a revolt among the allies, and in Euboea there were stirrings of rebellion. Some Euboeans sent envoys to King Agis at Decelea to plead for aid in a revolt, and he agreed to help them, but in the meanwhile, embassies came from other places seeking his intervention. Envoys from Lesbos came to him, hoping that he would help them to revolt too, and he put off intervening in Euboea. While this was happening, the Chians and Erythraeans made an appeal at Sparta itself for aid for their own revolt against Athens. With them they brought an ambassador from Tissaphernes, Persian satrap of Lydia, who governed western Asia Minor from his capital at Sardis on behalf of the Great King Darius II. Tissaphernes promised that if the Peloponnesians would cross over to Asia Minor, he would pay their army's expenses. The Great King, Thucydides says, had commanded him to deliver the tribute due from his satrapy, it being in arrears because Athens was preventing its collection from the Greek cities there. These cities and the money they had once contributed to Persian coffers had been lost as a result of the defeat of Persian invasions, and if the Athenians' control could be weakened, Tissaphernes reasoned, he could collect the tribute and send it along to his master. A Spartan alliance with Persia might also have the benefit of putting down the rebellion of Amorges in Caria.[5] This rebellion may have been of great significance in the Persians coming forward to aid Sparta more strongly after so many years of remaining on the sidelines. Athens had uncautiously given some type of aid to Amorges, whose father Pissuthnes, the former satrap of Lydia, had begun a rebellion against the Great King Darius II around 420. It is not clear what the Athenians did, but they did do something that seriously upset Persia. The Athenian orator Andocides, in his speech *On the Peace with the Spartans*, which was delivered around 392 in the context of another war, mentioned that it had been Athenian assistance to Amorges, who had carried on with the rebellion from his base at Iasus in Caria after Tissaphernes had defeated his father Pissuthnes in 415, that had so angered the Great King that he decided to side with the Spartans in the earlier (i.e., Peloponnesian) war and bring about the destruction of the Athenian Empire.[6]

Still another proposal for anti-Athenian action came to Sparta from Pharnabazus, the Persian satrap of the Hellespont. He too wished to see the cities in his satrapy revolt from Athens so that he could procure the tribute due from them, as well as secure an alliance with Sparta on behalf of the Great King. The Spartans, spoiled for choice as to which proposal to support, decided on the Chian option. Alcibiades, still in exile, had argued in favour of this move. But before the Spartans made a definitive move, they sent an envoy named Phrynis to Chios to make certain that the Chians had just as many triremes as they claimed, and that their city was as wealthy as they said it was. When Phrynis returned and confirmed both things, the Spartans entered into an alliance with Chios and Erythrae, pledging to send forty triremes under Melanchridas to Chios to join the sixty or more that were already at the island. The sizeable Chian fleet was likely the deciding factor in choosing the Chian option, as such a large force of triremes could form the core of the great navy that the Spartans wished to create if the revolt succeeded.[7] The Spartans had planned to send ten of their own ships as part of the forty, but an earthquake struck, and superstitious as ever, they replaced Melanchridas as admiral with Chalcideus, and instead of the planned ten ships sent just five from Laconia.[8]

With 412 opening, the Chians pressed for the departure of the League fleet, fearful that the Athenians might learn of the planned uprising. The Spartans sent a delegation to Corinth, where the allied ships had gathered, to drag them across the Isthmus to the other side, with all to set sail for Chios once this was accomplished. The League plan, agreed to in a council at Corinth, was to intervene first at Chios, then go to the aid of the rebels in Lesbos, and then sail for the Hellespont. To make the sailing of the fleet less observable by the Athenians, they would first send across the Isthmus just half of their ships, twenty-one of the total of thirty-nine, with the rest to be hauled over the Isthmus later. Operational security had been disregarded by the Peloponnesians by this time, as 'no care had been taken to keep this voyage a secret through contempt for the impotence of the Athenians, who had as yet no fleet of any account upon the sea'.[9]

The Peloponnesians were courting trouble by their delay and laxity. It was perhaps inevitable that word of the mission to Chios would leak out and find its way to Athens; it was a hard thing to keep the fitting out of a fleet hidden, but the manner in which the Athenians learned of the voyage was certainly avoidable. The Corinthians would not go on the expedition until after they had completed the celebration of the Isthmian Festival which was taking place at the time. This held up everyone else involved in the expeditionary force, and meanwhile, the Athenians grew suspicious that a revolt was brewing on Chios. They sent a general, Aristocrates, to Chios, where he accused them of planning to rebel, an accusation that they denied. Most of the Chians had no knowledge of the plot, and when Aristocrates demanded that they prove their good faith as allies by sending ships back with him, they delivered seven triremes, with crews. Those Chians aware of the simmering plot said nothing, as they were unwilling to show their hand until they were sure that the Peloponnesians were on their way, something that seemed ever more doubtful the longer the delay.[10]

The Isthmian Festival took place, and the Athenians, who had been invited to participate under truce in this panhellenic celebration, saw while there that some kind of operation had been planned for Chios. Once they had returned home to Athens, they kept a watch on Cenchrae so that the enemy could not sail out without being spotted. When the Peloponnesian fleet of twenty-one ships did finally sail, under the command of Alcamenes, the Athenians moved against them with a fleet equal in size. The Peloponnesians turned back toward shore, unwilling to engage the Athenian fleet in open waters. The Athenians turned around too, as they did not fully trust the Chian vessels in their fleet. They next manned thirty-seven ships and went back on the attack, chasing the Peloponnesian fleet into the abandoned Corinthian port of Spiraeum. The Athenians landed some troops ashore, and in a combined attack by land and sea, the Athenians crippled most of the Peloponnesian ships and killed Alcamenes while losing just a handful of their own men. The Athenians left a number of their triremes behind to blockade the surviving Peloponnesian warships, anchored the remainder at an island not far off, where they built a camp, and summoned additional support from Athens. A day later, some Corinthians had joined the Peloponnesians and were trying to help the trapped ships. Keeping up a constant guard over their ships proved very difficult, and at last they hauled them onto the beach and kept a watch over them with their land forces, where they would wait for an opening to escape.[11]

The Spartans, hearing of the defeat of the fleet at Spiraeum, were disheartened by the news, and scrapped their plans to send out their own ships to join the allies. Alcibiades stepped forward to plead with Endius and the other ephors that the expedition should still be made. It would arrive at Chios before news of the defeat at Spiraeum did, he said, and he could convince the Ionian cities to revolt by telling them of Sparta's zeal and the weakness of Athens. He further told Endius that he would win glory by securing an alliance with Persia instead of King Agis. The five Spartan ships therefore set sail under Chalcideus, with Alcibiades aboard.[12]

Along the way, Chalcideus and Alcibiades seized every ship they came across at sea to prevent word of their voyage escaping, and then deposited their captives at Corycus on the mainland of Asia Minor. There were Chian accomplices waiting for them, and on their advice, the Spartans sailed on to Chios without delay. At Chios, their arrival was a complete surprise to the inhabitants, as Alcibiades had predicted. Alcibiades assured them that other ships were coming behind him, and leaving out any word about the fleet trapped at Spiraeum, he convinced the Chians to revolt, and they were followed quickly afterward by the Erythraeans. Three of the Spartan ships sailed on to Clazomenae, which also rose in revolt.[13] The Athenians, hearing of the uprising on Chios, were alarmed, sensing that other allies might follow suit. They feared that the empire could crumble altogether if the defection of these states was not halted right away. Money again became an issue. Despite their dire financial straits after the collapse of the position in Sicily, the Athenians had steadfastly refused to touch the reserve fund of 1,000 talents that had been put in place in 431. With the crisis at Chios, and trouble brewing elsewhere in the Aegean, they voted to use the money to pay for crewing a large number of triremes. A squadron of eight ships withdrawn from the blockading force at Spiraeum was sent to Chios under Strombichides, to be followed shortly afterward by twelve more under Thrasycles. The seven Chian warships were also called back from the blockade at Spiraeum, and the slaves on these ships were freed, while the native Chians themselves were arrested. The Athenians next manned ten other ships and sent them to Spiraeum to maintain the guard over the Peloponnesian fleet ashore. To supplement these vessels, they voted to man thirty more ships.[14]

Chalcideus and Alcibiades sailed to Miletus with their fleet to stir up a revolt there before other ships from the Peloponnesus could show up. Alcibiades wanted to gain the honour of bringing over so many Ionian Greek cities by himself, together with the Chians, and Chalcideus the fleet admiral, and thus for Endius, as he had pledged. The Spartans arrived at Miletus and brought about a revolt. Not long after, the two Athenian squadrons under Strombichides and Thrasycles, with nineteen ships, came up to the city to find it shut against them, and they took their small fleet to anchor off the island of Lade.[15]

With Miletus in rebellion, the Spartans and Tisspahernes entered into a very one-sided treaty in which the Spartans and their allies and the Persians would carry on the war against Athens. By the terms of the agreement, the Spartans recognized the Great King's claims to the cities that had been lost in the aftermath of the failure of the Persian invasions decades before.[16] Back at Spiraeum, the Peloponnesians had waited long enough, made a sudden sortie against the blockading squadron and defeated it, capturing four of the Athenian triremes. This fleet returned to Cenchrae, and with the Spartan Astyochus taking up the command as navarch of the Peloponnesian fleet, made ready to set sail for Chios and Ionia. The anti-Athenian revolt was spreading, with uprisings occurring at Methymna and Mytilene on Lesbos. Astyochus left Cenchrae with four triremes and sailed to Chios. Three days later, he sailed again, with his four ships and one Chian vessel, to Lesbos, where an Athenian fleet of twenty-five ships had shortly before appeared. Seeing that the Athenians were back in control of the situation on Lesbos, he returned to Chios, where he was joined by six more Peloponnesian ships.[17]

At the island of Lade there was still the twenty-strong Athenian squadron that had been keeping up the blockade over Miletus. These ships made a descent on Panormus in Milesian territory. Chalcideus was slain when he moved against them with some troops. In a tremendous achievement for a city that had been without ships or crews just a year before, a fleet of forty-eight ships, including transports, sailed under the command of Phrynicus, Onomacles and Scironides, carrying with it a force of 3,500 troops culled from Athens, Argos and the allies to Samos, and thence to Miletus, where they made camp.[18] The Milesians came out to fight with 800 hoplites, the Peloponnesians troops who had come with Chalcideus, Persian cavalry under Tissaphernes and some of the satrap's mercenaries. Though the Argives on their wing were routed, the Athenians had the better of the fighting overall and the Milesians hurried back into their city for safety, while the Athenians celebrated their triumph by grounding their arms beneath Miletus' walls.[19]

As the sun was setting, news came to the Athenians that fifty-five Peloponnesian and Sicilian ships were on their way and would be showing up shortly. In this fleet were twenty-two ships from Sicily, twenty from Syracuse and two from Selinus, despatched at the insistence of Hermocrates to help deliver a killing blow to Athens. These ships first stopped at the island of Leros, before moving on to the Iasic Gulf to gather more intelligence about what was happening at Miletus. Alcibiades rode up on horseback and told them what had transpired in the battle outside Miletus, and urged them to move quickly to relieve Miletus if they did not want to see both Ionia and Tisspahernes lost to them. On the next morning, they agreed, they would make their attempt to lift the siege.[20]

On the other side, Phrynicus, one of the Athenian commanders, received news of the arrival of the enemy fleet at Leros, and when the other commanders with him wanted to fight a battle at sea against it, he refused. Not only would he himself not stay to fight; he would not allow anyone else to fight either. To Phrynicus' mind, the risk of the battle outweighed the reward, and there would be no disgrace to not fight when a defeat might result in the loss of Athens' precious few remaining ships and leave it defenceless in the face of a naval attack. The fate of the Sicilian Expedition and the parlous state in which Athens now found itself made going into battle willingly at sea when not forced to do so an unjustified risk to themselves and the state. They collected their troops and their supplies, and departed for Samos. Thucydides approved of this decision, saying that Phrynicus on this occasion and at all other times did 'show himself to be a man of sense'.[21]

Thucydides acknowledged that the Athenian victory had been left 'incomplete' and that the Argives, aghast at their losses, left for home once they had reached Samos. With the Athenians gone, the Peloponnesians sailed to Teichioussa, where they had stowed their tackle in preparation for the battle, it being a common practice for war galleys to strip themselves of non-essential weight when battle was imminent. While there, Tissaphernes met up with them and requested that they sail against Iasus, which was held by Amorges. The Iasians were taken by surprise, never thinking that ships appearing on the horizon might be anything other than Athenian vessels. Iasus, a wealthy city, was sacked, Amorges was captured, and the mercenaries serving with Amorges, most of whom were of Peloponnesian origin, were taken into Peloponnesian service. The captives were given to the satrap at the price of one Daric *stater* (a Persian gold coin of recognized high purity) per person.²²

In the winter of 412/1, Tissaphernes brought a month's pay to the crews of the Peloponnesian ships on the agreed rate of one drachma per day. However, in the future, he said he would be reducing the pay rate to just three obols a day, equal to half a drachma, until the Great King should approve the payment of a full drachma. This caused the Syracusan general Hermocrates to complain, and the disagreement was resolved only when Tissaphernes agreed to give five ships' worth of pay in excess of the three obols that were to be paid to each crewman. The satrap would thus pay thirty talents for fifty-five triremes, and for any above that number he would pay at the same rate.²³

The Athenian fleet based at Samos was reinforced over the winter of 412/1 by thirty-five additional ships under the command of Charminus, Strombichides and Euctemon. Thirty ships were sent against Chios with some hoplites, while seventy-four ships were sent to Miletus. The Spartan navarch Astyochus took twenty ships – ten Peloponnesian and ten Chian – and made an attack on Pteleum, which failed. He then moved on to Clazomenae, which he also attacked. Though the city lacked a wall, this attack as well failed, and a powerful gale drove the navarch's ship to Phocaea and Cyme, with others of his fleet being blown to the islands of Marathoussa, Pele and Drymoussa, near to Clazomenae. These plundered the territory of the Clazomenians for eight days while waiting for favourable winds to arise. When they did, the ships sailed away to rejoin Astyochus at Phocaea and Cyme.²⁴

While at Phocaea and Cyme, some men of Lesbos came and expressed their desire to revolt once more against Athens. Astyochus was sympathetic, but the Corinthians and the other allies with him were unwilling to lend their support. So Astyochus and his squadron of sixteen ships sailed to Chios, where he tried to enlist the help of Pedaritus and the Chians in a venture to Lesbos. He was again rebuffed, with Pedaritus, the Spartan commander at Chios, denying him the use of any Chian ships. After warning the Chians that they could expect no help from him in the future, Astyochus and his squadron sailed for Miletus. Stopping for the night at Corycus, the much larger Athenian fleet of thirty triremes coming from Samos also put in for the evening nearby, with the two forces separated only by a single hill standing between them. Neither became aware of the other's presence; Astyochus was called away by the rumour of an uprising at Erythrae, and by pure chance managed to avoid encountering the Athenians the next day.

The Athenian fleet itself encountered three Chian triremes off Arginus and pursued them. A storm arose and the Chian chips found safety in Arginus' harbour, while the leading three Athenian ships were wrecked by the storm and cast ashore near the city of Chios. Their crews were either killed or taken captive. The rest of the Athenian fleet found safety in the harbour known as Phoenicus, beneath Mount Mimas, and then moved on to Lesbos, which they began to fortify.

Also during the winter of 412/1, Hippocrates of Sparta, with ten Thurian triremes, together with one Laconian and one Syracusan ship, made call at Cnidus, which had revolted with support from Tissaphernes. Six of these ships were detailed to guard Cnidus, while the other six were to take up station around the Triopium promontory to intercept all merchant ships coming from Egypt. The Athenians sent ships from Samos to Triopium, and captured all six of the enemy ships there, though their crews escaped. The Athenians then mounted an attack on Cnidus, and came close to capturing it, but a stout defence repulsed them, and after plundering Cnidian territory they returned to Samos.[25]

Astyochus and his squadron reached the rest of the Peloponnesian fleet at Miletus at about this time, finding that it was well supplied with money and the loot recently taken at Iasus. Politically, there was friction because the Peloponnesians were unhappy with the terms of the first treaty that had been concluded with Persia by Chalcideus, seeing it as too favourable to the Great King. Formally recognizing Persian dominion over Greek cities had never sat well with the Spartans. So a second treaty was made with Tissaphernes by Therimenes in which the requirement that Persia pay for the Greek forces was made explicit; the language which stated that the Greek cities of Asia belonged to the Great King was left out, and the clause that had obligated the Spartans to help suppress revolts by cities in the Great King's domains was dropped. This new treaty, though cloaked in language less offensive to the Spartans, was not in substance a major departure from the first. Amorges' revolt had already been put down, so further assistance of that sort would not be needed. Moreover, the pay due to the Peloponnesians from Persia was not specified in writing, and the pay that was to be delivered was itself restricted to the size of the forces called up by the Great King.[26]

With the second treaty concluded, command of the Peloponnesian fleet was transferred to Astyochus by Therimenes, who departed Miletus in a small boat and was lost at sea. The Athenian fleet had made the crossing from Lesbos to Chios, and the fortification of

Delphinum was begun. Chios was slow to react to this move, the city being divided after so many losses. Pedaritus had executed some Chians on the suspicion of having Athenian sympathies, and his imposition of an oligarchic government made all suspicious of each other. Consequently, they did not consider either their own forces or Pedaritus' mercenaries capable of taking on the Athenians. They asked Asytochus for aid, which he, still smarting from their refusal to help him instil a revolt at Lesbos, refused to provide. Pedaritus made a complaint to his government in Sparta that Astyochus was a traitor, which was nonsense, but such was the poisonous relationship between the Spartan commanders that such an accusation could be made. The Athenian fleet operating out of Samos would sail now and again to Miletus to see if the Peloponnesians would emerge to do battle, but were refused each and every time and would go back to Samos.[27]

The Spartans had not forgotten about Pharnabazus' proposal to bring the war to the Hellespont. Twenty-seven triremes were outfitted and despatched under the command of Antisthenes, with the fleet sailing for Ionia. Aboard were eleven commissioners meant to advise Astyochus. The venomous letters sent by Pedaritus had also damaged Astyochus' reputation, to the extent that the advisers also had been given the power to relieve him of command of the fleet and replace him with Antisthenes if they deemed it necessary. The twenty-seven ships proceeded from Malea across the Aegean, touching at Melos, where they encountered ten Athenian ships. They took three of the ships empty and burned them. The rest escaped, and fearful that the fleeing Athenians would alert their compatriots at Samos, the Peloponnesians turned south and made for Crete. From Crete, they then sailed to Caunus, in southeastern Asia Minor, and sent a message to Miletus to request the sending out of ships to convoy them along the coast.

At Chios, Pedaritus and the Chians had continued to badger Asytochus with requests for help. The Chians were having difficulty keeping their slaves in line with the Athenians besieging the city. The slave population on Chios, Thucydides tells us, was the highest of any city in Greece besides Sparta, and the punishments they experienced were very harsh on account of their large numbers. When the Athenians had established a fortified position on the island at Delphinum, many of them deserted and provided valuable intelligence to the invaders.[28] The Chians saw that the Athenians were still busy with their works at Delphinum, and implored Astyochus to come and help before they could finish. Astyochus relented, despite his earlier threats not to help them, once he saw that his allies were of the opinion that they should go to Chios' aid.

The twenty-seven ships bearing the Spartan commissioners had arrived at Caunus, and Astyochus put off going to the aid of Chios until he had safely convoyed the new fleet to Milietus. Coasting southward with his own ships, Astyochus came upon Cos, a city that had recently experienced a massive earthquake that had wrecked its structures. The people had fled into the high country, and he landed and plundered what he could, and then made for Cnidus, which he reached that night. The Cnidans came out to meet him, telling him not to disembark his crewmen, but to move against a squadron of twenty Athenian triremes under the command of Charminus that was operating in the area. The Athenians at Samos had been told of the movement of the twenty-seven-strong Peloponnesian fleet by those of their own vessels that had survived the encounter with the Peloponnesians at Melos, and the squadron was on the lookout for this new fleet carrying the commissioners, lying in wait for it off Syme, Chalce, Rhodes and Lycia, having learned that it had reached Caunus.

Astyochus sailed on to Syme, intending to intercept the enemy before his approach was known to them. His fleet encountered fog and rain, lost coherence as it moved and his ships straggled. As he rounded the island of Syme in disorder, only the Peloponnesian left wing was visible to the Athenians, who mistook it for the fleet of twenty-seven they were expecting from Caunus. The Athenians, under the command of Charminus, were beached, but on spotting Astyochus' ships they quickly boarded, and in their haste they put to sea with fewer than their full strength of twenty triremes, sinking three of the Peloponnesian ships and crippling others. The appearance of the laggard main body of the Peloponnesian fleet coming round the island turned the tables on the Athenians, who found themselves surrounded. The Athenians ran, losing six of their vessels, making first for the island of Teutloussa and then for Halicarnassus. The victorious Peloponnesians put back into Cnidus, where they were met by the twenty-seven ships coming up from Caunus.[29]

The Athenians still at Samos sailed to Syme, where they recovered the valuable ships' tackle that had been left ashore by Charminus' squadron, and then returned to Samos without encountering the Peloponnesians at Cnidus. At Cnidus, Astyochus repaired his ships while the eleven commissioners from Sparta met with Tissaphernes, who had come to speak with them. One commissioner, Lichas, was especially critical of the previous treaties concluded between

Chalcideus and Theramines, arguing that it was unacceptable that the Great King should be asserting his ownership of so many lands, the islands, Thessaly, Locris and everything up to Boeotia, that had been out of his or his ancestor's possession for so long. The prior treaty, he contended, made the Spartans give to the other Greeks a Persian master instead of their freedom.[30] This was of course directly counter to the stated Spartan wartime goal of bringing liberty to Greece, and it made no sense to replace Athenian domination with that of the Persians. Lichas refused to accept Persian money on such terms, and insisted that a new treaty be made, but Tissaphernes, having had his fill of the Spartans and their endless haggling, was so offended that he rode off without a new agreement of any kind.[31] The satrap's frustration with the obstreperous Spartans is easy to understand. He had been dealing with them for more than a year now, and they were always dissatisfied with whatever agreement had previously been made with Persia. They were unwilling to recognize the Great King's suzerainty over his former possessions, and made nonstop complaints about pay.

Astyochus next took his fleet on an expedition to Rhodes, after learning from some of the leading men there that the island was ripe for revolt from Athens. Bringing Rhodes into the fold was an attractive option, as it had many seamen and troops, and by its addition the Peloponnesians would be able to maintain their own fleet from amongst their own members, and not have to rely upon Tissaphernes for money. They sailed in the winter of 412/1 from Cnidus, arriving at Rhodes with ninety-four ships. They persuaded the people of Rhodes to rebel, and the Athenians, hearing of the Peloponnesian movement, sailed themselves to Rhodes but came too late to prevent its defection. The Peloponnesians next extracted a thirty-two talent contribution from Rhodes, and after beaching their ships, remained on the island for the next eighty days.[32]

Alcibiades and Tissaphernes

Thucydides at this point reintroduces Alcibiades into his narrative. The Athenian exile's relations with the Spartans had begun to sour ever since the death of Chalcideus and the Battle of Miletus. So bad did things become that Astyochus was sent instructions by Sparta to execute him. Alciabiades had been busy making both friends and enemies, with Plutarch writing that the lusty Athenian had seduced Timaea, the wife of King Agis, and gotten her with child.[33] Alcibiades got wind of the order before it could be carried out, and fled to Tissaphernes, becoming, Thucydides says, 'his adviser in everything', doing 'all that he could ... to injure the Peloponnesian cause'.[34]

It had been Alcibiades, Thucydides writes, who had earlier advised Tissaphernes to reduce the pay to the Peloponnesian seamen to just three obols a day, or half a drachma, telling him that this was all that the Athenians paid their own sailors, who were far more experienced. Alcibiades said that Athens limited the pay to prevent the crewmen from becoming corrupted by being too well off. He also counselled Tissaphernes that such payments that he did make should be irregular, the idea being that the seamen would be less likely to desert while they were still owed money by their paymaster. Alcibiades' advice went further, with him telling the satrap that he should pay bribes to the fleet captains and the generals of the cities so that they would not make a fuss about the reduced pay. This plan had worked with everyone except Hermocrates of Syracuse, who objected vehemently to the cut, which had resulted in the slight revision upwards in the pay due to the Greeks.[35]

Alcibiades also turned away those cities who had come to the satrap's door to ask for money, saying that the Chians, the wealthiest of all the Greeks, were impudent to request funds from Tissaphernes while they were at the same time being protected by foreign military forces. To the other cities, he declared that they must pay at least as much for their own defence as they had previously contributed to Athens. The satrap was even now paying for the war against Athens out of his own treasury, and thus his thrift was justified, assuring the cities that once more money arrived from the Great King he would pay them in full.[36]

Alcibiades' strategic advice was also shrewd. He told Tissaphernes not to be too eager to bring the war to a conclusion, or to bring into the fight the Phoenician fleet that he was in the process of fitting out, or to increase the pay of the Greeks. In Alcibiades' opinion, it would be damaging to Persia if both land power and seapower were to become combined in one of the contending sides. One side should be left dominant on land, and the other on the sea. This power would be impossible to overcome, and the Great King would have no one to employ to fight it unless he himself chose to do so with his own forces, which would entail great risk and heavy financial costs. It would be much less expensive to let the warring Greeks exhaust themselves, which could be achieved at small cost to the Great King in blood and treasure.[37]

Alcibiades saw Athens as being the preferable partner for Persia, telling Tissaphernes that the Athenians did not wish to conquer territories ashore, but wanted only a naval empire, while the Spartans were seeking the liberation of the Greeks, which threatened Persian possessions deep inland from the sea. Tissaphernes' ultimate aim, Alcibiades counselled, should be to weaken Athenian power, and once this was achieved, to expel the Spartans from Asia. This was the advice, Thucydides writes, that had underlain the pattern of haphazard payments of the Peloponnesian fleet that had hindered it in fighting at sea. Its efficiency was further sapped because the satrap falsely informed the Peloponnesians that the Phoenician fleet would be coming to join them, which made them hold back in the belief that they would soon be going into battle with the odds weighted heavily in their favour.[38]

Thucydides claimed that Alcibiades had an ulterior motive for giving the advice that he did to Tissaphernes, 'not merely because he thought it really the best, but because he was seeking means to bring about his restoration to his country, well knowing that if he did not destroy it he might one day hope to persuade the Athenians to recall him'.[39] The best way to persuade his countrymen, he felt, was to demonstrate that he had the favour of Tissaphernes. Alcibiades' instinct was correct. The leading men in the Athenian fleet at Samos were convinced, Thucydides writes, mainly of their own accord, but also at Alcibiades' prompting, that if the democracy of Athens were to be replaced by an oligarchy, Alcibiades would return from exile and bring with him the valuable friendship of Tissaphernes. Phrynicus, the general at Samos, was dead set against the idea of doing away with the democracy, and saw through Alcibiades, saying that his motive was only to have himself recalled to Athens, and that he did not care at all whether Athens was governed by an oligarchy or by a democracy. It made no sense, Phrynicus argued, for the Great King to side with the Athenians just when the Peloponnesians, who had never harmed his empire, had achieved naval parity with the Athenians. Further, Athens' allies would not like her any more if she became an oligarchy, and it would certainly not lure rebellious states back into the imperial fold. What mattered to them was their own freedom, not the type of government at Athens that kept them in servitude.[40]

Fearing, rightly, the consequences that might befall him if Alcibiades were to be restored at Athens, Phrynicus opened communications with Asytochus, who was currently in the area of Miletus, informing him by a secret letter of what Alcibiades had been telling Tissaphernes, and how he was damaging Spartan interests in his role as the satrap's adviser. Instead of moving against Alcibiades, who was in any case out of his power to harm, Astyochus told them everything that Phrynicus had said in his letter. Thucydides says that 'if the report may be trusted', Astyochus then became a paid informant of Tissaphernes, and that the bribes that he took had also bought his acquiescence concerning the earlier cut in pay for the fleet.[41]

Book 8, in which these events are related by Thucydides, is unfinished, and has been called 'the workshop of Thucydides' to convey its less than polished nature.[42] It is almost certain that it would have undergone revision after it was completed. As the book exists, the precise chronology of Alcibiades' machinations with Tissaphernes is difficult to follow. Thucydides explores his advice to Tissaphernes and its consequences at 8.45–46, but he makes it plain that Alcibiades had been advising the satrap for some time beforehand, and had been behind the cut in pay mentioned in 8.29. This makes determining whether Astyochus' refusal to come out to fight the Athenians outside Miletus at 8.38, when they made repeated challenges with their fleet, was attributable simply to his own fearfulness, or a sound strategic decision – if he believed that fighting was not worthwhile – such as if he thought that the Phoenician fleet would soon arrive and he would have overwhelming numbers on his side, or because the Peloponnesian fleet had already begun to decline in efficiency on account of Tissaphernes' irregular payments to his crews. Thucydides is telling much of this strand of the story retrospectively, and not in a linear manner. His assertion that Astyochus had been bought by the satrap further clouds the picture. The movement of the Peloponnesian fleet to Rhodes, and their desire to find a source of oarsmen for their ships so they would not have to rely on Tissaphernes for money, together with the feud of Lichas with Tissaphernes at Cnidus, suggests that Astyochus and the Spartans were still fully independent of the satrap. The eighty days in which their fleet remained inactive at Rhodes bears the hallmarks of a strike. According to Thucydides, the execution order for Alcibiades and his involvement as adviser to Tissaphernes had taken place 'during this time, and even earlier, before [the Spartans] went to Rhodes'.[43] This makes it very hard to know how much weight to give Thucydides' allegations of bribery of the Peloponnesian city commanders and trierarchs, apart from Hermocrates, at 8.45, since they do not seem to have acted as if they had been bought, if their constant complaining about Persian pay and their refusal to fight is any indication.

Similarly, placing the alleged turning of Astyochus is problematic. He was 'still in the neighbourhood of Miletus' when the letter for him from Phrynicus arrived, not at Rhodes, where the Peloponnesian fleet was beached and would remain for the winter. It would be a startling thing for the fleet to be without its admiral for such a long time. Had there been a split among the Spartans so severe that the fleet departed Miletus for Rhodes, leaving its navarch Astyochus behind? Thucydides does not mention such a division, and if it existed one must wonder why he did not, but the puzzling events of the winter of 412/1 can be read that way.

Alcibiades informed the other Athenians at Samos of what Phrynicus had communicated to Astyochus, and Phrynicus, in deep trouble, sent another message to Asytochus; after berating him for not keeping the previous letter in confidence, he said that he was prepared to give him the chance to destroy the Athenian force at Samos, which was unfortified, including in his letter a detailed plan as to how to go about it. But this Astyochus also conveyed to Alcibiades, and Phrynicus, at last aware that Astyochus was in league with Alcibiades, and expecting that another letter from Alcibiades would soon be reaching Samos, began to strengthen Samos, warning his men that the enemy would be attacking shortly. The Athenians took up the task with alacrity, and the base at Samos was rapidly fortified. When the second letter to the Athenians from Alcibiades arrived, laden with the accusation that they had been betrayed by Phrynicus, Alcibiades was not believed, as his warning of the impending attack only seemed to confirm Phrynicus' own, seemingly accurate, intelligence.[44]

Alcibiades continued with his efforts to bring Tissaphernes over to the Athenian side. The Peloponnesian fleet was still at Rhodes, and its use against the Athenians appeared doubtful, once Lichas had objected so strongly to acknowledging Persian suzerainty over lands that had once belonged to the Great King. Alcibiades' warning that the Spartans were more of a danger to Persian territories than the Athenians seemed to have been borne out.

A delegation from the Athenian force at Samos, led by Pisander, went to Athens and spoke before the Assembly. They argued in favour of replacing the democracy with an oligarchy, but there were strong objections to their proposal. Pisander then spoke to each of the opponents in turn, and laid out in stark terms the dangers that threatened Athens. The Peloponnesians had as many ships at sea as they did, he said, more allies and funding from Tissaphernes and the Great King, while Athens' treasury was empty. Their only hope of salvation was to bring Persia over to the side of Athens. The government would have to be put in the hands of fewer men, which would reassure the Great King, and Alcibiades, the only person who could deliver a Persian alliance, had to be recalled from exile.

At last persuaded, the Assembly voted to have Pisander and ten colleagues sail to Asia to meet with Tissaphernes and Alcibiades to form an alliance. Phrynicus and his colleague in command at Samos, Scironides, were relieved on the basis of a false charge levelled by Pisander – that they had betrayed Iasus and Amorges. In their place, new commanders, Diomedon and Leon, were appointed.

Still in the winter of 412/1, Diomedon and Leon led an attack on Rhodes. The Peloponnesian fleet's warships were ashore, and the Athenians landed and defeated the Rhodian troops sent out to meet them. After this, the Athenians withdrew to Chalce, where they kept a watch on the enemy fleet. Around this time a messenger arrived from Pedaritus at Chios with the news that the Athenian fortifications on the island had been completed, and that if the entire fleet was not sent immediately to the rescue, Chios would fall. The Peloponnesians agreed to go to the aid of Chios, but in the interim an initially successful assault led by Pedaritus on the fortified Athenian encampment turned sour, and the Athenian counter-attack saw him and many of the Chians slain, with famine taking root in Chios as the city began to suffocate under a siege maintained by land and sea.[45]

Pisander opened negotiations with Tissaphernes, but here they found their hopes of an alliance dashed. Tissaphernes was not nearly as willing to enter into an agreement with them as they had been led to believe by Alcibiades. The satrap was still more worried about the Peloponnesians than he was about the Athenians, and further, Thucydides says, wanted to see both sides tire themselves out, in accordance with the strategic advice that Alcibiades had himself given to him. Alcibiades, seeing that Tissaphernes was not interested in concluding an agreement of any kind with his countrymen, wanted to evade being blamed for the failure of the talks because he could not persuade the satrap. Instead, he made it appear that the negotiations had failed because the Athenians had not made enough concessions, despite Tissaphernes' openness to an alliance. Negotiating on behalf of Tissaphernes, he made demands of such extraordinary magnitude that they would, as he intended, be rejected by the Athenians and make it seem as if it were the Athenians' fault, and not his, that the talks had foundered. These demands included that they cede Ionia in Asia Minor to Persia, as well as the adjacent islands. Astonishingly, the Athenians, in their desperation, agreed to them both. But they balked when Alcibiades put forth another demand, that the Great King be permitted to build warships of his own and sail them along his shore whenever he wished. This term, which would have been a drastic revision of the peace treaty that had seen Persian warships banned from the Aegean, the Athenians could not stomach, and finally seeing through Alcibiades' deceptions, they quit the negotiations and went to Samos.[46]

With the Athenians out of the picture, Tissaphernes had to heal the breach with the Peloponnesians and get them back into the war. The satrap worried that if the Peloponnesians were left unpaid, their fleet would be either forced to fight and lose, or if the crews abandoned their ships for lack of pay, the Athenians would win without his help. There was also the threat that the Peloponnesians might turn to raiding his territory to acquire necessary supplies. Going to Caunus to meet them, he agreed to pay them, and entered into a new treaty in which the grandiose claims of Darius II to Greek lands once held by his ancestors were not present. Apart from the immediate payment due to the Peloponnesians, Tissaphernes also agreed to call up the Phoenician fleet, after which time any money taken by the Peloponnesians from Tissaphernes to pay for their ships would have to be repaid by them to the Great King.[47] Thucydides notes that after the treaty was made, Tissaphernes began to prepare 'to bring up the Phoenician fleet ... and to make good his other promises, or all events wished to make it appear that he was so preparing'.[48] Tissaphernes was still playing his double game, and his move to reconcile with the Peloponnesians was a shrewd one.

At the end of winter, the Peloponnesians at Rhodes sailed on a rescue mission to Chios, encountering off Triopium the Athenian fleet based at Chalce, where it had been keeping watch on Rhodes. Neither fleet moved to engage the other, with the Spartans, observing that they could not relieve Chios without a fight, putting in at Miletus, while the Athenians continued on to Samos. In the spring of 411, a small force under the command of the Spartan Dercyllidas marched by land to instigate a revolt at Abydos in the Hellespont. Meanwhile, the Chians, receiving no help from Astyochus, and straining under the siege, had to fight the Athenians at sea. They had received a new commander to replace the fallen Pedaritus, a Spartan named Leon, who brought with him twelve triremes from Miletus, comprising five Thurian ships, four Syracusan, one Anaian (Anaia being the base of the Samian exiles), one Milesian and the last being one of Leon's own vessels. These twelve ships, combining with thirty-six Chian triremes, emerged to do battle with thirty-two Athenian triremes in the blockading force. The Chians and their Peloponnesian allies had 'rather the best' of the hard fighting, but with darkness approaching, they withdrew to the city.[49]

Not long after this, Dercyllidas came to Abydos after having marched there from Miletus, and his appearance incited a revolt there against Athens. The revolt of Abydos was followed by one at Lampsacus just two days later. Strombichides, hearing of the twin rebellions, took a squadron of twenty-four ships, including in that number some transports bearing hoplites, and retook Lampsacus, which was unfortified. At Abydos, however, he was repulsed by the stubborn resistance of its people, and he next made for Sestos in the Chersonese, where he established a base. With the Chians gaining the upper hand at sea, and Strombichides' departure from Samos with his ships, the Peloponnesians at Miletus saw a glimmer of hope. Astyochus combined the ships of Chios with those of his own fleet, and they sailed together against Samos, seeking a fight. The Athenians would not come out, however, as their fleet was riven by discord occasioned by political strife that was engulfing both Athens and the overseas fleet.

The Athenian democracy had by now been undone, with an oligarchical system of government put in its place. A coup in Athens in early 411 resulted in power being vested in only a relative handful of citizens known as the Four Hundred, and this narrow and thoroughly undemocratic government, which would exist for just four months, sought an end to the war, only to see their desire frustrated when Sparta made the cost of peace too high. King Agis, who was nearby at fortified Decelea, responded negatively to their overtures by insisting that peace would only come if the Athenians 'surrendered their maritime empire'.[50]

Agis next moved against Athens with his army, reinforced heavily by troops recently brought in from the Peloponnesus, thinking perhaps by a show of force to compel a surrender or at least capture the Long Walls. But the Athenians were far better prepared to resist than expected, and Agis, seeing that there was still fight left in the enemy, returned to Decelea and sent the reinforcements back home.

The dissolution of the democracy at Athens caused immense strains within the Athenian force at Samos, with the crewmen and soldiers there coming down squarely against the oligarchy now in power. Significantly, they swore that they would reject any intercourse with the oligarchs, and additionally resolved to carry on the war against the Peloponnesians on their own. The men reassured themselves with the knowledge that they had the entire Athenian fleet with them at Samos, a strong city in itself, and the fleet was enough to compel the other cities of the empire to contribute money to them, which would be no different than if it had been based back at Athens. The impoverished capital was lacking money to send to them, in any case, and so the severance of relations with Athens made little material difference to the force at Samos. Furthermore, in the event of a defeat, they could retreat to many other locations in their ships. There was still a desire among the soldiers to recall Alcibiades, whom they saw as the key to winning an alliance with Tissaphernes.[51]

There was also dissension among the Peloponnesian seamen at Miletus, where the mood was testy. They blamed Astyochus and Tissaphernes for 'ruining their cause', seeing that Astyochus had been unwilling to fight a naval battle when the Athenian fleet had been much smaller and the Peloponnesian crews were 'in full vigour', and now, when the Athenians were 'in a state of sedition'.[52] Tissaphernes' much-promised Phoenician fleet had yet to appear, and the Peloponnesian crews had since lost their edge through inactivity while waiting. The pay due from Tissaphernes was, as ever, irregular, and not being made in full. The Peloponnesians, and foremost among them the Syracusans, insisted on taking on the Athenian fleet in a decisive battle.

Astyochus and the commanders of the allied ships had already decided that they would have to fight, and learning of the secession of the Athenians at Samos from their home government, sailed with 110 ships to Mycale, while a land force of Milesians marched to meet them. Eighty-two Athenian ships were cruising off Glauce in Mycale, and seeing that they were outnumbered, went back to Samos. The Peloponnesians put in at Mycale for the evening, and would have attacked Samos, but when they received news that the squadron under Strombichides that had recently sailed to Abydos had come back to Samos, they returned to Miletus. With Strombichides' ships added to their total, the Athenians had 108 ships and sailed against Miletus, desiring to fight a major battle, but the Peloponnesians refused to come out, not liking their chances against a fleet that so closely matched them in numbers. The Athenians returned to Samos.

With Tissaphernes still underpaying them, the need to find money led the Peloponnesians to send forty triremes north under the command of Clearchus to try to secure an agreement with Pharnabazus, the Persian satrap at the Hellespont. Pharnabazus, it should be remembered, had earlier asked the Peloponnesians at Sparta to help him in the Hellespont, before they had decided to cast their lot, at least initially, with the Chians and Tissaphernes. He again promised to provide pay for the Peloponnesians, and around this time overtures came from Byzantium offering to revolt over to them. The forty ships travelled across open sea to evade detection by the Athenians, but en route encountered a storm that forced most of them to seek refuge at Delos. After returning to Miletus, Clearchus went by land to the Hellespont to take up the command. In the meantime, ten of the ships of his storm-tossed fleet, under a Megarian commander named Helixus, succeeded in reaching the Hellespont and brought about the revolt of Byzantium. The Athenians at Samos, hearing of the defection, sent a squadron against the city, and there was a minor battle between eight ships on either side.[53]

The Athenian fleet at Samos at this juncture recalled Alcibiades and gave him amnesty. To them, Alcibiades had said that Tissaphernes wished to bring up the Phoenician fleet, which was now based at Aspendus, to join the Athenians, and that they would be well-furnished with supplies by him, but that he had to be able to trust the Athenians completely, and the only way to do that was if they recalled Alcibiades 'to be his security for them', Thucydides says. Alcibiades exaggerated his influence with Tissaphernes so that he might make the oligarchy of Athens afraid of him. The troops elected him general to serve alongside the others currently holding command. Many in the force on the island were of a mind to sail immediately for Piraeus, ready to disregard the Peloponnesians nearby. But Alcibiades was squarely against this proposal, and instead told the men that he would go to Tissaphernes and make plans for a combined effort against the Peloponnesians. Alcibiades then sailed to see Tissaphernes and demonstrated that he was now an Athenian general. He was playing both sides against each other, Thucydides writes, wishing as he did to 'frighten the Athenians with Tissaphernes and Tissaphernes with the Athenians'.[54]

The news that Alcibiades was in command of the Athenian fleet at Samos caused an upswelling of loathing among the Peloponnesians for Tissaphernes, who had become even more remiss with his payments. In the Peloponnesian camp, many again grumbled that they had never been fully paid, that whatever they had obtained from Tissaphernes was very limited and that the payments that they did receive were irregularly made, something that must have been a constant irritant when the sailors and soldiers had to pay for their own food. The crewmen demanded that they either sail out to fight a decisive battle against the Athenians or go to some other destination where they could find provision, or else they would desert.

Among the Peloponnesians, Astyochus was blamed first and foremost for the deplorable state of affairs, believing that he was privately profiting from his cozy relationship with the satrap. In the fleet, Thucydides says, the crews from Syracuse in Sicily and Thurii in Italy were comprised mostly of free men, and they, as the 'freest crews in the armament', pressured Asytochus strenuously on the matter of their pay. It had been Hermocrates of Syracuse who had objected most heavily when Tissaphernes proposed to cut the pay due to the fleet in half, and Thucydides also pointed out that, alone of all the captains, Hermocrates had not taken a bribe from the satrap. As free men, it would only be natural for the Syracusans and Thurians, unimpeded by bribed officers, to be more vocal in their complaints over pay. When they confronted Asytochus over their money, they were backed up by Dorieus, one of their officers. Astyochus was arrogant in his response and made threats against them. Astyochus even raised his baton against Dorieus, a stupid and thoughtless act, and the men, seeing this, rushed upon Asytochus, seeking to stone him, with the Spartan surviving only because he saw them moving against him and found refuge at an altar.[55]

The Milesians were angry as well. Tissaphernes had built a fort at Miletus and this was seized by the Milesians, who threw out the garrison. This act garnered much support from amongst the Peloponnesians, especially the Syracusans, but Lichas the Spartan criticized the move, saying that the Milesians should show more respect to Tissaphernes, in whose satrapy they dwelled until the war was 'happily settled'.[56] This was a surprising opinion coming from Lichas, who had recently been so adamant in his refusal to accept Persian domination of the Greek cities of Asia Minor. When he died some time later due to illness, the spiteful Milesians refused him burial where his Spartan compatriots wished.

Astyochus was replaced as navarch of the fleet by the Spartan Mindarus, and he, along with an agent of Tissaphernes named Gaulites, sailed back to Sparta. Tissaphernes had sent Gaulites with Astyochus in the knowledge that the Milesians were themselves sending a delegation to complain about his actions, and Gaulites was to complain on the satrap's behalf about the Milesian capture of the fort and defend his master against the claims made by the Milesians. With the Milesians was Hermocrates, Tissaphernes' bitter enemy, who was going along to argue that Tissaphernes had been in league with Alcibiades and had played a 'double game' that had ruined the Peloponnesian war effort.[57] Hermocrates had himself been recalled by his own government after a democratic revolution in Syracuse, and new officers – Potamis, Myscon and Demarchus – had been appointed to command the Syracusan ships already at Miletus For whatever reason (though it is certain to have had something to do with the ascendance of the democratic faction in Syracuse), Hermocrates found himself exiled, and the vengeful Tissaphernes shamelessly levelled the charge against him that the Syracusan had previously approached *him* for a bribe, and had then declared himself an opponent of the satrap when he had been refused.[58]

Yet it is clear that Hermocrates had acquitted himself very well while in service with the Peloponnesian fleet. Xenophon, who incorrectly dates the recall of Hermocrates to later in the war, writes that the marines, the ship captains and the helmsmen of the Syracusan vessels all insisted that the generals should remain in command of them, but the dismissed generals would not hear of disobeying the edict, though it meant their own exile. They told the men that they must 'remember how many sea battles you yourselves have won through your own efforts, and how many ships you have captured, and how often you, with your allies, have been undefeated under our command'.[59]

The greater part of all the captains present swore that they would undo the exile of the generals once they had returned home. Hermocrates would be much missed. He was a careful and dedicated commander, each day having over to his tent the best of the trierarchs, the helmsmen and the marines, telling what was on his mind and seeking out their advice. Such collegiality was welcomed by the men under his command, and in the council of the generals he was considered to be the best speaker and finest adviser. He had been at odds for a long time with Tissaphernes, due to his incorruptibility, but his relations with Pharnabazus were much better. When he went to see the satrap, Pharnabazus had money ready for him, without Hermocrates having to make a request for it first, and with these funds he hired mercenaries and readied triremes for his return voyage to Syracuse.[60]

Alcibiades had returned to Samos from his visit to Tissaphernes, and a delegation from the Four Hundred government at Athens arrived. The envoys addressed the hostile fleet crews, pleading that they were trying to save Athens, not hand it over to the enemy. Their property would not be touched, they said, and a much larger and more representative body, the Five Thousand, would have a 'proper share in the government'. The men were not persuaded, and were of a mind to sail for Piraeus then and there. But Alcibiades convinced them otherwise, saying that if they were to abandon their position at Samos all of Ionia and the Hellespont would fall to the enemy. This prevention of an attack on Piraeus, Thucydides writes, was a service rendered by Alcibiades to the state of 'the most outstanding kind'.[61] Had the Athenians given up the war to chastise their political enemies back home, the Peloponnesians, despite the hindrances they faced with

Tissaphernes, would have quickly seized the Hellespont and gained control of the vital waterway through which food flowed to Athens. Maintaining the war in the Aegean, no matter the political differences with the home city, was the only sensible strategic decision that could have been made, but only Alcibiades, Thucydides says, could have convinced the men to stay put instead of immediately going home.

Tissaphernes attempted a reconciliation with the Peloponnesians, who were now under no illusion that he was in cahoots with the Athenians, and invited Lichas to come with him to the Phoenician fleet that was massing at Aspendus. While he was to be away, Tissaphernes appointed Tamos to be his lieutenant to oversee payment of the Peloponnesian crewmen. Tamos was an unhappy choice, as he turned out to be even more lax in making payments than his master. As for the Phoenician fleet, Thucydides says that 147 ships were collected at Aspendus, but that they went no further. He advances theories as to why the fleet was never brought into the war, with one being that Tissaphernes had never intended to use the Phoenicians, and called them up to Aspendus only so that he could demand money from them for their discharge from service. Another theory holds that his intention to get the ships at Aspendus was real, and occasioned by the desire to prove to the Spartans that he was not to blame for the faltering war in the Aegean. Thucydides himself held that Tissaphernes had not brought the Phoenician fleet into the war because he was content to allow the evenly matched Greeks to wear themselves out fighting one another, and that the efficiency of the fleet's crews would decline while he was away at Aspendus. 'Had he wished to finish the war, he could have done so,' Thucydides writes, 'assuming of course that he made his appearance in a way which left no room for doubt; as by bringing up the fleet he would in all probability have given victory to the Spartans, whose navy, even as it was, faced the Athenians more as an equal than as an inferior.'[62] The excuse that the satrap gave for not bringing up the ships, that fewer of them had appeared than had been ordered by the Great King, was not credible to Thucydides. Their numbers would still have been sufficient to tip the scales in favour of the Peloponnesians, and he would have done so by spending less money, which would surely have won him credit for achieving more with less.[63]

Deciphering Tissaphernes' genuine motivations is less tricky than often thought. Some have seen him as being something of a 'psychological riddle' for both Alcibiades and Thucydides himself which neither were able to solve.[64] Tissaphernes was almost certainly enacting the strategy, as Alcibiades had previously advised, of letting the Greeks exhaust themselves by fighting each other. While they were doing so they were less of a threat. It does not follow that Tissaphernes could not have thought of such a plan on his own, even though Thucydides gives Alcibiades the credit for it. The repeated delays in calling up the Phoenician fleet, the endless skimping on pay for the Peloponnesian crews and the dalliance with the Athenians are all signs of a cagey imperial governor keeping both his friends (a word used very loosely in relation to Tissaphernes) and enemies off balance to reduce the threat to the empire. Alcibiades had made the case that Persian interests would have been better served by an Athenian victory as opposed to a Spartan one, but there is no real reason to believe that Tissaphernes saw things that way. If both Athens and Sparta could have lost, then Tissaphernes would probably have seen Persian interests served just as well. Alcibiades, according to Thucydides, had all along been playing a double game with Tissaphernes by giving seemingly good advice as to how to keep the Greeks busy fighting one another while at the same time trying to secure his recall from exile to Athens. Tissaphernes was at least as subtle a man, and was willing to support the Peloponnesian fleet just enough to keep the Athenians occupied without allowing victory to go to the Spartans.

At the request of Tissaphernes, the Spartans sent two triremes under the command of Philip to bring back the Phoenician ships. The Spartans seem to have kept up their hopes that Tissaphernes might finally come through with his long-promised pay and Phoenician ships, despite his failure to deliver on so many earlier occasions.

Alcibiades went on his own voyage to Aspendus with thirteen triremes to meet with Tissaphernes, promising that he would do a 'great and certain service for the Athenians', as he would either bring the Phoenician ships over to the Athenian side or prevent them from joining with the Peloponnesians. Thucydides is sceptical about Alcibiades' motive, believing that Alcibiades never had any hope that Tissaphernes would bring the ships into the war, and that instead he was seeking to make it appear that the satrap and he were on good terms so as to make the Peloponnesians ever more distrustful of the Persian and make it more probable that Tissaphernes would take the side of Athens.[65]

Alcibiades' determination to carry on the war against the Peloponnesians encouraged the members of the Athenian oligarchy who were disappointed with the new regime, and they sought to empower the much larger body of the Five Thousand. They had opponents in Athens, especially in the form of Phrynicus, the enemy of Alcibiades, as well as Aristarchus, Pisander, Antiphon and many other powerful men. This anti-democratic faction began the construction of a wall at the Eetionia breakwater in Piraeus, the purpose of which was to create a fortified position from which they could control access to the port. It was their intention, Thucydides says, to use this fortified section, once completed, not to keep the democratic Athenian fleet at Samos out, but to allow the enemy fleet and army *in*. The oligarchs feared most of all that if the democracy were to be restored they would be subject to the vengeance of the commons. They would, in the last resort, call in the Peloponnesians and make peace with them if their own lives and control of the government were guaranteed. A Peloponnesian fleet of forty-two ships under the command of Agesandridas was on its way to Euboea, having been invited there by the Euboeans, and had currently anchored at Las in Laconia. In Athens there was a fear, voiced strongly by Theramenes, that it was meant to join the oligarchic party fortifying Eetionia and capture the city.[66]

Theramenes went down to the works at Eetionia in Piraeus and, with his encouragement, the hoplites there pulled the wall down. The hoplites then marched from Piraeus to Athens, where they were met by delegates of the Four Hundred, who asked for the chance to hold an assembly on a later day, promising that they would make the larger and more democratic body of the Five Thousand a reality. Thus mollified, the hoplites desisted from their mission. When the day came to hold the promised assembly, word arrived that Agesandridas' fleet was on its way to Piraeus from Megara. The Athenians rushed to Piraeus to man their ships and took to sea.

The Peloponnesians went on their way to Euboea, and the Athenians had to follow after them, since Euboea was the source of so much of their food now that access to Attica had been denied to them by the year-round presence of the Spartans at Decelea. Their ships' crews were poorly trained, and sailed for Eretria in Euboea, and with the triremes already present on the island numbered just thirty-six. Agesandridas, sailing out of Oropus, came up right after his men had had their dinner and caught the Athenians off-guard while they were busy finding their own food. He had an enormous advantage in the Eretrians themselves. The Eretrians wished to be rid of the Athenians, and had made sure that no provisions were on sale in the marketplace, which caused the Athenian crewmen to go far from their ships to find food and be delayed when they tried to get back on their ships. The Eretrians also signalled to Agensandridas to let him know precisely when the Athenian crewmen were away from their ships. The Athenians were hastily recalled, but the unlooked-for appearance of the Peloponnesians forced them to put out to sea haphazardly and without full preparations.

In the ensuing battle fought off Eretria, the Athenians held their own for a time, then fled and were chased onto the shore by the pursuing Peloponnesians. Some of their ships escaped back into Eretria, where they were set upon by the hostile inhabitants and slaughtered. Some ships found safety at the Athenian fort in Eretrian territory, while others made their way to Chios where they found refuge. The Peloponnesians captured twenty-two triremes, for no losses given by Thucydides. Euboea was now in Peloponnesian hands with the exception of Athenian-held Oreus, and this development caused a panic in Athens when word of the disaster came. The sense of distress was worse than that which had arisen after the defeat of the Sicilian expedition in 413. The fleet at Samos had rebelled against the home government, they had lost all of their ships, they were bereft of crews to make good their losses in manpower and Euboea had been lost. There was, on top of these hurts, the threat that the enemy might make an immediate attack on Piraeus while they had no fleet to protect it. Thucydides notes that this could have been achieved by the Spartans with 'a little more courage'. A move against Athens would have forced the fleet at Samos to sail to the aid of the city, despite the hostility that it felt for the government of the Four Hundred, and in doing so would have left the Hellespont, Ionia, the Aegean islands and all the lands up to Euboea, which Thucydides notes was 'the whole of the Athenian empire', wide open to seizure by the Spartans. The opportunity to deal a deathblow to Athens was not taken, with the historian writing that 'here, as on so many other occasions, the Spartans proved the most convenient people in the world for the Athenians to be at war with. The wide difference between the two characters, the slowness and want of energy of the Spartans contrasted with the dash and enterprise of their opponents, proved of the greatest service, especially to a maritime empire like Athens.'[67]

The Athenians responded to the fall of Euboea by manning twenty triremes, and then held an assembly in the Pnyx. The government of the Four Hundred was deposed and in its place was established the government of the Five Thousand, with the criterion for membership being the possession of a panoply of hoplite armour. Among its first acts, Alcibiades was recalled, and the new government requested that the fleet at Samos continue the war against the Peloponnesians.[68]

Back at Miletus, the situation regarding Persian funding had not improved, with the Peloponnesians receiving no money at all; the Phoenician fleet had not budged from Aspendus, and Tissaphernes was likewise absent. Philip, who had been despatched to Aspendus with a couple of ships to bring back the Phoenician fleet, and his colleague Hippocrates, another Spartan, reported now to Mindarus at Miletus on the unsatisfactory situation, and that they were being subjected to abuse by the satrap. Pharnabazus, in the meantime, had been repeating his request for the Peloponnesian fleet to sail to his own satrapy in the Hellespont to bring about anti-Athenian revolts in the cities there. Exasperated with Tissaphernes' double game, Mindarus agreed to Pharnabazus' pleas, and in the summer of 411 he sailed with seventy-three ships from Miletus, where he would be joining sixteen other triremes that had sailed northward and taken possession of part of the Chersonese. Mindarus' fleet, however, ran into a storm along the way, and was forced to put into Icarus. After waiting for five or six days there because of poor weather, it moved on and reached Chios. Mindarus' decision to move north to join Pharnabazus was to have a profound impact on the strategic complexion of the Ionian naval war. When the Peloponnesian fleet had been based at Miletus, and hobbled by Tissaphernes haphazard funding, the Athenian fleet base at Samos was sufficient to protect Athens' Aegean trade routes. But with the Peloponnesians now at the Hellespont, Athens' food supply from the Black Sea was more definitely threatened.[69]

Hearing of the movement north, a fleet of fifty-five ships under the command of Thrasyllus put out from Samos, hoping to reach the Hellespont before the Peloponnesians did. When information came that Mindarus was at Chios, Thrasyllus posted lookouts on Lesbos and across from it in Asia Minor to keep watch for him. If the Peloponnesian fleet were to stay for any length of time at Chios, he planned to attack it from his base at Lesbos. In the interim, he mounted a seaborne attack on Eresus, a Lesbian city that had rebelled against Athens. Off Eresus, he was met by a squadron of five ships under Thrasybulus, two others which were in transit home to Athens from the Hellespont and five Methymnian ships, which brought his fleet up to a strength of sixty-seven vessels.[70]

The Battle of Cynossema

At Chios, Mindarus' ships spent two days taking on supplies, with the Chians paying each crewmen three coins of the island's currency. On the third day, Mindarus moved out as quickly as he could to slip past the Athenian ships lying at Eresus, sailing first along the mainland coast to Carteria, and from there to Arginousae, then to Harmatus and after that to Rhoeteum in the Hellespont, with some of the ships being distributed to other ports, including Sigaeum. The Athenian squadron of eighteen ships at Sestos was alerted to the Peloponnesian fleet's approach by signal fires and the rapid surge of fires on the enemy shore. At night, the Athenians hurriedly sailed out, staying close to the coast of the Chersonese, going to Elaeus so that they could then sail into the open sea to avoid being sighted by the Peloponnesians. They escaped detection by the Peloponnesian squadron of sixteen ships at Abydos, but ships from Mindarus' fleet spotted them, and pursued. Fourteen of the Athenian ships evaded the Peloponnesians and found refuge at islands of Imbros and Lemnos, but four were overhauled by the enemy, with three being taken as prizes and the fourth burned on the shore of Imbros.[71]

The strength of the Peloponnesian fleet rose to eighty-six ships when Mindarus' fleet was joined by the sixteen coming from Abydos. They besieged Elaeus for a day, and, meeting with no success, put into Abydos. The main Athenian fleet was blissfully ignorant of Mindarus' movements, with their lookouts having failed to warn them of his sailing, and were busy with their siege of Eresus. When word came at last that the Peloponnesians were close, they dropped everything at Eresus and rushed to the Hellespont. On the way they captured two Peloponnesian ships that had become separated from the main body during the pursuit of the Athenian squadron from Sestos, and anchored at Elaeus. There they were joined by five ships that had earlier found safety at Imbros, and for five days they readied themselves for the expected battle. Diodorus says that the Peloponnesians, seeing the Athenians 'rehearsing for the battle', likewise used the five-day lull to put their oarsmen through a regimen of intensive practice.[72]

The Athenians made the first move, sailing in line of column along the shore north from Elaeus toward Sestos. The Peloponnesians, stationed at Abydos further inside the Hellespont, came out to engage them off Point Cynossema. The seventy-six Athenian triremes formed a battle line stretching from Idacus to Arrhiana, along the European side of the strait, with the Peloponnesian line of eighty-six warships running from Abydos to Dardanus on the Asian side. The Athenian left wing was commanded by Thrasyllus, and its right by Thrasybulus. Across the strait, the Syracusans were placed on the Peloponnesian right wing, while its left was commanded by Mindarus with the finest crews in his fleet.[73]

Mindarus on the left attempted a *periplous* manoeuvre around the Athenian right wing, hoping to keep it from escaping from the Hellespont and to push the Athenian centre against the coast, which was close behind. The Athenians recognized the enemy's intention and reacted quickly, and using their superior rowing skill and consequent speed, extended their right wing to prevent it from being outflanked. This, however, left the centre of their line relatively weak, and further difficulty was created by the presence of Point Cynossema directly behind them, which intruded far into the strait and thus into the Athenian battle line making it impossible for them to see what was occurring on the other side of the point. The Athenian centre was driven onto the beach, with the Peloponnesians disembarking to capture the stranded enemy ships and crews. The Athenian right under Thrasybulus was so hard pressed that he could render no assistance to the centre, while Thrasyllus' left wing could not see what had happened because the view was obstructed by Point Cynossema, and was also itself fully engaged with the Syracusans and other Peloponnesian vessels.

Overconfidence doomed the Peloponnesians. They became disordered, thinking that the victory was theirs, just as they had outside Naupactus back in 429 BC. This was noticed by the ships of the right wing under Thrasybulus, which halted its slide southward and turned around. Their attack routed the Peloponnesians to their fore, and then they fell like wolves upon the out-of-formation enemy ships in the centre. These they drove off, sometimes without needing to land a blow against them. On the left wing, the Athenians under Thrasyllus had gained the upper hand over the Syracusans opposite them, and when these saw the flight of the other Peloponnesian ships, they too turned and fled.[74]

Diodorus explains in his account of the battle that the Peloponnesians had more ships and braver marines, and that these took part in ferocious boarding actions for the possession of ships. These advantages were, however, negated by the superior manoeuvring ability of the Athenian ships. When a Peloponnesian ship would surge forward to ram, the more talented Athenian pilots would manoeuvre so as to present the prow of their ships to the enemy, thus offering only an unappealing ram against ram attack. Mindarus, seeing this, it is said, then ordered his ships to attack either individually or in small groups, but this tactic proved ineffective and exposed the Peloponnesian ships to strikes in the sides.[75] The Athenians' edge in manoeuvring was a decisive factor in their victory once again.

The Athenians captured relatively few enemy ships, since with the Hellespont being so narrow the Peloponnesians did not have far to flee to find safety. Of the twenty-one ships taken by them, eight were Chian, five Corinthian, two Ambraciot, two Boeotian and one each from Leucas, Sparta, Syracuse and Pellene; the Athenians lost fifteen triremes themselves. The comparative loss tally, twenty-one to sixteen, might not seem to have been too lopsided, but the victory was of immense psychological importance for the Athenians. Up until the Battle of Cynossema, Thucydides says, they had been afraid of the Peloponnesian fleet because of the carnage in Sicily and a handful of small-scale defeats. After the battle, they had regained their old swagger.[76] The news of the triumph at Cynossema was also an enormous boost to the morale of the people of Athens, instilling in them a belief that if they could hang on, grimly determined, they would win the war.

Four days after the fight in the Hellespont, the Athenians sailed against Cyzicus, which was in rebellion and had gone over to Pharnabazus.[77] Eight Byzantine ships were lying at anchor off the unfortified city, and the Athenians, coming up, landed their troops and defeated the enemy soldiers ashore. They took the Byzantine vessels as prizes and then captured Cyzicus itself. On its citizenry the Athenians imposed a levy. While the Athenians were going about their business at Cyzicus, the Peloponnesians sailed from Abydos to Elaeus and recaptured some of the triremes they had lost in the battle, though a few had previously been set afire by the people of Elaeus. The Athenians would have been far better served, strategically, to have either towed away or destroyed the remaining Peloponnesian ships that had been left ashore. But the need for funds had impelled them to restore order at Cyzicus and obtain money from it.[78]

Alcibiades during this time had been away on his mission to Tissaphernes, and returned presently with his squadron of thirteen triremes to Samos. He claimed credit for having convinced the satrap to refrain from bringing up the Phoenician ships from Aspendus to combine with the Peloponnesians, a great service to Athens if he is to be believed. After crewing nine additional ships, he sailed to Halicarnassus where he levied money from the inhabitants. After this he moved on and fortified Cos, where he installed a governor. He then went back to Samos in the autumn of 411. His erstwhile employer, Tissaphernes, hearing the news that the Peloponnesian fleet had decamped to the Hellespont, sailed from Aspendus to Ionia in western Asia Minor. There was other trouble brewing in his satrapy. The people of Antandrus, in northwestern Asia Minor, had rebelled against Arsaces, Tissaphernes' governor in the city, and expelled the Persian garrison, just as had been done earlier at Miletus, and a similar insurrection was also occurring around this time with the garrison at Cnidus. Tissaphernes awoke to the seriousness of the breach between him and the Peloponnesians, and was irritated too that Pharnabazus was making use of their ships and might succeed against the Athenians more quickly and more cheaply than he had. He sailed off to the Hellespont to explain why he had been so tardy in calling up the Phoenician fleet and to lodge a protest concerning the expulsion of his troops from Antandrus.[79]

The Battle of Abydos

Xenophon, taking up the history of the war where Thucydides had left off in 411 BC, albeit with some lapse of time between the events last described by Thucydides and the point at which he begins his own narrative, states that the Athenians and Peloponnesians under Agesandridas fought another naval battle that year, in which the Peloponnesians were victorious, but does not say where. At the start of winter 411, Dorieus departed Rhodes for the Hellespont with fourteen ships. On the way, enemy lookouts saw them, and the Athenians sailed forth with twenty ships, but Dorieus evaded them and beached his triremes near Rhoiteion. The Athenians came up and there was fighting on the ships and the land, but the Athenians, having no success, withdrew and went to Madytos, where the rest of their forces were stationed.[80]

Dorieus tried to continue on his way to the Hellespont but the Athenians were already alert to his presence, and when he sailed again they sent out their full fleet of seventy-four ships, and Dorieus ran for safety to Dardanus. He disembarked his soldiers from the ships and handed them large numbers of missile weapons, and arranged them in strong defensive positions on the land and in the bows of his ships. The Athenians, coming up, and having the benefit of superior numbers, threw cables around the Peloponnesian triremes and began to haul them off the beach. Mindarus was at Abydos when he learned of the fighting at Dardanus, and with his entire fleet of eighty-four ships he sailed out to the rescue.[81]

Pharnabazus had brought troops to Dardanus, and these were fighting alongside Dorieus when Mindarus arrived. Adding Dorieus' ships to his fleet, Mindarus now had ninety-seven ships at his command. He placed the Syracusans on the left wing of his line, with himself in command of the Peloponnesian right. The Athenians opposite him formed a line too, with Thrasybulus commanding their right wing and Thrasyllus in command of the left. With trumpets sounding the attack, the two fleets hurled themselves at each other, Diodorus saying that as 'the rowers showed no lack of eagerness and the pilots managed their helms with skill, the contest which ensued was an amazing spectacle'. Diodorus gives enormous credit to the pilots, who displayed great expertise in steering their ships. '[W]henever the triremes would drive forward to ram,' he writes, 'at that moment the pilots, at just the critical instant, would turn their ships so effectively that the blows were made ram on.'[82]

At times the pilots could also prevent enemy ships from getting to grips with their own ships by skillful manoeuvring. Boarding actions could not be avoided altogether; Diodorus says that marines onboard 'kept up a stream of arrows and soon the space was full of missiles, while others, each time that they drew near, would hurl their javelins'. Their targets on opposing craft were often enemy marines and the pilots. '[W]henever the ships would come close together, they would not only fight with their spears but at the moment of contact would also leap over on the enemy's triremes and carry on the contest with their swords.'[83]

The battle hung in the balance, when in the distance an unidentified squadron appeared, each side hoping that it was friendly reinforcements. It was Alcibiades with a squadron of twenty ships brought up from Samos. Running up a purple flag from his personal ship, as had been agreed prior to the battle, Alcibiades signalled to the Athenians his identity. The Peloponnesians, seeing that the enemy had been strongly augmented by these new ships, turned and fled. The Athenians tried to pursue, capturing ten triremes, but further efforts were stymied by a storm that came up, making it impossible to ram effectively in the high waves. The Athenians tried to make off with those Peloponnesian ships that had beached themselves, but after hard fighting on land they were driven off by Pharnabazus' troops and withdrew to Sestos. Diodorus explains that the Persian troops put up a stubborn defence against the Athenians because Pharnabazus wished to demonstrate his commitment to the cause, with the satrap explaining to the Peloponnesians that the 300-ship Phoenician fleet had had to be sent back to Phoenicia because of the threat posed to that country by 'the king of the Arabians and the king of the Egyptians'.[84] Some thirty Peloponnesian triremes were captured by the Athenians, and all of their own wrecks were taken in hand and brought back to port.

After Abydos, the Athenian fleet despatched all but forty of its ships on missions outside the Hellespont to collect money, while Thrasyllus was sent to Athens to bring news of what had occurred at Abydos and to ask for more ships and troops. Tissaphernes re-entered the picture here, arriving in the Hellespont region. Alcibiades went to meet with the satrap in a single ship, and despite bringing gifts, was thrown into prison in Sardis by Tissaphernes. The reason for this, the satrap explained, was that the Great King Darius II had given him orders 'to make war on Athenians'. Alcibiades' confinement cannot have been too strict, since he escaped thirty days later, and finding a horse, made his way from Sardis to Clazomenae.[85]

The Battle of Cyzicus

Alcibiades brought five ships with him on his return to Sestos, and not long after there came Theramenes with twenty ships brought from Macedonia, and Thrasybulus next came with twenty more ships from Thasos, after having completed their money collection missions. In 410 BC, the Athenians learned that Mindarus was bringing sixty ships against them, and they sailed to Cardia, and after removing their mainsails and stowing them ashore in preparation for battle on Alcibiades' order, the Athenian fleet of eighty-six triremes sailed on to Parium. On the next night they sailed for Proconnesus, which they reached in the morning about breakfast time. Mindarus and his fleet, they discovered, were now at Cyzicus, and ashore was Pharnabazus with his land troops. Remaining at Proconnesus for a day, Alcibiades addressed his fleet, warning them of the tough fight that lay ahead. They would have to fight a decisive battle on the sea, as well as one on the land, even 'at the very walls' of Cyzicus. At root, it was a matter of money. The Athenians lacked it, he said, 'while our enemies have unlimited resources from the [Great] King'.[86] The Athenians could not afford to delay, or they would find themselves running out of money for their crews and see their naval strength dwindle.

For the upcoming battle, operational security was of great importance for Alcibiades. He kept all of the ships, including the small boats, with himself, in one place, to prevent the enemy from learning their numbers, and also let it be known that he would put to death anyone who was spotted crossing the Hellespont to the enemy side in order to prevent a leak.[87]

Cyzicus itself had been placed under siege by the Peloponnesians, and with the help of Pharnabazus' Persians the city was captured.

The Athenians arrived, with their fleet divided into three parts. Alcibiades had the command of one squadron of twenty ships, which according to Diodorus took the lead against the Peloponnesians, seeking to lure Mindarus' ships out of Cyzicus. Once this had been accomplished, the two other squadrons that followed behind, under Theramenes and Thrasybulus, would enact *periplous* manoeuvres around the flanks of the Peloponnesian fleet. Mindarus, Diodorus writes, took the bait, and his fleet of eighty eagerly pursued Alcibiades' squadron, not seeing the rest of the Athenian fleet from his vantage point. As the Peloponnesians closed with Alcibiades, his squadron turned in feigned flight, as planned, drawing the enemy ships away from Cyzicus for some distance. The Peloponnesians thought that since the enemy was fleeing, they were winning, but then at a signal, Alcibiades' ships turned around to fight, and the other two squadrons under Theramenes and Thrasybulus came up behind the Peloponnesians and interposed themselves between them and the city, cutting off their avenue of retreat.[88]

Xenophon's account of the engagement at Cyzicus differs greatly. In his, it was raining heavily as Alcibiades came up to Cyzicus, which then stopped, and Mindarus' fleet of sixty ships was already out of port a far distance, undergoing exercises. Alcibiades' appearance cut off the Peloponnesians from Cyzicus, and Mindarus' ships immediately beached themselves and prepared to fight on land.[89]

To return to Diodorus' narrative, Mindarus found himself surrounded. He landed his ships and disembarked his men around Cleri, close to where Pharnabazus and his troops were stationed. Alcibiades followed them to shore, and after sinking a few and capturing some others, he threw grappling irons onto their beached triremes, attempting to pull them away. A fierce fight broke out as the Persians ran down to the beach to help the Peloponnesians defend their ships from the Athenians, who though outnumbered, were fighting furiously to take possession of the ships. Seeing the lopsided nature of the encounter, Thrasybulus delivered his marines ashore to support Alcibiades, and called upon Theramenes to land his own marines to take part in the battle.[90]

The Athenians under Thrasybulus were being worsted when Theramenes' men, now on land, rushed up to reinforce them. The fight was long and bitter, but at last the Athenians succeeded in pushing Pharnabazus' troops from the field, and these were followed not long after by the Peloponnesians, who had suffered heavily in the combat. Theramenes' men then moved to aid Alcibiades' troops. Mindarus' Peloponnesians struggled against the attack of Theramenes, while still trying to fend off Acibiades' attempts to haul away their ships, with the Spartan admiral dying bravely in the ensuing fighting. When he fell, the Peloponnesians and their allies took to their heels. The Athenians took possession of the enemy ships and the city of Cyzicus, which had been abandoned by the Peloponnesians.[91]

Cyzicus was, in all ways, an extraordinary victory. It demonstrated once again the nautical skill of the Athenians, and its strategic impact was vast. The threat of a closure of the Hellespont to Athens' grain traffic was averted in a single day, and the Athenian fleet was once again unchallenged as master of the sea.[92] Another beneficial result of the victory was that, soon afterward, the Athenians were able to establish a fortified customs station at Chrysopolis in Chalcedon to extract a 10 per cent toll on all sea traffic coming through the Bosphorus. We may assume that this supplemented the money garnered as a result of the 5 per cent tax imposed on seaborne trade in 413 BC in place of the failing tribute system. Prior to the battle, the Athenians had been starved for cash, while the Peloponnesians had access to Persian funds. With Chrysopolis in operation, Athens now had another, comparatively secure, source of money for its war effort. A fleet of thirty ships was left in place to defend that station, under the command of two generals, Theramenes and Eumachus.[93]

The people of Athens were overjoyed when they learned of the triumph, and this made them ever more confident in their chances of winning the war. The Spartans, once more suffering a disaster, sought peace, sending Endius, Alcibiades' old friend, to speak to the Athenians. He offered a peace in which each side would keep the cities it possessed, surrender the holdings it maintained in each other's territory and exchange prisoners. He reminded the Athenians that Sparta still held several advantages. Sparta had gained many allies during the war, while Athens had lost many. It also had the financial backing of 'the richest king to be found in the inhabited world' to pay for the 'cost of the war', while the 'poverty stricken' Athenian people had to shoulder the burden themselves. 'Consequently, our troops, in view of their generous pay, make war with spirit, while your soldiers, because they pay the war-taxes out of their own pockets, shrink from both the hardships and the costs of war.'[94]

Endius went on, noting that 'when we make war at sea, we risk losing only hulls among resources of the state, while you have on board crews most of whom are citizens'. A defeat at sea would hurt Sparta far less than it would Athens. 'Even if we meet defeat in our actions at sea, we still maintain without dispute the mastery on land … but you, if you are driven from the sea, contend not for the supremacy on land, but for survival.' This was a cogent analysis of the far more severe consequences facing Athens if it met with defeat at sea than that which would accrue to Sparta. Endius assured his audience that while the Spartans were not benefiting from the war, they were 'suffering less than the Athenians'. He urged them to agree to peace, saying: 'Only fools find satisfaction in sharing the misfortunes of their enemies, when it is in their power to make no trial whatsoever of misfortune.'[95]

Many Athenians were swayed by Endius' words, but those who favoured war, foremost among them Cleophon, argued that the extent of their current military successes against the enemy made peace inadvisable. The Assembly voted against peace, but Diodorus writes: '[T]he Athenians after taking this unwise counsel, [later] repented of it when it could do them no good, and deceived as they were by words spoken in flattery, they made a blunder so vital that never again at any time were they able to truly recover.'[96] The Athenians had, once again spurned a chance for peace when offered to them.

The Peloponnesians were in a terrible condition after Cyzicus. A message from Hippocrates, vice-admiral under Mindarus, was intercepted by the Athenians. It read: 'Ships gone, Mindarus dead, men starving, don't know what to do.'[97] Pharnabazus stepped in to reassure them. They were not to lose heart, he pleaded, over timber. They were still alive, and more ships could be built with timber taken from the Great King's lands. To each of the Peloponnesians he gave a cloak and money sufficient to pay for two months' rations. Giving weapons to them, he employed them to protect the coasts of his satrapy. Gathering together the Peloponnesian generals and trierarchs, he had them begin to build replacement ships at Antandrus, giving them money to pay for the construction with wood cut from the slopes of Mount Ida.

In Attica, King Agis was still at Decelea and made a raid against Athens, taking his army right up to the city's walls. Thrasyllus was in Athens at the moment and took out soldiers to meet the Spartans. Agis retreated, and some amongst his rearguard were slain by Athenian light troops. The attack had the effect of convincing Agis that it was pointless for him to have his troops keep the Athenians from farming the land of Attica while grain freighters were able to sail unmolested through the Hellespont. It would be better to send ships to intercept this traffic. Clearchus was despatched to Chalcedon and Byzantium with fifteen troop transports manned by Megarians and other allies. These encountered a small Athenian squadron of nine ships that were shepherding the freighters through the strait, and three were sunk, with the rest escaping to Sestos before continuing on to Byzantium.[98] Among the Athenians, the repulse of the raid inspired them to send reinforcements back to Ionia with Thrasyllus, comprising 1,000 hoplites, 100 cavalry and fifty triremes. Endius, when he had highlighted the personal cost to the Athenians of continued war, had not been exaggerating. The armament that was to sail with Thrasyllus in 409 included, in addition to the ships and troops aforementioned, 5,000 oarsmen equipped as peltasts (javelineers). All told, the entire force would have comprised some 11,100 men, and if they were being paid at the half-rate of three obols per day, which had come into being after the failure of the Sicilian venture, the fifty ships and the soldiers going with them would still have cost the Athenian treasury about thirty talents per month. Additional money would have had to be embarked on the ships to pay the men their salaries for several months thereafter.[99] It should also be borne in mind here that, between Thrasyllus' return to Athens in or before 410 (having been sent back to Athens sometime after the Battle of Abydos in 411) and his expedition to Ionia in 409, about a full year had passed. The reason typically given for the extended delay by modern commentators is that money was so scarce in Athens that much time was required to collect and outfit the reinforcements that eventually sailed with Thrasyllus.

Thrasyllus' expeditionary force sailed to Samos at the start of the summer of 409, and from there began to conduct an assault against Pygela. The Athenians next went to Notium, and then to Colophon, which came over to them. On the following night they raided Lydia, collecting plunder, money and slaves. Thrasyllus' next target was Ephesus, but Tissaphernes foresaw this and sent a strong force of infantry and cavalry to protect it. They met the Athenians advancing on Ephesus and routed them, killing about 400 of their troops. Thrasyllus withdrew his force after this and sailed for Notium, where they buried their dead, and then made for the Hellespont. Anchored off Methymna in Lesbos, the Athenians spotted a squadron of twenty-five Syracusan ships sailing past that had previously been at Ephesus. The Athenians struck, capturing four of the enemy ships and chasing the remainder back into Ephesus. Thrasyllus resumed his voyage north, going to Sestos to link up with the rest of the Athenians in the region, and from there the whole force crossed the Hellespont to Lampsacus.[100] From their base there, the Athenians mounted plundering raids into Persian territory.

Crucially, the Spartans made good use of the diversion of Athenian resources and attention to Asia Minor by launching a campaign to capture Pylos, which was still being held by a Messenian garrison. With six Spartan triremes and five more from Sicily, they landed troops and began a siege. The Athenians sent thirty triremes under the command of Anytus to the rescue, but a storm kept them from rounding Cape Malea, and the fleet went back to Athens. The Messenians held out as best they could, but with aid not now coming, men dying and food growing scarce, they gave up the fort under a truce.[101] Pylos, which had been a thorn in the side of the Spartans since 425, had fallen at last, and the Athenians were deprived of both a secure naval base from which to harry the Peloponnesus and a desirable piece of real estate that could have been traded back to the Spartans as part of a future peace deal.[102] About this time (409), Sparta also sent a new admiral, Cratesippidas, to take command of its fleet. He was despatched with twenty-five ships as reinforcements. Diodorus says that he operated for a while around Ionia 'without accomplishing anything worthy of mention'. He was then given money by the Chian exile community, and with it he was able to put them back in power in Chios.[103]

Alcibiades and Athenian Plundering Expeditions

Lack of funds had an effect on Athens' conduct of operations, which increasingly revolved around getting money and supplies to continue fighting, notwithstanding the inflow of money from the custom house at Chrysopolis. Plundering was an option that the Athenians turned to out of desperation, their prime targets being the Greek states of Asia Minor and the Hellespont region.[104] Alcibiades raided the lands of the Persian satrap Pharnabazus in 410/409 BC against no opposition. He next moved on in 409 to Chalcedon, which had defected from alliance with Athens and had installed a Spartan governor and garrison. Preparing to assault it, he learned that the city's people had sent all of their plunderable property to Bithynia, whose people were friendly, for safekeeping. Alcibiades marched to the border and despatched a herald to the Bithynians holding it. Overawed, they turned it all over to Alcibiades and entered into a treaty of friendship with him too.[105]

Back at Chalcedon, he was building a wall to cut it off when Pharnabazus appeared with troops to lift the siege. Hippocrates, the Spartan governor inside Chalcedon, also brought out his garrison troops, and they attacked in concert. Alcibiades arrayed his troops so that he could fight both enemies at the same time. The Athenians drove off the Persians and smashed the Spartans, slaying many of them, including Hippocrates himself. Alcibiades then sailed to the

Hellespont to collect money from the cities there, and took Selymbria by bluff. He spared the city from a sack on the payment of money and acceptance of a garrison.[106]

Alcibiades returned to Chalcedon, and in exchange for money from Pharnabazus, he agreed to lift the siege. Chalcedon would again become subject to Athens, and Pharnabazus' own satrapy would no longer be raided. With his operations at Chalcedon finished, in winter 409/408 Alcibiades went to Byzantium, where he erected a wall around the city. It had revolted against Athens, but there was a party within that was willing to hand it over on the condition that it not be sacked. Alcibiades made a grand display of weighing anchor and sailed off with all of his ships, letting the Byzantines believe that he had departed for good. He returned quietly at night and brought his troops up to the walls while the fleet attacked the harbour and made a huge clamour. The Byzantines were surprised and distracted by the assault, and this gave the pro-Athenian group the opportunity to let Alcibiades and his troops inside while the fighting raged at the harbour. There were Peloponnesian, Boeotian and Megarian troops inside Byzantium, and these defeated the Athenian ship crews, pushing them back to their ships, but by this time Alcibiades' soldiers were already within, and after a hard fight the Athenians were victorious. Alcibiades was true to his word and spared the city from sack, and no Byzantines were either killed or banished.[107]

Plutarch says that Alcibiades, flush with success, wanted to go home to Athens, and he sailed back there in the spring of 408 with 'Athenian ships of the line decorated from stem to stern with the shields and trophies of war'. Behind them they towed the prize ships taken and at least 200 figureheads removed from the enemy triremes that his warships had sunk.[108] His return electrified the populace, with large numbers of people coming down to the docks to see his ships, festooned with gilded arms and garlands, pull in. Prominent Athenians, Diodorus says, saw in the exile a 'strong man capable of opposing the people openly and boldly, while the poor had assumed that they would have in him an excellent supporter who would recklessly throw the city into confusion and relieve their destitute condition'. Alcibiades was, in other words, all things to all people, and they believed that his return boded well for Athens.[109]

The tearfully joyful people of Athens, Plutarch writes, wished that they had kept Alcibiades in command, and perhaps then they would have avoided the great catastrophe in Sicily. He had taken up the Athenian cause once more while still an exile, and finding 'Athens all but driven from the seas, while on land she was mistress of little more than the ground the city stood on … he had raised her up again, and not merely restored her dominion over the seas, but made her victorious over her enemies everywhere on land'.[110]

Alcibiades' confiscated property was restored; the stelae upon which his sentence and other acts had been inscribed were tossed into the sea; the curse set upon him was revoked; and he was made the supreme commander of all Athenian land and sea forces. He continued with his piratical raids in search of booty. He took 100 triremes and sailed for Andros, where he seized Gaurium and made it into a stronghold. The Andrians and Peloponnesians garrisoning the city emerged to do battle with him, and were defeated, but Alcibiades' subsequent attempts to take the city failed. He left behind a garrison to hold the fort at Gaurium and sailed on to Cos and Rhodes, both of which he plundered for loot with which to support his forces.[111] Another operation saw an Athenian flotilla of fifteen triremes under Thrasybulus make a landing at Thasos. He defeated its army, forced it to accept back pro-Athenian exiles and placed a garrison in it. Thrasybulus sailed next to Abdera, which he brought over to the side of Athens.[112]

After their pummelling at Cyzicus, the Peloponnesians had been largely quiescent at sea for two years. Now the Spartans decided to try to make another effort, choosing Lysander as their admiral in late 408 to succeed Cratesippidas. Diodorus writes that he was 'a man who was believed to excel all others in skill as a general and who possessed a daring that was ready to meet every situation'. He raised another fleet, collecting as many oarsmen from the Peloponnesus as he could. He sailed to Rhodes and added its ships to his fleet, and from there sailed to Ephesus and Miletus. With the ships of these cities, and those of Chios, he gathered at Ephesus a force of about seventy triremes. The 17-year-old Prince Cyrus the Younger, son of the Persian Great King Darius II, having been appointed in 408 as the commander of Persian forces in the maritime satrapies, arrived there with money in 407, and gave to Lysander 10,000 darics to pay his troops. Xenophon reports that Cyrus told Lysander that he had 500 talents on hand to pay for the war effort, and if more were to be needed he would delve into his private funds, pledging to 'mint coins using the throne on which he sat', which was significant as it was 'made entirely of silver and gold'. The young prince told the Spartan not to hesitate to ask for more money in the future. Lysander and other Spartans with him are said to have asked the prince for some more money just then, so that he could afford to pay one drachma per day to each of their crewmen.

Doing so, the Spartans said, would lure away many of Athens' rowers to their side, and so Persia would spend less money altogether since the war would be over faster. This the prince would not do, since the treaty between Persia and Sparta called for the payment of thirty minae, or a half-talent, to pay for the upkeep of one trireme. Lysander persisted, and at dinner that evening Cyrus asked him what he could do to 'please him most'. Lysander quickly replied: 'You could add one obol to the [daily] pay for each sailor.' Cyrus agreed, and so now the crewmen of the Peloponnesian fleet were better paid, if only slightly, than those of Athens, with Plutarch writing that because of this pay raise 'he all but emptied the Athenians' ships' of oarsmen.[113] Cyrus also undertook to pay the wages of the Peloponnesian seamen that had fallen into arrears, and gave them a month's advance too.

Cyrus' openhandedness with money stands in stark contrast to the penny-pinching ways of Tissaphernes. Like Tissaphernes, Cyrus would never bring up the fleet from Phoenicia, probably because he was unable to do so, but otherwise he was ready and willing to help the Spartans however he could. He also spent much of his own personal money on the Peloponnesian fleet over and above the funds he had received from his government. He was not being altruistic. The real reason for his desire to defeat Athens had its roots in Persian dynastic politics. Cyrus' father had another son, older than Cyrus, who had been born prior to the Great King's accession to the throne. Cyrus, though younger, had thus been born royal, and he believed that his claim to kingship was therefore superior, but he anticipated that he would not be named as heir. The teenage prince was already thinking ahead to the day when he would have to march inland and challenge his brother for the throne. When this day came, he would need thousands of Greek hoplites, the finest heavy infantry to be had, to form the hard core of his army of rebellion. He was also aware that the Spartans had the reputation of being the toughest soldiers among the Greeks, and wanted them especially for his army. Only a prompt end to the war would release Spartan and other Greek soldiery from their current duties and make them available for hire by Cyrus.[114] When taken in conjunction with the shift in Spartan naval operations to the Hellespontine area, in effect since 411, Cyrus' eagerness to subsidize the Peloponnesian navy meant that a large, powerful and well-funded enemy fleet now threatened Athens' Black Sea lifeline to a greater degree than ever before.

Lysander continued to build up his fleet in this period. To the leading men of the allied cities, Lysander said that he promised that if his venture was successful, he would put them in control of their own cities. So each of them had a motive to do his utmost to help Lysander, and in this way the crafty Spartan collected all of the military equipment he needed and amassed a fleet of ninety triremes at Ephesus.[115]

When Alcibiades heard of Lysander's preparations at Ephesus, he sailed against it (the year was now 406) with his entire fleet. No ships emerged to challenge him as he waited outside its harbours; he had his ships drop their anchors at Notium, leaving them under the command of his personal helmsman, or *kybernetes*, Antiochus, with specific orders not to give battle until he returned. Alcibiades hurried off with his troop-triremes to Athenian-allied Clazomenae, which was under attack from some of its own exiles. Antiochus, whom Diodorus calls 'an impetuous man … eager to accomplish some brilliant deed on his own account', immediately forgot his orders and took ten of his best triremes out against the enemy, with the intent of drawing the Spartans into battle. His remaining captains were told to be prepared to do battle if the Spartans responded. Lysander had been informed by deserters that Alcibiades himself was elsewhere, along with his best troops, and decided that he would go on the offensive. Lysander's ships rowed out to meet the Athenian vanguard, sinking the lead ship that Antiochus was on and putting the rest to flight. The other Athenian trireme captains hastily got their own crews aboard their ships and came to help, but they were disordered by the rush and were utterly unready for battle. They paid for their lack of formation, losing twenty-two ships. If there was a silver lining it was only that most of the crews of these vessels were able to make their escape by swimming to shore. Alcibiades came back to Notium once he had heard of the debacle, got his ships together and again placed them off Ephesus, hoping that Lysander would once more come out to fight. Lysander was pleased with his accomplishment, and stayed put. With no one to fight, Alcibiades withdrew his fleet to Samos.[116]

Xenophon's account of the action at Notium differs from that of Diodorus in that Antiochus is said to have taken only two triremes, his own and another, and, much more provocatively, sailed right into the harbour of Ephesus, where 'he passed by the very prows of the ships of Lysander'.[117] Lysander responded to the challenge by getting a few of his own triremes into action, and this was followed by the arrival of more Athenian triremes that came to the assistance of Antiochus. Lysander then ordered the whole of his fleet to be manned and put to sea, which turned into a general engagement between both fleets, with the Athenians losing fifteen ships.[118]

The Oxyrhynchus historian may add a small but interesting insight on the understanding of the battle as set forth by Diodorus and Xenophon. In his telling, which Diodorus appears to largely follow, Antiochus conceived a plan to use his ten fastest triremes to draw the Peloponnesian fleet out of harbour by sailing for Ephesus, while the rest of the Athenian fleet, as per the plan, was to keep watch and then spring into action once the Peloponnesians had taken the bait and sailed out after the squadron of ten ships. This they did, but they were nonetheless set upon more quickly, it seems, than they had expected, and they could not get all of their triremes crewed before contact was made with Lysander's warships, and the ones that did make it out were not in formation for battle.[119]

There is a lacuna in this particular Oxyrhynchus fragment which suggests that Antiochus had sought initially to engage three Peloponnesian triremes by enticing them into battle. These three ships may have formed a small reconnaissance squadron that Lysander routinely sortied to keep tabs on the Athenian fleet and its state of readiness. Antiochus may have tried some sort of gambit to get these ships to come out to fight by baiting them with just two ships, which would then be set upon by the remaining eight ships of his squadron. This plan went awry and led to the general engagement in which the Athenians were worsted.

The two variant traditions concerning this fight, that of Xenophon, followed by Plutarch, and Diodorus, who follows the Oxyrhynchus historian, agree that Alcibiades had forbidden Antiochus from doing battle. So Antiochus was operating against his commander's direct orders whatever spin that we may wish to place on the reasoning behind his actions. Further, if the Athenian fleet had been alerted by Antiochus to be ready to launch their ships in case Lysander came out to fight, they were inexcusably slow to get moving once the Peloponnesian fleet had sortied in full strength. Indeed, Lysander seems to have been waiting for an opportunity to take on the Athenian fleet while Alcibiades was away from the scene. Knowing that Alcibiades was temporarily out of the picture, Lysander, Diodorus says, 'hoped to strike a blow worthy of Sparta'.[120] How else to explain the speed with which the Peloponnesian seamen launched their ships in pursuit of the overconfident Antiochus, except that Lysander was waiting for just such a moment to go on the offensive?[121]

Defeated, Alcibiades unwisely pushed his luck when he moved against Cyme. Cyme was an Athenian ally, but Alcibiades, Diodorus says, 'hurled false charges against the Cymaeans, since he wished to have an excuse for plundering their territory'. But his operation against them turned disastrous when the Cymaeans surprised Alcibiades' troops and forced them to take refuge with their ships. The Cymaeans sent a delegation to Athens to protest Alcibiades' actions against a loyal ally. Their charges against Alcibiades were heard, along with others brought by some of his own soldiers at Samos, who disliked him, and his star again began to wane. The contingent from Samos alleged that Alcibiades was sympathetic to the Spartan cause and on overly good terms with Pharnabazus. They charged that after the war was over Alcibiades planned to 'lord it over his fellow citizens'.[122]

The fickle Athenians were discontented with Alcibiades because of the humiliating outcome of the Battle of Notium, and now felt his daring to be a defect, where it had once been seen as a good thing in the man. Plutarch believed that it was Alcibiades' prior achievements that hurt him most. '[I]f ever there was a man destroyed by his own high reputation it was Alcibiades. His repeated successes had built him up into such a prodigy of audacity and intelligence that any failure was put down to a lack of will to succeed.' The Athenian people expected so much from him that they became irritated that he did not achieve everything all at once. 'In particular,' Plutarch wrote, 'they never stopped to consider his lack of money. He was fighting men whose paymaster was the king of Persia, and it was this fact which repeatedly forced him to leave his headquarters and sail off to look for money and rations for his men.' Plutarch assessed the problem facing Alcibiades correctly. Without money he could not keep his ships adequately manned, and this unceasing need to secure funds warped his strategic planning to the point that he could not always remain with his fleet as he should have.[123]

Alcibiades was stripped of his command and a new board of ten generals elected in his place. Finding no support among his troops, Alcibiades departed in a single trireme and went to his private stronghold in the Chersonese. The activities of his successor as admiral of the fleet, Konon, were not much different, since he was burdened just as Alcibiades had been by the constant need to collect money for his crews. Conon found the fleet at Samos unhappy, and he fitted out seventy triremes from of the 100 or so that he found there, presumably removing worn-out ships from service, or perhaps because he lacked enough rowers to crew them all. With these he conducted raids against enemy lands.[124]

Despite his great success against the Athenians, Lysander was replaced after his term in command was up, as was Spartan custom.

When Callicratidas, his successor, met him at Ephesus, Lysander told him that he was handing over the fleet as 'master of the sea' and as a man who had defeated the enemy in a naval battle. Callicratidas responded by saying that if Lysander should first sail to Miletus, where the Athenian fleet was anchored, and give over his warships there, then he would agree that Lysander was a master of the sea. Lysander thought better of accepting the challenge, saying that he would not do such a thing while Callicratidas was in command. The new navarch took the ships from Lysander and fitted out a further fifty with crews from Chios and Rhodes. Altogether, with ships from the allies, he assembled a fleet of 140 triremes.[125]

But it was now the Spartans' turn to run into money troubles. Lysander may have even given back some of the money previously disbursed by Cyrus simply to hinder Callicratidas. Prince Cyrus was much less generous bankrolling the Peloponnesian fleet with his good friend Lysander gone, and told Callicratidas to wait for two days to see him. Disgusted by his meeting with the prince being repeatedly postponed, and also by the need for Greeks to go to a 'barbarian' to ask for money, Callicratidas sent ships back to Sparta to obtain it, and promised that if he ever returned he would do whatever he could to bring about a reconciliation between Athens and Sparta. He also faced dissension within his command. There were friends of Lysander still serving with the fleet, and these men were outspoken with the allies about their belief that it had been a mistake for Sparta to replace Lysander with another man as admiral. Callicratidas acted quickly to end the dissent, and called together a meeting of the Spartans with the fleet. If there were any, he said, who were more experienced with naval matters than he, then he would step aside. Should he not, he asked them, obey the commands of Sparta to command the fleet? Should he stay on as admiral, he wondered, or go back home to make his report on the state of affairs in Ephesus? The other men present, stunned and ashamed, could only answer that he should stay and remain in command.[126]

Still needing money, Callicratidas went to the Milesians for it. From them he received a grant, and private contrbutions too, and from Chios he obtained enough to pay each of his crewmen five drachmae. He sailed then to Methymna in Lesbos, which was allied to Athens and had an Athenian garrison in the city. They would not switch their allegiance to Sparta, and Callicratidas took the place by assault. The Spartans collected the booty they could, but Callicratidas refused categorically to sell any of the Methymnaians into slavery, saying that 'while he was commander, not one of the Hellenes would be enslaved if he had anything to do with it'. The Athenians he captured in the city, though of course Hellenes too, were not so fortunate, and them he sold as slaves. Full of confidence, he sent a message to Conon that soon 'he would put an end to his illicit love affair with the sea', a pointed statement meaning that the sea belonged now to Sparta, and not Athens.[127]

Action off Mytilene

Conon arrived too late to be of assistance at Methymna, and anchored his fleet of seventy triremes in the Hundred Isles. Of these ships, Diodorus says that they had been 'fitted out with everything necessary for making war at sea more carefully than any other general had ever done by way of preparation'. At dawn he saw the Peloponnesian fleet of some 140 ships approaching, and not wanting to face a force twice his size, he retreated from the Hundred Isles, hoping to draw a portion of the enemy fleet away so that he could attack them off Mytilene in Lesbos. This would allow him to give chase to the Peloponnesian ships if he should be successful, and if things went badly he could find shelter in the friendly harbour of Mytilene.[128]

Conon had his oarsmen row at a sedate pace so that the Peloponnesians would believe that they had a chance to catch them. The Spartans took the bait, and their fastest ships hurried to overtake the rearmost Athenian triremes. But this exertion depleted their rowers while at the same time taking them far away from the trailing ships of the main part of the Peloponnesian fleet. Just off Mytilene, Conon raised a red banner on his ship, giving the signal for his captains to turn about and attack. The Athenian crews began to sing their battle song, and trumpets blared. The Peloponnesians were out of formation, so incautiously had they pursued the Athenians. Conon's ships struck them ferociously, while they were in no semblance of order, ramming ships and smashing oars. The Peloponnesians fought back, steadfastly refusing to flee. They backed water long enough to give the rest of their fleet time to come up to their aid. Seeing that he would soon be outnumbered, Conon withdrew to the safety of Mytilene with forty of his triremes, but on the Athenian left wing, matters had soured. The Athenians had driven off the enemy ships opposite them, but had unwisely set off in pursuit. They found themselves surrounded and cut off from Mytilene when the bulk of the Peloponnesian ships arrived in support. The crews abandoned their ships on the beach and then fled on foot to Mytilene.[129]

Callicratidas had inflicted a heavy defeat on the enemy, taking thirty ships despite his fleet having been caught out of formation at the outset of the engagement. Conon was holed up in Mytilene with his remaining triremes, and a siege ensued. Conon sank small craft in the shallower parts of the harbour, and above deeper spots he anchored merchantmen 'armed with stones'. Callicratidas came up with his fleet, put his troops ashore and made camp. With his best ships he led an assault on the harbour entrance to break through the barrier placed there by the Athenians. Conon put some of his soldiers on triremes, and placed these ships before the openings within the barrier, their prows facing outward. The Peloponnesians advanced in a large mass against the harbour and Conon brought his own triremes into the fight. A ferocious ship-to-ship action ensued, with the ships colliding at their prows and marines leaping from one ship to another to fight in close combat. From the yardarms of the merchantmen, Athenian soldiers tossed stones down upon the enemy triremes. Other troops guarding the harbour's breakwaters prevented the Peloponnesians from making a landing on them. The stones thrown by the Athenians took a heavy toll on the Peloponnesian warships, but Callicratidas at last succeeded in pushing his way through the barriers at the harbour entrance. He brought his ships inside and began a siege of the city.[130]

Conon required aid from Athens quickly to survive the siege. He outfitted his two fastest triremes with his best oarsmen from his fleet and despatched them to get help. One sailed toward the Hellespont, while the other raced for the open sea. Conon had timed their departure for when the Peloponnesian crews in the blockading force were ashore taking their meals and not particularly vigilant. It took them a while to get back aboard their ships to pursue the running Athenian triremes. They chased after and caught the ship that had made for the open sea and took it after a fight, but the one that had headed for the Hellespont escaped and brought word of Conon's plight to Athens.[131]

While the Athenian sailors were making their report in Athens, a squadron of twelve Athenian ships under Diomedon arrived at Mytilene, but this force was roughly handled by Callicratidas, who captured ten of the enemy triremes. Diomedon escaped with the remaining two ships. Back at Athens, the Assembly voted to outfit a rescue fleet of 110 ships. Every man whom they could put aboard, whether free or slave, was given a place in the crews. Xenophon notes that even some of the 'Knights', members of Athens' wealthiest class of citizens who would ordinarily serve as cavalrymen, went aboard. Together with the military recruitment of slaves, this demonstrated that the city was suffering severe manpower problems at a time of dire emergency. Diodorus relates that the metics and foreigners in Athens were given citizenship if they were willing to fight. This force was readied for war in thirty days, and it sailed out to Samos to pick up ten Samian ships. Over thirty more ships were supplied by the allies, bringing its total to a little above 150 triremes.[132]

Callicratidas sailed against this force with 120 of his own triremes, leaving behind fifty others under the command of Eteonicus to keep up the blockade of Conon at Mytilene. He put in at Cape Malea on Lesbos so that his men could take their meals. At the same time the Athenians were taking their own meals in the Arginusae Islands not far distant. Callicratidas could see their campfires from where his own ships were bivouacked, and attempted a night raid against them to catch them by surprise, but this was foiled by heavy rainfall and a thunderstorm.

Battle of Arginusae

The next morning, Callicratidas put his ships to sea again and sailed for the Arginusae Islands. Diodorus reports that the pre-battle omens had been especially bad for Callicratidas, and the Spartans' seer would not approve giving battle on that day. The head of the victim was covered by the inrushing waves as it lay upon the beach, and this, the seer predicted, meant that the admiral of the fleet, Callicratidas, would die in the battle that day. Callicratidas would not be dissuaded from going out to fight. 'If I die in the fight,' he said stoically, and very much in keeping with the proud traditions of his homeland, 'I shall not have lessened the fame of Sparta.'[133] To his men, Callicratidas spoke to encourage them just before fighting: 'So eager am I myself to enter battle for my country that, although the seer declares that the victims foretell victory for you but death for me, I am nonetheless ready to die.' Since it was common for forces to be tossed into confusion by the deaths of their commanding officers, he told them, he had taken the precaution of appointing Clearchus to be his successor as admiral if he should fall.[134]

The Athenian seer had also found ill-omens and forbade battle that day too. The supreme commander of their fleet that morning was Thrasybulus, and he had had a dream during the night that he was in Athens in a theatre, where he and six of the other generals were playing roles in Euripides' *Phoenician Women*, while the competing troupe were performing the *Suppliants*. The result of the competition was a 'Cadmean victory', in which the Athenian generals all died, in the same way as had those who had fought at Thebes. The Athenian seer interpreted this to mean that seven of the generals on the Athenian side would be killed in the battle. Yet because the omen had promised a victory, the generals suppressed any word of their own fates, allowing only it to be known that victory had been foretold.[135]

The Athenians emerged and moved against Callicratidas, with their left wing extending out into the open sea. Though the Athenians were more numerous, their ships were in poorer condition, and in an inversion of the norm that had held for much of the war, their rowers were inferior to those of the Peloponnesians. It is not difficult to see why this was so. The Athenians were desperate to man their rowing benches, and had resorted to enfranchising non-citizens to find bodies for the fleet. They had little or no experience pulling an oar in time. To overcome this skill deficit, they made tactical use of the 1,600 yard-long western Arginusae Island, which was in the centre of the Athenian fleet.[136] On the far left was a fifteen-strong squadron under the command of Aristocrates. Next to him was Diomedon's squadron of fifteen ships. In a second line behind Aristocrates was a squadron of fifteen under Pericles, the illegitimate son of the great statesman of the same name, and behind Diomedon was a further fifteen commanded by Erasinides. To their right was the westernmost Arginusae Island. Directly in front of these were the ten Samian warships, and behind them were ten ships captained by the taxiarchs, a designation relating to the tribes of Athens. Behind the ships of the taxiarchs were three triremes of the fleet commanders and some other allied ships. Altogether there were thirty ships in front of the island in the centre of the line. On the right wing were another four squadrons, each with fifteen triremes, under Protomachus, Thrasyllus, Lysias and Aristogenes, mirroring the deployment of the left, with two in the front and two to the rear.[137] The purpose of the double lines on the wing was to prevent the Peloponnesians from enacting the *diekplous* manoeuvre. With the second line stationed in the rear, it was ready to pounce upon any enemy ship that might break through and try to ram the sterns of the Athenian triremes.

Callicratidas' own helmsman is said to have advised him to forego an attack on the much more numerous Athenians, but the Spartan would hear none of it. It would be a shameful thing to flee, he said.[138] He also seems to have desired a worthy end for himself, now that he had heard the seer foretell his death. He drove his own trireme directly at that of the Athenian general Lysias, which he rammed and sank. Several more he rammed and disabled, and a few others he struck and sheered away their oars, leaving them immobilized. The final trireme he attacked was that of Pericles, which he rammed and holed. The bronze ram was embedded so firmly that the Spartan oarsmen could not get their ship back out again. Pericles' men hurled an 'iron hand' grapnel onto Callicratidas' galley and boarded, killing the entirety of its crew. In the boarding action, Diodorus says, Callicratidas fought 'brilliantly' defending his ship, but in time was overcome by weight of numbers and killed.[139]

The fighting at Arginusae was especially fierce. The ships of both fleets battled with a desperate fury, first in a crowded melee, and then as the battle wore on it devolved into many local combats between small groups of ships. With Callicratidas dead, the Athenian right wing gained the upper hand over the Peloponnesian left. The Spartan ships broke and fled to Chios and Phocaea. All told, Callicratidas' fleet lost nine Spartan triremes, while their allies lost sixty. Athenian losses, pegged by Xenophon at twenty-five triremes, were much lighter, despite the hastiness of their preparations and the inexperience of their crews.[140]

Aftermath at Arginusae

The aftermath of the battle was to have a greater impact on the course of the war than the battle itself. Though victorious, numerous Athenian ships had been wrecked in the fight and many of the seamen aboard were in trouble and in need of rescue. There were also many Athenian corpses floating in the bloodwashed sea, and it was an imperative of Greek religious culture that these too be retrieved for proper burial. Though the Peloponnesian fleet at Arginusae had been trounced, this grim duty was complicated by the nearby presence of fifty enemy triremes under Eteonicus currently besieging Conon at Mytilene. This necessitated that the Athenian fleet not disperse to pick up any survivors, along with the dead, but remain grouped in a body so as to retain its fighting power. The surviving seamen in the stricken ships were not to be abandoned altogether, however. The generals of the Athenian fleet ordered Theramenes and Thrasybulus, who were serving as lower-ranking trierarchs in this engagement, not as generals, to go to their aid. This was the wisest decision that could have been made under the circumstances. But then the weather turned foul and the massive storm that came up prevented the Athenians from either going to the support of Conon at Mytilene or attempting a rescue of the survivors of the battle. Instead they sought safety in Arginusae.[141]

The people of Athens were delighted to hear the news of the victory at Arginusae but aghast at the failure to collect the bodies of the dead. The majority of these would have been ordinary rowers, friends and relatives of lower-class men of the Assembly. It was their kind who had been left to die by the upper-class generals. The Assembly voted to depose all of the generals, with the exception of Conon, Adeimantos and Philocles. Six of them – Pericles, Diomedon, Lysias, Aristocrates, Thrasyllus and Erasinides – returned to Athens, while two others – Protomachus and Aristogenes – Diodorus says, 'fearing the wrath of the populace, sought safety in flight'.[142]

Theramenes and Thrasybulus had arrived back home in Athens before the generals had, and they put the onus for the failure to retrieve the dead on the generals. The generals, upon their return, defended themselves at trial, saying that 'simply because they accuse us ... we will not falsely accuse them by saying they are guilty but, rather, it was the magnitude of the storm that prevented the rescue of the shipwrecked'. They had properly given the job of picking up the survivors and the dead to men, they said, to Theramenes and Thrasybulus, who had previously been generals themselves, and some other competent officers.[143]

Hasty justice prevailed in the trial of the generals. The unhappy people 'gave attention to the accusation and to those who spoke to gratify them, but any who entered a defence they unitedly greeted with clamour and would not allow to speak'.[144] The Assembly voted to find the eight generals guilty. The six who were physically present in Athens were quickly put to death and their property was confiscated. As was often the way with such rushes to judgment, the people, almost as soon as the generals had been executed, had second thoughts, repented of their actions and blamed others in the Assembly for having deceived them. Their reconsideration, however sincere, came too late to save the generals who had won Athens such a signal victory.

The Athenians would come to repent their decision in time, but the damage was done. The sheer bloodymindedness of the Assembly has puzzled and horrified readers ever since. Was the decision an example of radical democracy gone haywire, as it has often been characterized? There can be no doubt that the Assembly, a deliberative body composed of the citizenry, was subject to excesses of passion, and vulnerable to the speechifying of demagogues. It was also prone to wild mood swings, and capable of making great errors when anger overwhelmed reason. The decision to execute the Arginusae generals would seem to be an example of the latter. Not to exonerate the Assembly in any way for its self-defeating and ungrateful decision, it should not be forgotten the genuine religious feelings of the ancient Greeks, and the true horror that they must have felt at the thought that so many bodies had gone unrecovered. But religious scruples can neither explain nor excuse the harsh sentence against generals who had a valid justification of their decision to act as they had. We must not forget that the bulk of the lost drawn from the lower class *thetes*, the 'naval mob', as Aristotle would disparage them in the following century. The men of the Assembly judging the well-born generals would have been the relatives of the poorer citizens who had perished at Arginusae, and an element of class resentment may have influenced the harsh decision imposed on officers who had won such a signal victory for Athens.

After the drubbing at Arginusae, the Peloponnesian fleet had gathered at Chios, and there spent the summer, with the men making do with the food available on the island and farming the land for pay. When winter came, food became scarce, and the men, poorly clad and shoeless, looked upon the friendly city of Chios and saw a rich prize ripe for the taking. Some of them formed a plan to seize it, but this conspiracy was quashed by Eteonicus when he heard about it. To keep the soldiers contented, he went to the Chians and demanded that they hand over money so that his men would stop plotting to take the city for themselves. When presented in this manner, the Chians wisely obeyed, and Eteonicus gave each of his men a month's pay to placate them, pretending that he himself knew nothing of their intentions regarding Chios.[145]

Later in 406 BC, the Chians and the other allies met together at Ephesus in council and made a request to Sparta to reappoint Lysander, the much-admired victor of Notium, as admiral of the fleet. Their plea was supplemented by Cyrus, who also asked for Lysander to take command once more. Spartan law held that the same man should not be navarch more than once, so they sent Lysander out as the deputy to the admiral Arakos, but actual command of the fleet was vested in Lysander.[146]

Battle of Aegospotami

In the following year, 405, Lysander made the voyage to Ephesus, to which he recalled Eteonicus and the ships from Chios. He concentrated all the other ships in the theatre under his command at the city and began to repair them. To augment these older triremes, he had new ones constructed at Antandrus. He also made a request to Cyrus for more money, and Cyrus handed it over, reminding Lysander of just how much had already been delivered to the Spartans by the Great King. The full allotment originally given to Cyrus by his father had already been spent, he told the Spartan, together with additional money, and to prove his point the prince gave Lysander an accounting of all of the money which had been given to previous Spartan admirals. Nevertheless, Cyrus found more funds, and with this money Lysander appointed captains for his ships and paid all of the wages to his men that were in arrears.[147]

While Lysander was busy rebuilding his fleet, and the Athenians were readying their own for battle, Prince Cyrus again sent for Lysander, telling him when he came that his father, the Great King, was sick, and that he was being summoned to his side in far-off Media. Lysander was forbidden to fight a naval battle against the Athenian fleet until he had many more ships ready. There was much more money available, the prince assured the Spartan admiral, and with it the Peloponnesians could build and crew many more triremes. In addition, the tribute due from the cities that were Cyrus' own personal property was assigned to Lysander, along with extra money from his treasury.[148]

It was not bad advice. With Persian financial backing, the Spartan advantage in money could in time be translated into an overwhelming numerical superiority in ships. If Lysander would only wait long enough, he would be able to crush the cash-strapped Athenians at little risk to his own fleet. There was no hurry in seeking out a decisive battle, and Cyrus, cognizant of the tremendous advantage that the full coffers of Persia gave him, understood this.

Lysander made another distribution of pay and then sailed to the Ceramic Gulf in Caria in southwestern Asia Minor. He launched an attack on Cedriae, an Athenian ally, and took the town on the second day. After enslaving the townsfolk, he sailed to Rhodes. At the same time at Samos, the Athenians were conducting their own raids on Persian lands. Their fleet, with Menandros, Tydeus and Cephisodorus picked as generals to supplement the others on hand, moved against Chios and Ephesus in preparation for a naval engagement. Lysander took his fleet north from Rhodes up the Ionian coast to the Hellespont to interdict the Athenian freighters making their passage through the strait and threaten the cities that had bolted from the Peloponnesian alliance. The Athenians were at the same time sailing to Chios, and Lysander moved on to Abydos, where he collected some troops, and with them attacked and sacked Lampsacus. The Athenians, with their 180 ships, had followed after Lysander's ships but missed them. When they were moored at Elaeus, they learned of the fall of Lampsacus while the crewmen were disembarked and having their breakfast. Getting back aboard ship, they sailed to Sestos, took on supplies, and next sailed to Aegospotami on the European side of the strait, just across from Lampsacus on the Asian side. For the Athenians, the seizure of Lampsacus was a mortal threat, as a large and powerful Peloponnesian fleet was now situated at the chokepoint of their maritime food supply.

The two fleets waited through the night, and before sunrise, Lysander ordered his men to have their breakfast and board their ships. He erected screens aboard his triremes as defences against missiles, but told his men not to move from where their ships had been positioned or take to the sea. The Athenian fleet came up in challenge, forming a line of battle, but the Peloponnesians would not come out to fight, and with the sun setting, the Athenians turned back. Lysander ordered a few of his fastest ships to tail the Athenians back to Aegospotami, where they had made their encampment, and find out what they did when they got there. His own sailors he kept aboard his triremes, and only let his men get off and eat when the reconnaissance ships had come back. For four days this sequence of events played out again and again, with the Athenians on each day sailing close to Lamspacus to fight and Lysander declining to accept their challenge.[149]

There was one important observer to these goings-on who could have made a difference had he been in command of the Athenian fleet. Alcibiades, Xenophon reports, had been keeping watch over all that had been happening between the rival fleets. He immediately saw that Aegospotami, which was not much more than a beach, was an unacceptable place at which to station the Athenian ships, since there was no port nearby. The Athenians were forced to bring in their supplies from Sestos, which was roughly 12 miles distant, making it a logistical nightmare to try to provision the crews of 180 triremes – some 36,000 men – from a town so far away. Alcibiades pointed this out to the generals in command of the fleet and advised them to make their base instead at Sestos, which had a port and a city where supplies could be readily obtained. From a base at Sestos, he told the generals, they could 'fight a sea battle at any time of your own choosing'. Alcibiades warned the generals of another danger. Their crews, he criticized, were being allowed to wander about far from their camp, not even keeping a watch on the enemy, while the Peloponnesians exhibited much more discipline, and were 'trained to obey any order in silence at the word of one man'.[150] In an emergency it would take time to get these men back aboard their ships and at the oar.

This wise counsel, from one of the best commanders Athens had produced, was rejected outright by the Athenian generals, who reminded Alcibiades that they were in command of the fleet, not him. Tydeus was especially insulting, and told him to leave. So Alcibiades left the Athenian encampment, now thinking that some treachery was being planned. As he walked away, he told his friends that if he had not been so ill-treated he would in a few days have either destroyed the Peloponnesian fleet or compelled them to fight a naval battle on terms not of their own choosing. Alcibiades was right about the deficiencies of the Athenian position, and he also had a large body of Thracian mercenary peltasts under his personal command, together with some cavalry, and these could have caused chaos in the Peloponnesian encampment if they had attacked from the land. His intervention might well have proved decisive for the Athenians had they listened to him and been more considerate of his feelings.[151] Diodorus, interestingly, believes that the reason the Athenian generals turned down Alcibiades' offer of help was that if they won, the credit would all belong to Alcibiades, while if they lost, the blame for the defeat would accrue to themselves.[152]

On the fifth day of the stand-off, the Athenians came out once more, and then went back to Aegospotami again without fighting. Lysander again ordered ships to follow behind them to ascertain when the Athenian crews had disembarked from their ships. The Athenians had lost some respect for the enemy because of his continued refusal to fight, and with each passing day had begun to scatter ever more about the Chersonese in search of food.[153] The food problem seems to have become acute, as, according to Diodorus, the Athenians began to experience famine in their camp.[154] Lysander's scout ships once more waited for the enemy crewmen to get out of their ships and walk away, signalling to Lysander when this happened. Lysander gave the order for his own ships to row at full speed across the strait and attack the Athenian triremes that had been hauled onto the beach. In horror, Conon saw the Peloponnesians approaching, and signalled to his men to hurry back aboard their ships, but these were too widely dispersed to make it back in time and many of their ships lacked full complements of oarsmen when they put to sea, with some having rowers at only two levels and others having oarsmen at just one. Plutarch places the blame for the chaos in the Athenian camp squarely on the generals: '[B]ecause of their commanders' inexperience [the seamen] were utterly unaware of what was about to happen.'[155] Of the 180 triremes in the Athenian fleet, just nine, including Conon's flagship and the

Athenian state galley *Paralus*, managed to get underway with a full complement of rowers. What ensued was not a battle, it was a fiasco. Almost the entirety of the Athenian fleet was caught and captured on the beach, together with most of the foot soldiers.[156]

Diodorus has the battle unfolding in a very different manner. He relates that, with hunger gnawing at the Athenian fleet, Philocles, who was the commanding general on the day of the battle, sortied with thirty ships. He had in the meantime given orders to the rest of the fleet to ready itself and follow him. Lysander then pounced on Philocles' advance guard with the whole of his fleet, upon which the Athenians turned and fled. Lysander pursued, and fell on the remainder of the Athenian force which was not yet ready for battle. The Athenian fleet in Diodorus' account was for the most part captured ashore.

It is difficult, if not impossible, to reconcile Diodorus' account of the battle with that of Xeonophon. Xenophon says nothing about Philocles' mission, a glaring omission if it actually occurred. Philocles' sortie with thirty ships seems to have been designed to goad the Peloponnesians to come out to fight, but if that was the intention, then it is hard to see why the rest of their ships were so woefully unready to come to fight beside them if Lysander took the bait. Philocles approach echoes that of Antiochus at Notium, with a smallish force of triremes getting close to a much larger enemy fleet to entice it into battle. At Notium too, the Athenians had trouble getting their men aboard their ships once Lysander had himself taken his own fleet out to fight, and were punished heavily for their tardiness. At Aegospotami, if you believe Diodorus, the Athenians were likewise unprepared. Perhaps the Athenians had been lulled into the belief that Lysander would not emerge to fight no matter what they did, and this could perhaps explain the inability to have their full fleet prepared for battle. If it is believable, and there is little reason to doubt it, that the bulk of the Athenian fleet could have been caught unready at Notium despite a part of the fleet undertaking an action to get the enemy to come out to fight, it is at least plausible then that the same thing could have happened at Aegospotami. It may be that Philocles' ships were precisely those that Xenophon says did sail out on the fifth day. Xenophon seems to imply that it was the whole of the Athenian fleet that had gone out and then went back to its encampment, but it might not have been the whole, just Philocles' squadron. After waiting for it to go back, Lysander then gave the order to sail with his entire fleet against the Athenians. In this scenario, we still have Lysander's warships falling upon the greater part of the Athenian fleet while on the beach at Aegospotami. Yet even here there is a serious discrepancy that is hard to ignore. Diodorus has the Philocles' Athenians and the Peloponnesians engage in some kind of fight while still at sea, ending with the Athenians running away, whereas Xenophon mentions no such thing.

Seeing that all was lost, Conon escaped with his nine ships and made his way to Abarnis, a headland of Lampsacus, where he seized the mainsails of the Peloponnesian fleet that Lysander had left ashore prior to the battle. *Paralus* returned to Athens to inform the people of the defeat, but Conon dared not go home, 'fearing the wrath of the people', and went instead to Cyprus, where its ruler, King Evagoras, sheltered him.[157] Lysander sent news of the great victory to Sparta with Theopompus, a Milesian pirate, who reached the city just two days after the battle. Lysander took the ships, prisoners – which included the generals Philocles and Adeimantus – and booty that he had captured with him to Lampsacus. There he held a council with the allies to discuss what was to be done with the prisoners. Many of the allies favoured extreme harshness, reminding those present of all the ill things the Athenians had done 'contrary to custom and law'.[158] At the instigation of Philocles, the Athenian Assembly had previously voted to cut off the right hands (or thumbs) of those whom they took prisoner, a reprehensible act that now came back to haunt them. In another recounted atrocity, Philocles had tossed overboard the crews of a Corinthian and an Andrian trireme. The Peloponnesians voted to execute all of the Athenian prisoners, with the single exception of Adeimantus, who was known to have argued in the Assembly against the measure to cut off the hands of captured Peloponnesians. Philocles was brought before Lysander, who asked him 'what sort of punishment he thought he deserved for having advised his fellow-countrymen to treat other Greeks so outrageously'. Philocles told Lysander 'not to play the prosecutor in a case where there was no judge, but to deal out as victor exactly the same punishment as he would have suffered had he been defeated'. The bloodthirsty Philocles' throat was slit, and Plutarch says that 3,000 Athenians were put to death along with him.[159]

From Lampsacus, Lysander took his fleet to Byzantium and Chalcedon. Both cities surrendered immediately, with the Athenian garrisons leaving under terms of a truce. Lysander allowed the Athenian garrisons of Byzantium and other cities to sail home to Athens under a safe-conduct pass, but to no other place, his instinct telling him that the more Athenians who returned to the city, the sooner they would consume the provisions on hand there. He then went back to Lampsacus, where he repaired his ships.[160]

In Athens, the news of the catastrophe at Aegospotami initiated a wailing that began at the docks of Piraeus and continued onward via the Long Walls and thence into Athens. In the Assembly the next day, the people voted to repair the walls and put guards on all of them, to block up the harbours except for one and make the city ready for a siege.[161]

With his fleet now numbering 200 triremes, Lysander mopped up the low-hanging fruit first, taking control of the cities of Lesbos, while his subordinate Eteonicus was sent to Thrace with ten triremes to bring its cities over to Sparta. The Athenian Empire went into full-scale revolt once word of the disaster suffered by the Athenians filtered around the Aegean. All of these subject cities rebelled, with the exception of Samos, where the commons had killed the aristocracy and taken over the city. Lysander decided that it was the appropriate time to strike directly at Athens. He sent word to King Agis at Decelea and to the government at Sparta that he was going to sail against the city with his 200 ships. The Spartans and their Peloponnesian allies marched out in force against Athens from the Peloponnesus under Agis' co-king, Pausanias, who brought his army into Attica and encamped in the Academy, which lay a short distance from the city's walls.[162]

Lysander took the island of Aegina back from Athens and returned it to its native inhabitants, who had been expelled by the Athenians in 431. He also restored the people of Melos, so cruelly treated by the Athenians in 416, and other peoples who had been ejected by the imperialistic Athenians. He then raided the island of Salamis, and afterward moored his fleet, now numbering 150 triremes, off Piraeus, which he blockaded.[163]

The Athenians had no idea how to respond. They had no warships left, and famine had come as they had little grain because the Hellespont lifeline to the Black Sea had been severed. They were also without friends, as their allies had all deserted them after their defeat at Aegospotami. Their great worry, at the nadir of their imperial project, was that they would be forced to endure the same dire fate they had visited on so many others in the fullness of their power. They tried bravely to carry on, but when, as Xenophon writes, the 'grain supply was entirely gone', they sent word to King Agis to seek a negotiated peace, asking to keep only the Long Walls and the fortifications around the port of Piraeus. Agis told them to take their request to Sparta, as he did not have the authority to make a treaty with them. Before the Athenian ambassadors had made it to Sparta, and were still in Sellasia, which was near to Laconia, the Spartan government learned of the details of their offer, and told them to go back home and obtain authorization from their own government for a better peace proposal.[164]

In Athens there was much unhappiness with the firm line that the Spartans had taken, and the people believed that they would either be enslaved by the enemy or starve to death while a peace treaty was negotiated. Yet nobody, Xenophon says, would consider tearing down the Long Walls as the Spartans demanded. One man, Archestratus, who believed that peace on such terms was worthwhile, was even hurled into prison for simply suggesting it, and a decree was passed that made debating it impermissible.[165]

Theramenes came forward and addressed the Assembly, saying that he would go to Lysander to find out whether the demand for the destruction of the Long Walls was being made in order to render Athens defenceless, and thus make slaves of them, or if it was being insisted on as demonstration of Athenian good faith. Theramenes, Xenophon says, 'wasted more than three months' with Lysander, 'waiting for the moment when the Athenians would agree to any proposal because their entire supply of grain would have been consumed'.[166] This latter point is confusing, as Xenophon had just stated prior to this that the initial Athenian peace feeler had been put out to Sparta when their grain supply had already dwindled to nothing, so it is unclear if the Athenians were truly reaching the bottom of their food supply or acted out of fear of doing so. Be that as it may, after three months, Theramenes finally returned to Athens and told the Assembly that Lysander had made him wait all that time before informing him that he lacked the authority to negotiate and that the Athenians would have to deal directly with the Spartan government. The Athenians then selected Theramenes and nine other envoys with full powers to go to Sparta to talk peace. The Corinthians, Thebans and many other Greeks who distrusted the Athenians were against any kind of peace deal, and instead wanted the Spartans to crush Athens completely. The Spartans responded to such bloody-mindedness by saying that they would not enslave a city that had done so much good for Greece. Rather, peace would be made on certain conditions. These included the destruction of the Long Walls and the fortifications of Piraeus; the handover of the Athenian fleet but for twelve triremes; that Athenian exiles should be allowed to return to their native city; that Athens would have the same friends and enemies as Sparta; and that Athens would accept the leadership of Sparta whether on land or sea, and accompany the Spartans on campaign whenever so commanded.[167]

Famine was already daily claiming the lives of some of the people at Athens, and on the delegates' return a crowd gathered around them to find out what had transpired. Theramenes went before the Assembly and spoke of the peace terms, saying that there was no choice but to accept them, and the following vote was in favour of peace. Not all could accept the terms, and one young orator of the Assembly, Cleomenes, asked whether Theramenes was willing to undo the work of Themistocles, who decades before had built the walls for protection against the Spartans. Theramenes answered him sternly: 'I am doing nothing, young man, that runs counter to Themistocles' policy: the very same walls that he put up for Athens' security, we shall pull down for her security. If walls ever made cities prosperous, then Sparta would be the worst provided of all, for she has none.'[168]

With the peace terms settled, Lysander appeared with his fleet in the harbour of Piraeus. He called for flute girls, and as they played their music, he tore down the great walls of the city and burned the last ships of the once mighty Athenian navy. Lysander provided Athens with a government more to Spartan tastes, appointing thirty men to rule as an oligarchy over the city. These Thirty, as they became known, would come to rule tyrannically, and would be supported in their efforts by a Spartan garrison provided by Lysander.[169] The war was over.

CONCLUSION

The end of the Peloponnesian War in 404 BC left behind immense wreckage. Athens was prostrate, and the Greek states had spent their blood and treasure in enormous quantities to bring about the destruction of its empire. Though peace had come, happiness was not to be the lot of all of the grand characters that survived the war. Several came to unpleasant ends. Alcibiades would be assassinated shortly after the Athenian surrender on the orders of Sparta while he was living in Asia Minor. Gylippus, hero of the defence of Syracuse, would be disgraced when it came to light that he had skimmed off some of the remainder of Athens' public funds and Lysander's personal treasure for himself before delivering it to Sparta. Gylippus had opened the money-filled sacks at their bottoms and pocketed some of the silver, not realizing that inside, at the tops of the bags, were notes indicating precisely how much money was in each. When his theft was discovered, he was banished.[1]

Lysander himself, intoxicated by success, would become very arrogant in the years following his victory over the Athenians and then fall afoul of Pharnabazus. Lysander's men had carried out raids in the Persian satrap's territory, and Pharnabazus had made a complaint to the Spartan authorities. The ephors issued a recall order and Lysander returned home. Unable to adjust to life in Sparta, he departed the city. Lysander later joined King Agesilaus' expedition to Asia, but would find himself sidelined during operations there. He would be slain fighting the Thebans outside the walls of Haliartus in 395.

Politically, Sparta would prove to be a blunder-prone hegemon. Aristotle would sum up well the root cause of Sparta's imperial misfeasance: '[T]he Spartans always prevailed in war but were destroyed by empire because they did not know how to use the leisure they had won, because they had practised no more fundamental skill than skill in war.'[2] Sparta also never solved the problem of its long-term demographic decline. Though it could call upon non-citizen troops to fill out its armies in the fourth century BC, by 371, Sparta had barely 1,500 full citizens, hardly a stable base upon which to rest the weight of an empire. Spartan aggression would drive the formation of coalitions against them, and in that same year the great Theban general Epaminondas would crush the Spartans at Leuctra and bring an end to the short-lived Spartan imperium after a single generation.

Athens itself would return to democracy after just a year under the unpopular government of the Thirty Tyrants imposed on them by the Spartans. With a rebuilt fleet and repaired walls, it would become a leader of the anti-Spartan coalition of a number of Greek states. In the fourth century BC, it would also restore somewhat her system of alliances.[3] This Second Athenian Empire would not be as tight or lucrative as that of the fifth century, but it is a testament to the underlying strengths and abilities of the Athenians, as well as the maladroitness of the Spartans, that the city was able to recover so much of its former position in Greece.

There can be no doubt that the war had been decided at sea. Athens here had long held the advantage, but it was primarily the financial backing that Persia gave to Sparta that defeated Athens and brought down its empire.[4] Athens' rise to the status of imperial power had been exceptionally fast, and had been predicated upon its role as leader of the anti-Persian coalition and the concomitant agreement between both Athens and the other great power of Greece, Sparta, that the Persians had to be excluded from the Aegean Sea. With Persia out of the picture, and Sparta unconcerned with the sea, Athens had the Aegean to itself and could fashion a profitable maritime empire in a short span out of the Delian League. This was hardly a solid foundation on which to build a long-lived empire as it was vulnerable to a change of mind in Sparta, and when that occurred the Persian absence would prove only temporary. This came about when, as the war dragged on and victory required taking the war to Athens at sea, the Spartans sought Persian gold to subsidize the creation of a navy powerful enough to do battle with the Athenian fleet. Athens could not sustain its seapower indefinitely in the face of an enemy that had access to enough money to continually replace lost oarsmen and ships.[5]

This worst injury suffered by the Athenians was almost certainly self-inflicted. The attack on Syracuse was unnecessary and unjustified, but Athens was able to recover from it. The overweening arrogance that brought it about seems also to have led the Athenians astray in their relations with Persia. If the speech given by Andocides is accurate, and there is no reason to doubt that it is, the Athenians were themselves to blame for its decisive financial intervention. They supported the revolt of the satrap Amorges, for reasons not known, and thereby angered the Great King to such an extent that he was willing to devote vast sums of money to support the Peloponnesian fleet that brought about the fall of the Athenian Empire. Pericles had worried decades before the end that his countrymen would embark on some wild scheme of conquest against Carthage or Etruria, and warned them against such things. He seems to have overlooked that an aroused Persia itself was the greatest threat to Athenian dominion in the Aegean.

Time began to run out for Athens once the war shifted to the Aegean in its later stages. This area had always been the foundation of her imperial power, the region where the bulk of Athens' seaborne empire was to be found, and in particular, the vital maritime link through the Hellespont and Bosphorus to the Black Sea that ran through it. The Spartans recognized the centrality of these places to Athenian commerce, and thus her survival as a city. That it took so long before Athens was brought to her knees reflects both the inexperience of the Spartans in making war at sea and the extraordinary ability of the Athenians to rebuild their own fleet after it was shattered in Sicily. Some of the credit for the restoration of the Athenian position after 413 must go to Alcibiades, whose advice to Tissaphernes, however self-serving it was, spared Athens from having to face a well-funded enemy fleet until much later in the war, when Prince Cyrus replaced Tissaphernes as overseer of Persian aid to the Peloponnesians.

Yet the ordinary Athenian seamen in the fleet were more important than Alcibiades or any of their other generals. They demonstrated time and again that they were the superior rowers, and with them their helmsmen could execute manoeuvres that brought victories at Cynossema, Cyzicus, Abydos and Arginusae. That the Athenian fleet was defeated at Aegospotami was more the result of her generals beaching their triremes too far from good sources of supply, forcing her crewmen to wander far away to find food, which allowed the Peloponnesians to catch them unprepared to fight. The common oarsmen, upon whom the Athenian Empire had so much depended for its creation and its sustenance, hardly figured in the last battle that cost Athens the war.

The laxity of their generals ruined the effectiveness of the fleet on more than one occasion. Nicias may have complained about his seamen in Sicily, but it was his dithering outside Syracuse, especially his decision to bring his fleet inside the Great Harbour and effectively trap it there, that cost him any chance of taking the city. In one instance, in 413, he allowed his men to go off and take their meals while the enemy prepared for another sortie on the same day, leaving his fleet vulnerable to a sudden strike. At Notium in 406, Alcibiades' helmsman Antiochus disobeyed direct orders and engaged the Peloponnesian fleet. Lysander struck back, the Athenian crews that were supposed to come to the rescue were again slow to launch, and the result was a serious defeat for Athens.

Over time, Athens' enemies would narrow somewhat the gap in rowing skill as the quality of Athenians crews declined and their own increased. The Corinthians in particular deduced that to try to match the Athenians in rowing skill was not the best course, and instead sought to reduce the Athenian advantage through the implementation of prow-to-prow ramming using triremes with strengthened bows. This was highly effective at Erineus in 413, and even more so in the Great Harbour later that year. Where the Peloponnesians made the critical advance, however, was in overall command. Lysander in particular kept a tight leash on his men, and was more than a match as an admiral for the various Athenian fleet commanders that he faced. He did not blunder as the board of enemy generals did at Aegospotami, and he was a clever tactician who knew that whatever deficit in skills his seamen had as individuals compared to their Athenian counterparts, it was the aggregate quality of his fleet that mattered more.

Athens could be said to have won the Archidamian War, in the sense that it had outlasted her opponent, just as Pericles had envisioned. Yet Athens was fortunate that Persia did not intervene earlier than it did. It might well have done so, but if the letters from the Great King found on the Persian diplomat Artaphernes in 425 are indicative, the Spartans had no real idea of what kind of assistance they wanted from Persia or what they might be willing to do to obtain it.

In addition to Sparta's muddled diplomacy, Athens also benefited hugely from its blunder in trapping several hundred of its own hoplites on Sphacteria in 425. The accelerating demographic decline experienced by Sparta over the course of the fifth century made it extremely sensitive to the loss of just a relative handful of its citizen soldiers, and this gave Athens the upper hand during the later Archidamian War once it took some of them captive and held them as a surety against further Spartan invasions of Attica.

Athens had thus survived the storm from the Peloponnesus, and with the Peace of Nicias she had demonstrated that she would not be bullied by anyone, even Sparta. But then it made a terrible blunder of its own. The expedition to Sicily was not at all necessary, and was part of Athens' hubristic imperial ambitions, not her immediate security. Syracuse was not a threat to her. As for the specifics of the catastrophe in Sicily, the avoidance of Athenian tactical and operational miscalculations, almost all of which can be laid at the feet of Nicias, would likely not have been enough to secure victory. Nicias made his mistakes, but the great error was to undertake the ill-conceived expedition in the first place, and this was the fault of the Athenian Assembly. Had a stronger fleet been sent, it might have enabled Nicias to withdraw a portion of his ships at a time to let them dry out, and thereby keep a larger number of them in prime, combat-ready condition. But Nicias was also having trouble finding adequate numbers of rowers for his ships, since he was far away in Sicily and Athens failed to ensure that sufficient replacements reached him. A large-scale reinforcement did not come until near to the end, when Demosthenes sailed in with his relieving fleet, but by then it was too late. Though Athens would recover admirably from the bloodbath, and replace her lost ships and men, the defeat in Sicily encouraged her enemies to see her as badly weakened, and to consider and undertake a genuine challenge to her at sea. This was the last thing that Athens needed. Though Athens would fight on long afterward, the combination of Spartan determination and Persian money achieved, in time, the final defeat of Athens and the end of its empire.

NOTES

Part 1: Introduction

1. Thuc. 1.23.6
2. Zagorin, p.23
3. Grant, *Anc. Hist.* pp.115–16
4. Thuc. 1.22.2
5. Thuc. 1.22.4
6. Grant, *Anc. Hist.* p.80
7. Thuc. 1.22.1; Adcock, p.27
8. Grant, *Anc. Hist.* p.125
9. Grant, *Anc. Hist.* pp.131–32
10. Thomas, *The Landmark Xenophon's Hellenika*, xxix, 7.7
11. Thomas, *The Landmark Xenophon's Hellenika*, xxix, 7.2–4
11. Thomas et al., *Citadel* p.63
13. Thomas et al., *Citadel* p.62
14. Green, *Armada* p.359
15. Green, *Armada* p.16
16. Green, *TGPW* p.13
17. DeSantis, 'A Nomad Strategy of Persistence' p.25
18. Green, *Armada* p.30
19. Hdt. 5.102.1
20. Hdt. 5.105.1–2
21. Grant, *Class. Gr.* p.10
22. Hdt. 7.89.1; 7.97.2
23. Plut. *Them.* 4
24. Hdt. 7.144.1–2
25. Meier, *Athens* p.18; Gabrielsen, pp.28, 39; Green, *Armada* p.19
26. Plut. *Them.* 4
27. Plut. *Them.* 4
28. Plut. *Them.* 19
29. Plut. *Them.* 19
30. Kagan, *Pericles* p.80
31. Meier, *Athens* p.289
32. Meier, *Athens* p.300
33. Aris. *Pol.* 1291b24; 1304a 22; *Ath. Pol.* 27.1; Jordan, p.117
34. Cawkwell, p.7
35. Hdt. 8.14.1–2
36. Hdt. 8.17–18
37. Hdt. 7.89.3
38. Hdt. 8.60
39. Hdt. 8.62.2
40. Hdt. 8.86
41. Strauss, *Salamis* p.171
42. Diod. 11.19
43. Bagnall, *TPW* p.100
44. Strauss, *Salamis* p.247
45. McGregor, p.21
46. Thuc. 1.95.7
47. McGregor, p.32
48. McGregor, p.33
49. Thuc. 1.96.1
50. Thuc. 1.98.1–4
51. Plut. *Cim.* 12
52. Thuc. 100.1
53. Plut. *Cim.* 13
54. Meier pp.340–41
55. Thuc. 1.99.1–3
56. Plut. *Cim.* 11
57. Plut. *Cim.* 11
58. Finley, *Econ.* pp.43, 49
59. Finley, *Econ.* pp.51, 60
60. Turchin, p.167
61. Turchin, p.167
62. Plut. *Per.* 18
63. Plut. *Per.* 19
64. Plut. *Per.* 20

65. Plut. *Per.* 21
66. Plut. *Per.* 12
67. Plut. *Per.* 12
68. Kagan, *Outbreak* p.116
69. Kagan, *Outbreak,* p.180
70. Ste. Croix, p.48
71. Kagan, *Outbreak* p.119
72. Plut. *Per.* 11
73. Fields *Anc. Gr. Fort.* p.17
74. Thuc. 1.7.1
75. Fields *Anc. Gr. Fort.* p.17
76. Thuc. 1.93.3–4
77. Plut. *Cim.* 13
78. Fields *Anc. Gr. Fort.* p.19
79. Thuc. 4.51.1
80. Finley, pp.34–35
81. Grant, *Rise of the Greeks* p.98
82. Grant, *Rise of the Greeks* p.92
83. Thuc. 4.55.2
84. Thuc. 1.84.1–2
85. Thuc. 1.84.3
86. Thuc. 1.84.4
87. Woodhead, p.115
88. Thuc. 1.19.1
89. Hdt. 7.234.2
90. Thuc. 5.68; Cartledge, p.264
91. Cartledge, p.264
92. Aris. *Pol.* 1270a29–32; Cartledge, p.263
93. Van Wees, p.110
94. Kagan, *Arch. War* p.21
95. Thuc. 1.10.1–2
96. Cartledge, p.142
97. Grant, *Rise of the Greeks* p.97
98. Forrest, p.39
99. Lendon, *Song* p.59–60
100. Thuc. 1.101.3
101. Thuc. 1.102.3
102. Thuc. 1.105.2
103. Thuc. 1.105.5
104. Sealey, 270–71
105. Thuc. 1.108.3–4
106. Thuc. 1.110.4
107. Thuc. 1.103.4
108. Hdt. 8.94.1–4
109. Bury, 379
110. Plut. *Per.* 25
111. Thuc. 1.115.3–5
112. Thuc. 1.116.2
113. Thuc. 1.117.1–3

Part 2: The Trireme

1. Green, *Armada* p.359
2. Plut. *Per.* 20
3. Plut. *Per.* 11
4. Thuc. 3.115.4
5. Thuc. 1.13.2
6. Thuc. 1.13.5
7. Clem. *Stromateis* 1.16.76; Wallinga, p.48; Hdt. 1.166.2
8. Thuc. 1.14.2
9. Morrison et al., *Ath. Tri.* p.133
10. Blackman, p.227
11. Casson, pp.201–02
12. Morrison et al., *Ath. Tri.* 180
13. Morrison et al., *Ath. Tri.* 182
14. Casson, 211
15. Delgado, p.44
16. Delgado, pp.43–44
17. Coates, 'The Naval Architecture and Oar Systems of Ancient Galleys' pp.133–34
18. Thuc. 7.40
19. Morrison et al., *Ath. Tri.* pp.236–37
20. Thuc. 2.93.3
21. Blackman, p.227
22. Blackman, p.225
23. Casson, p.93
24. Morrison et al., *Ath. Tri.* p.156
25. Casson, p.93
26. Thuc. 2.56
27. Hale, pp.24–25
28. Casson, p.90, n. 68
29. Rodgers, p.10
30. Rodgers, p.10
31. Morrison et al., *Ath. Tri.* p.110

32. Thuc. 3.98
33. Thuc. 2.86
34. Thuc. 2.89
35. Plut. *Alc.* 36
36. Morrison et al., *Ath. Tri.* p.256
37. Thuc. 3.17
38. De Souza, *The Peloponnesian War* p.44
39. De Souza, *The Peloponnesian War* p.69
40. Gabrielsen, p.108
41. Thuc. 6.8
42. Morrison et al., *Ath. Tri.* p.119
43. Thuc. 8.45
44. Thuc. 1.121.3
45. Thuc. 1.143.1–2
46. Meiggs, p.439
47. Gabrielsen, p.78
48. Gabrielsen, pp.6–7
49. Gabrielsen, p.79
50. Gabrielsen, pp.227–28
51. Gabrielsen, p.39; Jordan, p.145
52. Jordan, p.117
53. Thuc. 6.44
54. Casson, p.91; Hale, p.25
55. Morrison et al., *Ath. Tri.* pp.235, 264
56. Morrison, 'The Trireme' pp.57–59
57. Coates, p.127

Part 3: The Archidamian War

1. Rodgers, pp.121–22
2. Thuc. 1.25.1–4; 1.26.1
3. Thuc. 1.27.2
4. Thuc. 1.29.1–5
5. Thuc. 1.33.2–3
6. Thuc. 1.36.3
7. Thuc. 1.42.3
8. Thuc. 1.44.1–2
9. Thuc. 1.45.3
10. Thuc. 1.49.1–3
11. Thuc. 1.50.1–5; 1.51.1–2
12. Thuc. 1.52.1–3
13. Thuc. 1.53.1–4
14. Rodgers, p.125
15. Plut. *Per.* 29
16. Thuc. 1.69.1
17. Thuc. 1.80.3
18. Thuc, 1.81.3–4
19. Thuc. 1.87.3
20. Thuc. 1.118.3
21. Thuc. 1.121.3–4
22. Thuc. 1.124.3
23. Lazenby, pp.18–19
24. Thuc. 1.140.2
25. Thuc.1.140.5
26. Lendon, p.103
27. Thuc. 1.141.5
28. Thuc. 1.141.6
29. Thuc. 1.142.5–7
30. Thuc. 1.142.9
31. Thuc. 1.143.5
32. Thuc. 1.144.1
33. Plut. *Per.* 8
34. Kagan, *Thuc.* p.78
35. Cawkwell, p.44
36. Thuc. 1.82.1; 2.7.1
37. Cook, p.79
38. Thuc. 1.145.1
39. Plut. *Per.* 29
40. Plut. *Per.* 30
41. Thuc. 7.18.2
42. Thuc. 2.7.2
43. Thuc. 2.8.5
44. Thuc. 2.8.1
45. Thuc. 2.9.4–5
46. Thuc. 2.9.2–3
47. Thuc. 2.13.3–5
48. Thuc. 2.13.8
49. Thuc. 2.24.1–2
50. Gabrielsen, *Financing* p.126; Kagan, *Arch. War* p.26 n. 38
51. Kagan, *Arch. War* p.37
52. Thuc. 2.25.1–5; 2.26.1–2

53. Lazenby, p.37
54. Thuc. 2.16.2
55. Kagan, *The Peloponnesian War* p.69
56. Hanson, pp.36–37
57. Thuc. 2.47.3
58. Thuc. 2.49.2
59. Thuc. 2.49.3–6
60. McNeill, p.120
61. Rhodes, p.8
62. Lazenby, p.38
63. Plut. *Per.* 34
64. Thuc. 2.54.2
65. Plut. *Per.* 35
66. Plut. *Per.* 35
67. Thuc. 2.56.1–2
68. Thuc. 1.142.4
69. Plut. *Per.* 35; Lazenby, p.39
70. Thuc. 2.59.2
71. Thuc. 2.62.2
72. Thuc. 2.62.3–4
73. Thuc. 2.63.1–2
74. Thuc. 2.65.7
75. Kagan, *Arch. War* pp.93–94
76. Thuc. 2.66.1–2
77. Lazenby, p.40
78. Plut. *Per.* 38
79. Thuc. 2.80.1–4
80. Thuc. 2.83.3
81. Thuc. 2.83.4–5
82. Thuc. 2.84.1–2
83. Thuc. 2.84.3
84. Thuc. 2.84.3
85. Thuc. 2.87.7
86. Thuc. 2.89.8
87. Thuc. 2.89.10–11
88. Thuc. 2.91.3–4
89. Thuc. 2.92.3
90. Thuc. 2.92.7
91. Thuc. 2.103.1
92. Lazenby, p.48
93. Rodgers, p.136
94. Rodgers, p.180
95. Kagan, *Arch. War* p.115
96. Kagan, *Arch. War* p.114
97. Thuc. 2.85
98. Hale, pp.114–15
99. Thuc. 2.93.3
100. Thuc. 2.93.4
101. Lendon, 165–6
102. Lendon, 166
103. Thuc. 3.2.3
104. Thuc. 3.4.1–5
105. Thuc. 3.15.2
106. Thuc. 3.17.1–2
107. Meiggs, p.315
108. Thuc. 3.19.1
109. Thuc. 3.31.1
110. Thuc. 3.69.1
111. Thuc. 3.78.1–3
112. Thuc. 3.98.4
113. Thuc. 3.91.1–6
114. Thuc. 3.87.1–3
115. Thuc. 3.115.4; 4.1.1
116. Thuc. 4.4.1–3; 4.5.2
117. Thuc. 4.8.6
118. Thuc. 4.10.5
119. Thuc. 4.11.3
120. Thuc. 4.13.1
121. Thuc. 4.14.1
122. Thuc. 4.14.3–4
123. Thuc. 4.16.1–2
124. Thuc. 4.21.2–3; 4.22.3
125. Thuc. 4.27.1
126. Thuc. 4.28.4
127. Thuc. 4.38.3–5
128. Thuc. 4.40.1–2
129. Thuc. 4.41.4
130. Hanson, pp.114–15
131. Thuc. 4.25.2–5
132. Thuc. 4.43.1–5
133. Thuc. 4.44.5
134. Thuc. 4.45.1–2
135. Thuc. 4.48.5
136. Thuc. 4.47.2
137. Kagan, *Thuc.* p.85
138. Meiggs, p.327
139. Meiggs, p.325

140. Meiggs, p.331
141. Meiggs, pp.324-25
142. Thuc. 4.50.1-3
143. Thuc. 4.52.1-3
144. Thuc. 4.53.1-3
145. Thuc. 4.55.2
146. Thuc. 4.55.1
147. Thuc. 4.53.2
148. Thuc. 1.108.5
149. Hanson, pp.117-18
150. Thuc. 4.56.1
151. Thuc. 2.27.1
152. Thuc. 4.57.1-4
153. Kagan, *Arch. War* p.164
154. Thuc. 4.60.1-2
155. Thuc. 4.65.4
156. Thuc. 4.66.1-3
157. Thuc. 4.67.1-5
158. Thuc. 4.68.1-5; 4.69.1
159. Thuc. 4.69.3
160. Thuc. 4.73.1-4
161. Thuc. 4.75.1
162. Thuc. 4.76.1-4
163. Thuc. 4.77.1-2
164. Thuc. 4.101.3-4
165. Thuc. 4.100.1
166. Thuc. 4.79.1-2
167. Thuc. 4.80.1
168. Thuc. 4.80.3
169. Thuc. 4.80.5
170. Thuc. 4.81.1-3
171. Thuc. 4.83.1-6
172. Thuc. 4.84.2
173. Thuc. 4.85.1
174. Thuc. 4.85.2
175. Thuc. 4.88.1-2
176. Thuc. 4.104.5
177. Thuc. 4.106.1-2
178. Thuc. 4.106.3-4
179. Thuc. 4.107.2
180. Thuc. 4.108.1-3
181. Thuc. 5.26.5; Lazenby, pp.93-94
182. Thuc. 4.108.6-7
183. Thuc. 4.117.1
184. Thuc. 4.118.1-14
185. Thuc. 4.128.5
186. Thuc. 4.129.1-4
187. Thuc. 4.130.1-6
188. Thuc. 4.131.1-3
189. Thuc. 4.132.1-2
190. Thuc. 4.135.1
191. Thuc. 5.3.2
192. Thuc. 5.3.3-5
193. Thuc. 5.6.4-5
194. Lazenby, 91
195. Thuc. 5.14.3-4
196. Thuc. 5.15.1-2
197. Thuc. 5.16.1
198. Thuc. 5.16.1; 5.17.1
199. Plut. *Nic.* 9
200. Plut. *Nic.* 9
201. Thuc. 5.18.1-11
202. Thuc. 5.21.2-3
203. Thuc. 5.23.1-3
204. Thuc. 5.25.1
205. Thuc. 5.26.1-2
206. Thuc. 5.34.1
207. Thuc. 5.34.2
208. Thuc. 5.53.1
209. Thuc. 5.74.3
210. Thuc. 5.80.2
211. Thuc. 5.82.2
212. Thuc. 5.83.4
213. Thuc. 5.89.1
214. Thuc. 5.90.1-2
215. Thuc. 5.95.1
216. Thuc. 5.97.1
217. Thuc. 5.98.1
218. Thuc. 5.99.1
219. Thuc. 5.101.1
220. Thuc. 5.103.1-2
221. Thuc. 5.105.4
222. Thuc. 5.109.1
223. Thuc. 5.110.1-2
224. Thuc. 5.111.1-4
225. Thuc. 5.112.1-2
226. Thuc. 5.116.2-4

Part 4: The Sicilian Expedition

1. Thuc. 6.1.1
2. Thuc. 5.4.5–6
3. Thuc. 6.8.2
4. Thuc. 6.8.1–2
5. Thuc. 6.8.3
6. Plut. *Nic.* 2
7. Plut. *Nic.* 2
8. Plut. *Nic.* 6
9. Thuc. 6.10.5
10. Thuc. 6.11.3
11. Plut. *Nic.* 6
12. Thuc. 6.11.4
13. Thuc. 6.12.1–2
14. Plut. *Per.* 20
15. Thuc. 6.17.2–3
16. Thuc. 6.17.8
17. Thuc. 6.18.3
18. Thuc. 6.18.6
19. Thuc. 6.20.4
20. Thuc. 6.22
21. Thuc. 6.23.1–3
22. Green, *Armada* p.110
23. Plut. *Nic.* 12
24. Thuc. 6.24.3
25. Plut. *Nic.* 12
26. Thuc. 6.25.2
27. Thuc. 6.26.2
28. Thuc. 6.27.1–3
29. Thuc. 6.28.1
30. Thuc. 6.28.2
31. Thuc. 6.29.1–3
32. Thuc. 6.31.2
33. Thuc. 6.31.3
34. Thuc. 6.32.1–2
35. Thuc. 6.33.2
36. Thuc. 6.33.4–6
37. Thuc. 6.34.2
38. Thuc. 6.34.1–5
39. Thuc. 6.36.1–4
40. Thuc. 6.37.1
41. Thuc. 6.38.1–2
42. Thuc. 6.41.1–4
43. Thuc. 6.42.1
44. Thuc. 6.43.1
45. Thuc. 6.44.1
46. Thuc. 6.44.2–3
47. Thuc. 6.46.3–4
48. Green, *Armada* p.105
49. Thuc. 6.47.1
50. Thuc. 6.48.1
51. Thuc. 6.49.1–4
52. Thuc. 6.50.1–5
53. Thuc. 6.51.1–3
54. Thuc. 6.52.1–2
55. Thuc. 6.53.1–3
56. Thuc. 6.60.1–5
57. Thuc. 6.61.6
58. Thuc. 6.62.1–4
59. Thuc. 6.69.1
60. Thuc. 6.70.1–3
61. Thuc. 6.74.1–2
62. Thuc. 6.76.3–4
63. Thuc. 6.82.4
64. Thuc. 6.83.1–4
65. Thuc. 6.84.3
66. Thuc. 6.85.2
67. Thuc. 6.88.6
68. Thuc. 6.88.7–10
69. Thuc. 6.90.2–4
70. Thuc. 6.91.3–4
71. Thuc. 6.93.2
72. Thuc. 6.94.1–4
73. Thuc. 6.96.1–3
74. Thuc. 6.97.1–5
75. Thuc. 6.102.2–3
76. Thuc. 6.103.1–2
77. Thuc. 6.103.3–4
78. Thuc. 6.104.1–3
79. Thuc. 6.105.1–2
80. Thuc. 7.1.1–4
81. Thuc. 7.2.1–4
82. Thuc. 7.3.1–4
83. Thuc. 7.41–5
84. Thuc. 7.4.6

85. Thuc. 7.5.1–4
86. Thuc. 7.6.1–4
87. Thuc. 7.7.1–4
88. Thuc. 7.8.1–3
89. Thuc. 7.12.1–4
90. Thuc. 7.12.1–5
91. Thuc. 7.13.1–2
92. Thuc. 7.14.1–4
93. Thuc. 7.15.1–2
94. Thuc. 7.16.1–2
95. Thuc. 7.17.1–4
96. Thuc. 7.18.1–4
97. Thuc. 7.19.1–5
98. Thuc. 7.20.2; 7.26.2–3
99. Thuc. 7.21.1–4
100. Thuc. 7.22.1–2
101. Thuc. 7.23.1–4
102. Thuc. 7.24.1–3
103. Thuc. 7.25.1–4
104. Thuc. 7.25.5–8
105. Green, *Armada* p.266
106. Plut. *Nic.* 16
107. Thuc. 7.27.3–5
108. Rodgers, 151; Thuc. 7.28.4
109. Thuc. 7.29.5
110. Thuc. 7.33.3–6; 7.35.1
111. Murray, p.20
112. Thuc. 7.34.3–7
113. Rodgers, p.163
114. Thuc. 7.36.1–5
115. Thuc. 7. 36.6–7
116. Thuc. 7.38.1–3
117. Thuc. 7.39.1–2
118. Thuc. 7.40.1–5
119. Thuc. 7.41.1–4
120. Thuc. 7.42.1–5
121. Thuc. 7.43.1
122. Thuc. 7.44.1–8
123. Thuc. 7.47.1–4
124. Thuc. 7.48.2
125. Thuc. 7.48.3–4
126. Thuc. 7.48.5–6
127. Thuc. 7.49.2–4
128. Thuc. 7.50.1–4

129. Plut. *Nic.* 23
130. Plut. *Nic.* 24
131. Thuc. 7.52.1–2
132. Thuc. 7.53.1–4
133. Thuc. 7.56.1–3
134. Connor, *Thucydides* p.176
135. Thuc. 7.60.1–2
136. Thuc. 7.60.4–5
137. Thuc. 7.62.1–3
138. Thuc. 7.63.1
139. Thuc. 7.64.1–2
140. Thuc. 7.65.1–2
141. Thuc. 7.66.1–3
142. Thuc. 7.67.1–4
143. Thuc. 7.68.1–3
144. Thuc. 7.70.1
145. Thuc. 7.70.2–3
146. Thuc. 7.70.4–6
147. Thuc. 7.70.7–8
148. Thuc. 7.71.1–4
149. Thuc. 7.71.5–7
150. Thuc. 7.72.3–4
151. Thuc. 7.75.5
152. Thuc. 7.86.1–4
153. Thuc. 7.87.5–6
154. Green, *Armada*, 141–4

Part 5: The Ionian War

1. Thuc. 8.1.1–2
2. Thuc. 8.1.3
3. Thuc. 8.2.1–4
4. Thuc. 8.3.2
5. Thuc. 8.5.1–5
6. And. *On the Peace* 3.29
7. Lazenby, p.173
8. Thuc. 8.6.1–5
9. Thuc. 8.8.1–4
10. Thuc. 8.9.1–3
11. Thuc. 8.11.1–2
12. Thuc. 8.12.1–3
13. Thuc. 8.14.1–3
14. Thuc. 8.15.1–2

15. Thuc. 8.17.1–3
16. Thuc. 8.18.1–2
17. Thuc. 8.23.1–5
18. Thuc. 8.25.1
19. Thuc. 8.25.1–4
20. Thuc. 8.26.1–3; 8.27.1
21. Thuc. 8.27.1–5
22. Thuc. 8.28.1–4
23. Thuc. 8.29.1–2
24. Thuc. 8.31.1–4
25. Thuc. 8.35.1–4
26. Thuc. 8.37.1–5; Kagan, *Fall* p.81
27. Thuc. 8.38.1–5
28. Thuc. 8.40.2
29. Thuc. 8.42.1–4
30. Thuc. 8.43.1–3
31. Thuc. 8.43.4
32. Thuc. 8.44.1–4
33. Plut. *Alc.* 23
34. Thuc. 8.45.1–2
35. Thuc. 8.29.2; 8.45.2–3
36. Thuc. 8.46.4–6
37. Thuc. 8.46.1–2
38. Thuc. 8.46.3–5
39. Thuc. 8.47.1
40. Thuc. 8.48.4–5
41. Thuc. 8.50.3
42. Cawkwell, p.7
43. Thuc. 8.45.1
44. Thuc. 8.51.1–3
45. Thuc. 8.55.1–3
46. Thuc. 8.56.1–4
47. Thuc. 8.58.5–6
48. Thuc. 8.59.1
49. Thuc. 8.61.3
50. Arist. *Athenaion Politaea*, 32.3
51. Thuc. 8.76.4–7
52. Thuc. 8.78.1
53. Thuc. 8.80.1–4
54. Thuc. 8.82.3
55. Thuc. 8.84.1–3
56. Thuc. 8.84.5
57. Thuc. 8.85.2
58. Thuc. 8.85.3
59. Xen. *Hell.* 1.1.28
60. Xen. *Hell.* 1.1.30–31
61. Thuc. 8.86.4
62. Thuc. 8.87.4
63. Thuc. 8.87.5
64. Adcock, *Thucydides and His History* p.85
65. Thuc. 8.88.1
66. Thuc. 8.91.1–3
67. Thuc. 8.96.4–5
68. Thuc. 8.97.1–3
69. Rodgers, 177
70. Thuc. 8.100.1–5
71. Thuc. 8.102.1–3
72. Diod. 13.39
73. Thuc. 8.104.1–3
74. Thuc. 8.105.2–3
75. Diod. 13.40
76. Thuc. 8.106.2
77. Diod. 13.40
78. Lazenby, p.199
79. Thuc. 8.109.1
80. Xen. 1.1.2–3
81. Diod. 13.45
82. Diod. 13.45
83. Diod. 13.46
84. Diod. 13.46
85. Xen. 1.1.9–10
86. Xen. *Hell.* 1.1.14
87. Xen. *Hell.* 1.1.15
88. Diod. 13.50
89. Xen. 1.1.16–17
90. Diod. 13.50
91. Diod. 13.51
92. Kagan, *Fall* p.245
93. Xen. *Hell.* 1.1.22; Lazenby, p.206; Sealey, p.371
94. Diod. 13.52
95. Diod. 13.52
96. Diod. 13.53
97. Xen. *Hell.* 1.1.23
98. Xen. *Hell.* 1.1.36

99. Kagan, *Fall* p.268
100. Xen. *Hell.* 1.2.11–13
101. Diod. 13.64
102. Kagan, *Fall* p.264
103. Diod. 13.65
104. De Souza, *Piracy* p.33
105. Plut. *Alc.* 29
106. Plut. *Alc.* 30
107. Plut. *Alc.* 31
108. Plut. *Alc.* 32
109. Diod. 13.68
110. Plut. *Alc.* 32
111. Diod. 13.69
112. Diod. 13.72
113. Plut. *Lys.* 4
114. Cawkwell, 49
115. Diod. 13.70; Xen. 1.5.1–7
116. Diod. 13.71
117. Xen. *Hell.* 1.5.12
118. Xen. *Hell.* 1.5.13–14
119. *Hell. Oxy.* Frag. 8
120. Diod. 13.71
121. *Hell. Oxy.* Frag. 8; Lazenby, pp.220–21; Kagan, *Fall* p.317
122. Diod. 13.73
123. Plut. *Alc.* 35
124. Xen. *Hell.* 1.5.16–20
125. Xen. *Hell.* 1.6.1–3
126. Xen. *Hell.* 1.6.5–6
127. Xen. *Hell.* 1.6.12–15
128. Diod.13.77
129. Diod. 13.78
130. Diod.13.78–9
131. Xen. *Hell.* 1.6.19–21
132. Xen. *Hell.* 1.6.22–23; Diod. 13.97
133. Diod. 13.97
134. Diod. 13.98
135. Diod. 13.97
136. Rodgers, p.187
137. Xen. *Hell.* 1.6.30
138. Xen. *Hell.* 1.6.32
139. Diod. 13.99
140. Xen. *Hell.* 1.6.33–4
141. Diod. 13.100; Xen. *Hell.* 1.6.34–5
142. Diod. 13.101
143. Xen. *Hell.* 1.7.4–6
144. Diod. 13.101
145. Xen. *Hell.* 2.1.5
146. Xen. *Hell.* 2.1.6–7
147. Xen. *Hell.* 2.1.10–12
148. Xen. *Hell.* 2.1.13–14
149. Xen. *Hell.* 2.1.22–4
150. Xen. *Hell.* 2.1.25; Plut. *Alc.* 36
151. Xen. *Hell.* 2.1.26; Plut. *Alc.* 37
152. Diod. 13.105
153. Xen. *Hell.* 2.1.27
154. Diod. 13.106
155. Plut. *Lys.* 11
156. Xen. *Hell.* 2.1.28
157. Diod. 13.106
158. Xen. *Hell.* 2.1.31
159. Plut. *Lys.* 13; Xen. *Hell.* 2.1.31–32
160. Xen. *Hell.* 2.2.1–2
161. Xen. *Hell.* 2.2.3–4
162. Xen *Hell.* 2.2.5–8
163. Xen. *Hell.* 2.2.9
164. Xen. *Hell.* 2.2.13
165. Xen. *Hell.* 2.2.15
166. Xen. *Hell.* 2.2.16
167. Xen. *Hell.* 2.2.17–20
168. Plut. *Lys.* 14
169. Xen. *Hell.* 2.2.23; 2.3.13–14; Plut. *Lys.* 15

Conclusion

1. Plut. *Lys.* 16; *Per.* 22
2. Forrest, p.126
3. Kagan, *Fall* p.413
4. Cawkwell, p.64
5. Meier, *Athens* p.404

SELECT BIBLIOGRAPHY

Adcock, F.E. (1970) *Thucydides and His History*. Cambridge.
Amit, M. (1965) *Athens and the Sea*. Brussels-Berchem.
Austin, M.M., and Vidal-Naquet, P. (1977) *Economic and Social History of Ancient Greece*. Berkeley.
Bagnall, Nigel (2004) *The Peloponnesian War*. New York.
Blackman, David, Naval Installations (2000). In Robert Gardiner (ed.), *The Age of the Galley*, pp.224–33. Edison, New Jersey.
Brouwers, Josho (2013) *Henchmen of Ares*. Rotterdam.
Bury, John Bagnell (1900) *A History of Greece*. Cambridge.
Campbell, Brian (ed.) (2013) *The Oxford Handbook of Warfare in the Classical World*. Oxford.
Cartledge, Paul (2002) *Sparta and Laconia*. London.
Casson, Lionel (1995) *Ships and Seamanship in the Ancient World*. Baltimore.
Cawkwell, George (1997) *Thucydides and the Peloponnesian War*. London.
Coates, John (1995), The Naval Architecture and Oar Systems of Ancient Galleys. In Robert Gardiner (ed.) (2000), *The Age of the Galley*, pp.127–41. Edison, New Jersey.
Connor, Robert W. (1984) *Thucydides*. Princeton.
Cook, J.M. (1983) *The Persian Empire*. New York.
Delgado, James P. (ed.) (1997) *Encyclopedia of Underwater and Maritime Archaeology*. New Haven.
DeSantis, Marc (2014) A Nomad Strategy of Persistence. *Ancient Warfare*, VII-3, pp.22–25.
De Souza, Philip (1999) *Piracy in the Graeco-Roman World*. Cambridge.
De Souza, Philip (2002) *The Peloponnesian War 431–404 BC*. London.
De Souza, Philip (ed.) (2008) *The Ancient World at War*. London.
De Souza, Philip (2013) War at Sea. In Campbell, Brian (ed.), *The Oxford Handbook of Warfare in the Classical World*, pp.369–95. Oxford.
De Ste. Croix, G.E.M. (1972) *The Origins of the Peloponnesian War*. Ithaca.
Fields, Nic (2006) *Ancient Greek Fortifications 500–300 BC*. Oxford.
Fields, Nic (2008) *Syracuse 415–413 BC*. Oxford.
Finley, M.I. (1981) *Economy and Society in Ancient Greece*. New York.
Fornara, Charles W. (ed.) (1983) *Archaic Times to the End of the Peloponnesian War*, Vol. 1, 2nd ed. Cambridge.
Forrest, W.G. (1968) *A History of Sparta, 950–192 BC*. New York.
Gabrielsen, Vincent (1994) *Financing the Athenian Fleet*. Baltimore.

Gardiner, Robert (ed.) (2000) *The Age of the Galley*. Edison, New Jersey.
Grant, Michael (1970) *The Ancient Historians*. New York.
Grant, Michael (1989) *The Classical Greeks*. New York.
Green, Peter (1970) *Armada from Athens*. Garden City.
Green, Peter (1996) *The Greco-Persian Wars*. Berkeley.
Hale, John R. (2009) *Lords of the Sea*. New York.
Hanson, Victor Davis (2005) *A War Like No Other*. New York.
Jordan, Borimir (1975) *The Athenian Navy in the Classical Period*. Berkeley.
Kagan, Donald (1969) *The Outbreak of the Peloponnesian War*. Ithaca.
Kagan, Donald (1974) *The Archidamian War*. Ithaca.
Kagan, Donald (1981) *The Peace of Nicias and the Sicilian Expedition*. Ithaca.
Kagan, Donald (1987) *The Fall of the Athenian Empire*. Ithaca.
Kagan, Donald (1991) *Pericles of Athens and the Birth of Democracy*. New York.
Kagan, Donald (2003) *The Peloponnesian War*. NewYork.
Kagan, Donald (2009) *Thucydides*. New York.
Kallet, Lisa (2001) *Money and the Corrosion of Power in Thucydides*. Berkeley.
Kennedy, Paul (1987) *The Rise and Fall of the Great Powers*. New York.
Lazenby, J.F. (2004) *The Peloponnesian War*. New York.
Lendon, J.E. (2010) *Song of Wrath*. New York.
McGregor, Malcolm F. (1987) *The Athenians and Their Empire*. Vancouver.
McNeill, William H. (1976) *Plagues and Peoples*. New York.
Meier, Christian (1998) *Athens*. New York.
Meiggs, Russell (1972) *The Athenian Empire*. Oxford.
Morrison, John (1995) The Trireme. In Robert Gardiner (ed.) (2000) *The Age of the Galley*, pp.49-65. Edison, New Jersey.
Morrison, J.S., Coates, J.F., and Rankov, N.B. (2000) *The Athenian Trireme, Second Edition*. Cambridge.
Rhodes, John (2013) *The End of Plagues*. New York.
Roberts, John (ed.) (2005) *The Oxford Dictionary of the Classical World*. Oxford.
Sealey, Raphael (1976) *A History of the Greek City States 700-338 BC*. Berkeley.
Strassler, Robert B. (ed.) (2009) *The Landmark Xenophon's Hellenika*. New York.
Strauss, Barry (2004) *The Battle of Salamis*. New York.
Thomas, Carol G., and Conant, Craig (1999) *Citadel to City-State*. Bloomington.
Thomas, David Introduction. In Strassler, Robert B. (ed.) (2009) *The Landmark Xenophon's Hellenika*, ix-lxvi. New York.
Turchin, Peter (2006) *War & Peace & War*. New York.
Van Wees, Hans (2008) Warfare in Archaic and Classical Greece. In De Souza, Philip (ed.) *The Ancient World at War*, pp.101-17. London.
Wallinga, H.T. (2000) The Ancestry of the Trireme 1200-525 BC. In Robert Gardiner (ed.) *The Age of the Galley*. Edison, New Jersey.
Woodhead, Geoffrey A. (1970) *Thucydides on the Nature of Power*. Cambridge.
Zagorin, Perez (2005) *Thucydides*. Princeton.

INDEX

Abdera, 16, 213
Abydos, 190–2, 201, 203–204, 206
Acanthus, 107
Acarnania/Acarnanians, 18, 29, 61, 71–2, 77, 79, 105, 156
Achaea, 29, 61, 72–4, 91, 156
Actian Naval Monument, 35
Adeimantus, 224, 230
Aegean, 2, 6, 10, 13, 17, 19–20, 65, 96, 177, 182, 190, 196, 199–200
Aegina, 8, 28, 56, 64, 99, 119, 133, 152, 231
Aegospotami, 5, 225, 227–9, 231, 237–8
Aeolian Islands, 86
Agatharchus, 154, 168
Agesandridas, 198, 204
Agis, 119, 155, 174, 177, 184, 191, 209, 231
agoge, 22
Agrigentum, 125
aitiai, 3
Alalia, 32
Alcamenes, 176
Alcibiades, 6, 41, 118–19, 126, 128–9, 131–2, 137–40, 142–3, 151, 175, 177–9, 184–90, 192–7, 199, 203, 205–208, 211–13, 215–17, 227–8, 235, 237
Alcidas, 84–6
Ambracia, 47
Amorges, 174–5, 179, 181, 189, 236
Amphipolis, 2, 108–109, 113–18
Anabasis, 5

Anaia, 104, 190
Anapus River, 143, 158, 160
anastrophe, 38, 158
Andocides, 175, 236
Andros, 213
Antandrus, 97, 104, 204, 209, 225
Antiochus, 215–16, 229, 237
Antisthenes, 182
apella, 23
Aphrodisia, 100
Arakos, 225
Archestratus, 232
Archidamus, 23–4, 54–5, 59, 61, 65, 114
Arginus, 181
Arginusae, 5, 221–5, 237
Argos, 25–6, 29, 61, 115, 117–19, 145, 151–2, 178
Aristocrates, 176, 222, 224
Aristogenes, 222, 224
Aristotle, 10, 24, 225, 235
Arrhabaeus, 107–108, 111
Artaphernes, 97, 238
Artaxerxes, 28, 97
Artemisium, 10–11
Aspendus, 193, 196–7, 200, 203
Assinarus River, 170
Asytochus, 178, 180–4, 186–8, 190–4
Athens,
   Areopagus, 9
   Assembly, 9–10, 48–9, 62–3, 68–9, 101, 126–32, 148–50, 162, 188–9, 198–9, 209, 220, 222–5, 230–3, 239

Attica, population of, 31
cleruchies, 20
democracy, 9-10, 12, 17, 123, 131-2, 173, 186, 188, 191, 198, 224, 236
Long Walls, 20-2, 58, 62, 231, 232
navy, 2, 9-10, 14, 19-22, 40, 42, 48, 51, 54, 70, 78, 84, 149, 167
thetes, 9, 135, 225
Thirty Tyrants, 9, 236
Athlit Ram, 34
atraktos, 92
Attica, 6-8, 10, 19-20, 31, 53-8, 61, 63-5, 67-8, 70, 82-4, 88, 93, 99, 116, 130, 151-2, 154-5, 161, 173, 198, 209, 231, 238
Aztecs, 66

Black Sea, 6-7, 19-20, 31, 47, 82, 200, 214, 231, 237
Boeotia, 17, 28, 61, 86, 103-104, 117, 155, 184
Bosphorus, 30, 47, 208, 237
Brasidas, 2, 63, 74-5, 80, 89, 103-104, 106-16, 118, 122-3
Bricinniae, 125
Budorum, 81
Byzantium, 12, 16, 30, 45, 192-3, 209-10, 212, 230

Cadmean victory, 221
Callias, 14
Callicratidas, 218, 220-3
Camarina, 101, 125, 138-42
Cape Iapygium, 134, 156
Cape Malea, 98, 211, 221
Cape Pelorus, 94
Cape Triopium, 181, 190
Cardia, 206
Caria, 30, 61, 174-5, 226
Carteria, 201

Carthage/Carthaginians, 18-19, 32, 37, 69, 128, 130, 134, 142, 171, 237
Carystus, 13
cash, 15-16, 208, 226
Catana, 138-40, 142-3, 149, 160, 162, 166
Caunus, 30, 182-3, 190
Cecryphaleia, 28
Cenchrae, 176, 178
Centoripa, 143
Cephallenia, 71, 99
Ceramic Gulf, 226
Cerdylium, 113
Chaeronea, 104-105
Chalce, 183, 189-90
Chalcedon, 208-209, 211-12, 230
Chalcideus, 175, 177-8, 181, 184
Chalcidice, 106, 110
Chalcis, 40, 71-4, 77-9, 85, 99, 156-7
Charicles, 152
Charminus, 180, 183
Chelidonian Islands, 14
Chersonese, 18, 94, 191, 200-201, 217, 228,
Chimerium, 48-9
Chios, 22, 30, 61, 67, 89, 112, 135, 175-8, 180-3, 189-91, 199-200, 211, 213, 218, 223, 225-6
Chrysopolis, 208, 211
Cimon, 5, 13-16, 21, 27, 49
Circle (fort), 144
Clarus, 85
Clazomenae, 177, 180, 206, 215
Clearchus, 192-3, 209, 221
Clement of Alexandria, 32
Cleomenes 233
Cleon, 92, 110-14, 116, 126
Cleophon, 209
Cleopompus, 64, 69
Cleri, 207
clinker-built, 33

Cnemus, 71–2, 74, 75, 80
Cnidus, 181, 183, 187, 204
Colophon, 210
Conon, 156, 217, 219–21, 223–4, 228, 230
Corcyra, 4, 25, 32, 37, 47–9, 52, 56, 61, 63, 82, 86, 88, 94–6, 132–5, 156
Corinth/Corinthians, 25–6, 28–9, 31, 39, 42, 47–56, 61, 71–2, 77, 79–80, 83, 94–5, 104, 117–19, 142–5, 147, 150–2, 156–7, 159, 165, 168, 170, 174–6, 180, 203, 230, 232, 238
Coronea, 18
Corsica, 32
Cortyrta, 100
Corycus, 177, 180
Cos, 183, 203, 213
Council of 500, 9
Cratesippidas, 211, 213
Cratippus, 6
Crete, 61, 74–5, 78–80, 82, 85, 131
Cromyon, 95
Cunaxa, 4
Cyanaean Islands, 14
Cybele, 7
Cydonia, 74, 79–80
Cyllene, 48, 74, 85, 142
Cynossema, 200–203, 237
Cynuria, 115, 118
Cyprus, 12, 35, 230
Cyrus, 16, 213–14, 218, 225–6, 237
Cythera, 98–100, 115–17, 126
Cyzicus, 16, 203, 206–209, 213, 237

Dardanus, 201, 204
Darius I (the Great), 6–8, 59
Darius II, 174, 190, 206, 213
Decelea, 143, 151–2, 154–5, 160, 173–4, 191, 198, 209, 231
Delian League, 13, 15, 19, 24, 117, 236
Delium, 104–106, 115

Delos, 13, 18, 42, 58, 193
Delphi, 47, 55
Demarchus, 194
Demodocus, 104
Demosthenes, 86–9, 92, 102, 104–105, 150, 152, 156–7, 160–2, 164, 168–70, 239
Dercyllidas, 190–1
diekplous, 38, 50, 157, 168, 222
Diodorus Siculus, 5, 12, 201–202, 205, 207, 209, 211–13, 215–16, 219, 221, 223–4, 228–30
Diomedon, 189, 220, 222, 224
Diphilus, 156–7
dolphins, 160
Dorians, 26, 67, 123, 125, 141, 161
Dorieus, 194, 204
drachma, 40
Dyme, 73

eclipse, 67, 163
Eetionia, 198
Egypt, 6, 10–11, 18–19, 27–8, 35, 65, 98–9, 181, 205
Eion, 13, 97, 108–109, 113–14
eisphora, 84
Elaeus, 201, 203, 227
elate (fir), 33
Elea, 48, 117–18
Elis, 49, 61, 64, 142
Embatum, 84
Endius, 177–8, 208–10
Epaminondas, 236
Ephesus, 97, 210, 213, 215–16, 218, 225–6
ephor, 23, 142, 177, 235
epibatai (marines), 39–40
epibatai, 39–40
Epidamnus, 47–8
Epidaurus Limera, 100, 145
Epidaurus, 47, 67–9, 95, 100, 119, 132, 151

Epipolae, 143–7, 161
epotides (catheads), 156–7
Erasinides of Athens, 222, 224
Erasinides of Corinth, 147
Eresus, 200–201
Erineus, 156–7, 159, 165, 238
Erythrae, 174–5, 177, 180
Eryx, 136
Eteonicus, 221, 223, 225, 231
Ethiopia, 65
Etruria, 18, 69, 171, 237
Etruscans, 142, 144, 164
Euctemon, 180
Euphemus, 141
Eurybiades, 10–11
Eurymedon (officer), 88, 95–6, 101, 125, 150, 156–7, 160, 162–3
Eurymedon River, 14–16,
Euthydemus, 150, 168
Evagoras, 230
exairetoi (selects), 37

finances, 2, 4, 9, 15, 41, 43, 54, 61–2, 96, 140, 155, 162, 177, 185, 208, 226, 236
Five Thousand, 195, 197–9
Four Hundred, 191, 195, 198–9
funds/funding, 8, 14–16, 19–20, 40, 42, 61–3, 96, 107, 114, 130, 155, 177, 185, 188, 195, 200, 203, 208, 211, 213–14, 217, 226, 235, 237

Gaulites, 194
Gaurium, 213
Gela, 101, 125, 133, 145, 210
gerousia, 23
Glauce, 192
gold, 2, 7, 61–2, 108, 133–4, 136, 180, 213, 236
Gongylus, 145
Great Harbour, 35, 138, 144, 146–7, 153–4, 157–9, 165, 167–9, 171, 237–8

Gulf of Corinth/Corinthian Gulf, 18, 29, 71–2, 77, 80, 82, 104, 156–7, 165
Gylippus, 143–8, 152–3, 158, 160, 162–3, 167–8, 170–1, 235
Gythion, 99

Hagnon, 69, 114, 132
Halieis, 27–8, 95
Harmatus, 201
Hellenic Navy, 36, 45
Hellenica Oxyrhynchia, 6
Hellenica, 5
Hellespont, 6–8, 19–20, 31, 47, 61, 96, 104, 175, 182, 190, 192–3, 195–6, 199–204, 206, 208–12, 214, 220, 226, 231, 237
Helots, 12, 17, 25–7, 72, 88, 91, 93, 99–100, 106, 114–15, 117–18, 152
Hermae, 131, 139
Hermione, 47
Hermocrates, 101, 133–4, 141, 143, 152, 179–80, 185, 187, 194–5
Herodotus, 3, 7–8, 11–12, 24, 29
Himera, 145
hippagogos, 37
Hippocrates of Sparta, 181, 200, 209
Hippocrates, 102, 104–105
homoioi, 26
hoplitogogos, 37
Hundred Isles, 219
Hybla, 140
Hycara, 139
hypozomata, 43

Iasus, 175, 179, 181, 189
ila, 23
Illyrians, 111
Imbros, 20, 201
Ionia/Ionians 7, 12–13, 16, 61, 84, 96, 123, 132, 141, 144, 177–9, 181–2, 189, 195, 199–200, 203, 210–11, 226

Ionian Sea, 132, 144
Isthmian Festival, 176
Isthmus of Corinth, 11, 80
Isthmus of Leucas, 86, 88
Ithome, 27, 29

Kantharos, 21, 36
keleustes, 43
Knights, 220
kybernetes, 39, 43, 215
kyklos, 10, 73, 78, 85-6

Lacedaemonius, 49
Laconia, 12, 63, 87, 98, 106, 145, 198, 231
Lamachus, 104, 126, 137-9, 144, 171
Lampsacus, 16, 191, 210, 226-7, 230
Laurium, 8
Lecythus, 109
leitourgia (liturgy), 43
Lemnos, 20, 30, 65, 201
Leon (Athenian), 189
Leon (city in Sicily), 143
Leon (Spartan), 190
Leontine War, 125
Leontini, 125-6, 131, 141
Leros, 179
Lesbos, 30, 61, 67, 82-5, 97, 104, 120, 174-5, 178, 180-2, 200, 210, 218-19, 221, 231
Leucas, 47-9, 61, 74, 86, 88, 144-5, 203
Leucimme, 47-8
Leuctra, 24, 26, 236
Library of History, 5
Libya, 65, 98-9, 130
Lichas, 183-4, 187-8, 194, 196
Locri (Italy), 93, 136, 145, 154, 157
Lycia, 183
Lydia, 7, 30, 174, 210
Lyncestis, 107, 111-12
Lysander, 6, 213-18, 225-33, 235, 238

Lysias, 222, 224
Lysicles, 84

Macedonia/Macedonians, 8, 17, 106-107, 111-12, 114, 119, 206
Madytos, 204
Magnesia, 10
Mantinea, 5, 118-19, 128, 135, 145
Marathon, 8
measles, 66
Megara Hyblaea, 138, 154
Megara, 28-9, 47, 49, 56, 60-1, 80-1, 101-104, 117, 138, 143, 154, 198
Megarian Decree, 56, 60
Melanchridas, 175
Melos, 61, 86, 120-3, 182-3, 231
Menander, 150, 168
Mende, 110-12, 116
Messana, 87, 93-4, 137-8, 140, 145
Messenia 12, 87
Methana, 95, 99, 116-17, 126
Methymna, 178, 210, 218-19
Miletus, 29, 98, 178-82, 184, 186-8, 190-4, 200, 204, 213, 218
Mindarus, 194, 200-202, 204, 206-207, 209
Minoa, 102, 116, 126
Molycrium, 73
money, 1-2, 4-5, 8-9, 13-16, 18-20, 31, 41-2, 44, 48, 54-5, 57-8, 61-3, 78, 84, 96-7, 103, 107, 126, 129-31, 133, 136-7, 139-42, 144, 149-50, 155-6, 160-2, 173-4, 177, 181, 184-5, 187, 190-2, 194-6, 200, 203, 206, 208-14, 217-18, 225-16, 235-7, 239
mortise and tenon, 33
Mount Ida, 209
Mount Istone, 87, 95
Mount Mimas, 181
Munychia, 21, 36
Mycale, 12, 192

Myrcinians, 113–14
Myscon, 194
Mysteries, 131, 139
Mytilene, 15, 45, 82–5, 97, 104, 178, 219–21, 223

Naupactus, 29, 61, 71–2, 74, 76–80, 85, 89, 93, 99–100, 104, 117, 151–2, 156–7, 202
navarch, 44, 178, 180, 188, 194, 218, 225
Navarino Bay, 88–9
Naxos, 13, 138, 140, 142, 149
Nemea, 18
Neodamodeis, 118, 152
Nicias, 86–7, 94, 98, 111–12, 115–16, 118, 126–31, 136–7, 139–40, 144, 146, 148–50, 154, 159, 160–4, 166–70, 237–9
Nicostratus, 85, 112
Nisaea, 29, 80, 91, 101–104
Notium, 6, 210, 215, 217, 225, 229, 237

Oeniadae, 29, 105
Oenophyta, 28
Olympia, 42, 55, 58
Olympias (trireme), 36, 45
Olympieum 147, 159–60
On the Peace with the Spartans, 175
Oracle of Delphi, 47, 55
Oreus, 199
Oropus, 86, 198
Oxyrhynchus historian, 216

paean, 49, 76, 161
Pale, 47
Pallene, 109–10
Pamphylia, 13
Panormus, 74, 178
Parallel Lives, 6
Paralus, 85, 229–30

Parthenon, 16
Patrae, 72–3
Pausanias (co-king with Agis), 231
Pausanias, 12
Peace of Nicias, 115–16, 118, 131, 238
Pedaritus, 180, 182, 189–90
Pegae, 29, 91, 101
Pellene, 61, 203
Peloponnesian League, 2, 24, 55, 57, 99, 100, 174
Peloponnesus, 11, 13, 18, 24–7, 29, 54, 57–9, 61, 63–4, 71, 74, 82, 84–7, 92–3, 97–100, 104, 106–107, 115, 117, 122, 139, 141–3, 145, 148, 150–2, 162, 178, 191, 211, 213, 231, 238
pentecontor, 32, 135, 144
Perdiccas, 106–108, 111–13, 119
Pericles (son of Pericles), 222–4
Pericles, 6, 10, 17–19, 25, 29–31, 37, 42, 52, 56–65, 67–71, 83, 100, 116, 128, 132, 155, 163, 237
perioikoi, 25, 27, 98
periplous, 39, 50, 157, 163, 202, 207
Persia/Persians, 1, 2, 4–19, 24–5, 27–32, 41, 47, 50, 54, 57, 59, 65, 70, 97, 120, 134, 141, 152, 165, 174–5, 177–8, 180–1, 184–90, 192, 194, 197, 200, 204–208, 210–11, 213–14, 217, 226, 235–9
peuke (pine), 33
Phaeax, 125
Phaleron Bay, 21
Phaleron, 21, 28
Pharnabazus, 175, 182, 192, 195, 200, 203–207, 209, 211–12, 217, 235
Pheia, 64
Philip, 197, 200
Philocles, 224, 229–30
Phocaeae, 125
Phocaeans, 32, 97

Index 259

Phoenicia/Phoenicians, 11–12, 14, 28, 30–2, 50, 185–7, 190, 192–3, 196–7, 200, 203–205, 214
Phoenician Women, 221
Phoenicus, 181
Phormio, 40, 53, 72–80, 85, 157
Phrynicus, 178–9, 186–9, 197
Phrynis, 175
Pillars of Hercules, 130
Piraeus, 8, 15, 21, 25, 28, 32, 36, 41, 45, 53, 62, 65–6, 78, 80–2, 108, 117, 132–3, 137, 173, 193, 195, 198–9, 231–3
Pisander, 188–9, 198
Pissuthnes, 30, 174–5
pitch, 34
plague, 2, 65–9, 71, 87, 99–100, 128, 131
Plataea, 12, 60–1, 151, 165
Plemmyrium, 146-7, 153, 156–8
Plutarch, 5, 8–9, 13–14, 17–18, 20–1, 52, 59–60, 67–8, 71, 116, 127–8, 130–1, 154, 163, 184, 212, 214, 216–17, 228, 230
Pnyx, 199
Potamis, 194
Potidaea, 4, 53–4, 56, 69, 110, 112, 132
Prasiae 145, 151
Priene, 29
Proconnesus, 206
prophasis, 4
prorates, 43
Prosopitis, 28
Prote, 89
Protomachus, 222, 224
Ptychia, 95
Pylos, 87–91, 93, 98–100, 103, 115, 117–18, 145, 151, 169, 211
Pythodorus, 101

ram/ramming, 32, 34–5, 38–9, 45, 50, 76–9, 88, 157–8, 164, 168, 202, 205–206, 219, 222–3, 238

Rhegium, 86–7, 93–4, 136, 138, 145
Rhium, 74
Rhodes 36, 135, 183–4, 187–90, 204, 213, 218, 236
Rhoeteum, 97, 201

Salaminia, 85, 139, 142
Salamis, 11–12, 29, 50, 54, 81, 165, 231
Salynthia, 105
Samos, 10, 29–30, 104, 178–83, 186, 188–93, 195, 198–200, 203, 205, 210, 215, 217, 221, 226, 231
Sardis, 7, 30, 174, 206
Saronic Gulf, 28
satrap, 5
Scandea, 98
Sciathus, 10
Scione, 110–13, 116–17
Scironides, 178, 189
Scyllaeum, 119
Scyros, 13, 20
Segesta, 125–8, 130, 133, 136–7, 139–40
Selinus, 126, 129, 137, 139, 145, 179
Sellasia, 231
Selymbria, 212
Sestos, 191, 201, 205–206, 210, 227
Sicily/Sicilians, 1, 18–19, 29, 32, 37, 47, 61, 69, 82, 86–8, 95–6, 98–9, 101, 118, 125–52, 155–7, 160, 162–4, 167–77, 179, 193, 199, 203, 210–12, 237–9
Sicyon, 18, 29, 61, 105, 152
Sigaeum, 201
Sikia Channel, 88
silver, 8, 41, 61, 126, 133–4, 136, 143, 150, 213, 215, 235
Siphae, 104–105
smallpox, 66
Solygia 94, 116
Sophocles, 95–6, 101

Sparta, 2, 13, 22-9, 44, 57, 59, 70, 87, 91, 93, 97-100, 107, 110, 114-15, 118, 122-3, 174-5, 208-209, 214, 235-6, 238
   apella, 23
   agoge, 22
   Council of Elders, 23
   ephor, 23, 142, 177, 235
   Equals (Sparta), 26
   gerousia, 23
   Helots, 12, 17, 25-7, 72, 88, 91, 93, 99-100, 106, 114-15, 117-18, 152
   navarch, 44, 178, 180, 188, 194, 218, 225
   Neodamodeis, 118, 152
   perioikoi 25, 27, 98
   Spartiates, 24-5, 115, 118, 143, 152
Sphacteria, 87-94, 96, 109-10, 114-15, 117-18, 127, 169, 238
Spiraeum, 176-8
Stagirus, 107, 113, 117
stater, 97, 180
Strait of Messana, 87, 93-4
strategoi (generals), 44
stratiotis (soldier ship), 37
Strombichides, 177-8, 180, 191-2
Strymon River, 13, 97, 108-109
Suppliants, 221
Sybota, 39, 49, 51-2, 56, 85
Syedra, 14
Syme, 183
symmachy, 24
Syracuse, 35, 44, 87, 93-4, 125, 127, 129, 133-40, 142-52, 154-57, 161-8, 170-3, 179, 185, 193, 195, 203, 235-6, 238

talent, 41
Tamos, 196
Tanagra, 28, 86-7, 116, 126
Tarentum, 134-6, 144-5
tax/taxation, 8, 16, 84, 208
taxiarch, 222
Teichioussa, 179
teredo navalis (shipworm), 33, 37
Terias River, 138, 143
thalamioi, 44
Thapsus, 143, 162
Thasos, 26, 108, 206, 213
Thebes, 5, 60, 221
Themistocles, 6, 8-11, 13, 19, 21, 233
Theopompus, 230
Theramenes, 198, 206-208, 223-4, 232-3
Therimenes, 181
Thermopylae, 11
Thessaly, 106, 112, 184
thetes, 9, 135, 225
Thirty Years' Peace, 29, 49, 52, 91, 151
Thrace, 27, 53, 61, 69, 104, 106-109, 113, 117-18, 127, 231
thranitai, 44
Thrasybulus, 200-202, 205-207, 213, 221, 223-4
Thrasycles, 177-8
Thrasyllus, 200-202, 205-206, 209-10, 222, 224
Thrasymelidas, 88
Thucydides, 1-6, 8, 10, 12-14, 21, 23-5, 30-1, 37, 39-41, 45, 47, 49-50, 56, 61-2, 64-5, 67, 70, 80-1, 83-4, 86-8, 92-3, 96, 99, 101, 104, 106-109, 115-20, 123, 125-6, 128, 131-3, 137, 139, 150-1, 153, 155-6, 159, 161, 163-4, 168-70, 173-4, 179, 182, 184-90, 193-9, 203-204
Thurii, 139, 142, 144, 156, 193
Thyrea, 64, 100
Timaea, 184
timber, 8, 33-5, 37, 81, 87, 89, 97, 109, 142, 154, 173, 209
Tissaphernes, 5, 41, 174-5, 178-81, 183-90, 192-3, 194-7, 200, 203-204, 206, 210, 214, 237

Tolnides, 17–18, 99
Torone, 109, 113
toxotai, 39
Tragia, 30
Treasurers of Hellas, 13
tribute, 13–14, 16, 18–20, 24, 27–8, 41, 53, 59, 61–3, 84, 96–8, 104, 109, 117, 123, 141, 155, 174–5, 208, 226
trierarch, 39, 41, 43–4, 78–9, 132–3, 195, 209, 223
trieres, 31
trireme, 9–10, 12, 15–16, 20, 31–45, 81, 84, 155, 157–8, 167, 171, 173, 205, 225–6, 238

Troezen, 29, 47, 91, 95
Trogilus, 146, 152

Xenophon, 4–6, 45, 195, 204, 207, 213, 215–16, 220, 223, 227, 229–32
Xerxes, 8, 11

Zacynthus, 61, 70–71, 78, 88–9, 99
Zea, 21, 32, 36
zygioi, 44